The 2006 Tour de France

by John Wilcockson and the Editors of *VeloNews*

D1315382

VELO press

BOULDER, COLORADO

Front cover jersey photograph: Brad Kaminski
Back cover image: AFP/Getty Images

Photography credits for 16-page insert, with respective page numbers and positioning:
Casey Gibson: 1, 4, 9, 15 *(bottom)*
Graham Watson: 14
Getty Images: 2, 5 *(bottom)*
AFP/Getty Images: 3 *(top)*, 5 *(top)*, 6, 7, 8–9 *(bottom)*, 10, 11, 12, 13, 16
Bongarts/Getty Images: 3 *(bottom)*, 8 *(top)*, 15 *(top)*

Distributed in the United States and Canada by Publishers Group West.

VeloPress®, a division of Inside Communications, Inc.
1830 North 55th Street
Boulder, Colorado 80301–2700 USA
303/440-0601; Fax: 303/444-6788; E-mail: velopress@insideinc.com

FIRST EDITION

Cover and interior design by Erin Johnson Design

Library of Congress Cataloging-in-Publication Data
Wilcockson, John.
   The 2006 Tour de France / John Wilcockson. — 1st ed.
     p. cm.
   ISBN-13: 978-1-931382-91-5 (pbk. : alk. paper)
   ISBN-10: 1-931382-91-3 (pbk. : alk. paper)
   1. Tour de France (Bicycle race) (2006)   I. Title.
GV1049.2.T68W547 2006
796.6'20944—dc22

                                                               2006029050

To purchase additional copies of this book or other VeloPress books, call 800/234-8356 or visit us at www.velopress.com.

Printed in the United States of America

10 9 8 7 6 5 4 3 2 1

Contents

Acknowledgments

R arely has there been a Tour de France that involved so many characters and incidents within (and without) its three weeks of racing. Reflecting the complexity of what was an enormously enjoyable as well as deeply disturbing event, this book has required the contributions of half a dozen *VeloNews* reporters to produce this comprehensive story of a special race. In particular, I would like to thank European correspondent Andrew Hood, who supplied much of the writing and background details on *Operación Puerto*, Oscar Freire, Denis Menchov, Oscar Pereiro, Michael Rasmussen, Carlos Sastre, David Millar, Damiano Cunego, and Robbie McEwen; editor Kip Mikler for early-stage reporting and profiles on Thor Hushovd and George Hincapie; and senior writer Neal Rogers for profiles of Matthias Kessler, Andreas Klöden, and Floyd Landis. I also appreciated the reporting contributions to Chapter 20 from velonews.com editor Charles Pelkey and *VeloNews* managing editor Ben Delaney.

Australian sportswriter Rupert Guinness provided background information and assistance on a day-to-day basis. Some of the historical details were inspired by the writings of the late French journalist Pierre Chany. I would like to thank all the athletes and teams for making this Tour such an exciting race; the staff of VeloPress, particularly Jade Hays, Renee Jardine, and Ted Costantino, for their patience and expertise; and my wife, Rivvy Neshama, for her love, and for understanding that the Tour is an annual highlight of a cycling journalist's life.

John Wilcockson
September 2006

Introduction

The Tour at its best, and worst.

The vacuum left by a retiring Tour de France superchampion has often been filled by a race that astonishes the world, such as those held in the years after five-time Tour champions Miguel Induráin, Bernard Hinault, and Eddy Merckx left the sport. The 2006 Tour seemed likely to follow that trend.

In the months after Lance Armstrong hung up his cleats on clinching his seventh consecutive Tour victory in July 2005 and in the weeks building up to the 93rd Tour de France, Armstrong's successor seemed likely to emerge from an elite group of riders who had finished on the Tour podium during the Armstrong era. At the front of this group were the 1997 winner Jan Ullrich of Germany, the runner-up from 2005, Ivan Basso of Italy, and the third-place finisher from the remarkable 2003 Tour (behind Armstrong and Ullrich), Alexander Vinokourov of Kazakhstan. Facing this trio were a dozen possible challengers who included two Spanish riders, Francisco Mancebo and Alejandro Valverde, three Americans, Floyd Landis, George Hincapie, and Levi Leipheimer, an Australian, Cadel Evans, and a Russian, Denis Menchov. That was the expected hierarchy.

The first few chapters of this book trace the stories of these prerace favorites from their training camps and team presentations in the winter, through a spring season of races that brought them varying form and mixed fortunes, before they began approaching their optimal form in June. But other forces were at play.

Another of these early chapters addresses the thorny subject of doping in cycling, and the 40-year history of drug testing at the Tour de France. While the likely main players were training hard and scouting the courses they would race in July, a special unit of Spain's Guardia Civil was running an undercover investigation into the activities of the former doctor of a Spanish cycling team. The repercussions of that investigation would reach out from Madrid and overwhelm several riders and teams before the 2006 Tour de France began in Strasbourg on July 1.

This book chronicles the sensational story of this embattled Tour, while following the fortunes of the principal players and the riders who emerge to challenge for the overall victory. In contrast to some of the Tours in the recent past, the 93rd edition produced a wealth of memorable images, both happy and sad.

Many amazing, joyful moments made this Tour de France as remarkable as any in the past four decades: the gutsy attack on the Cauberg climb that gave a support rider a remarkable solo stage win in Valkenburg; a 36-year-old veteran skipping off the winner's podium in the yellow jersey at Rennes after becoming the first Ukrainian to lead the Tour; an Australian sprinter extricating himself from an impossibly blocked-in position in the final 100 meters of the stage to Dax and then accelerating so fast that he raced to a photo finish decided by millimeters; one team bringing the Tour to life with an explosive mass attack on the Col de Portillon in the Pyrénées; two Americans lighting up the mountaintop finish at Pla-de-Beret with a surge that only one rider could follow; a marathon 200km breakaway on the Tour's longest stage that gained half an hour on the peloton and put a little-known Spaniard in the yellow jersey; an extraordinary, daylong breakaway by a skinny Danish climber on the toughest day in the Alps, to give him the stage win and the polka-dot jersey; and an even more outrageous, 130km solo effort by a top favorite on the mountain stage to Morzine, to recover seven minutes of the eight minutes he had conceded to the race leader the day before.

And then there were the sad, sometimes heartbreaking moments: learning that Spain's reprehensible doping ring, *Operación Puerto*, had lassoed all of the Tour's odds-on favorites the day before the start; seeing the race leader, his yellow jersey spattered with blood, crying out in pain after his arm was gashed in a

70kph collision with a spectator leaning over the barriers during the Strasbourg finishing sprint; watching the new race favorite sitting on a Dutch roadside, clutching a broken collarbone, his Tour hopes shattered; following another race favorite in the Rennes time trial and realizing after only 5km that there was something wrong, he was going too slow, and his dream of winning the Tour was disappearing with every pedal stroke; hearing a third race favorite at a news conference in Bordeaux give details of a degenerative hip joint that would have to be replaced by surgery after the Tour; seeing one of the top American hopefuls riding laboriously toward the stage 11 finish in Spain, knowing his chances of winning had also gone south; and then watching the race leader after L'Alpe d'Huez seeing his chances of overall victory apparently disappearing from sight after he blew up and could ride at only a painfully slow pace to the alpine summit of La Toussuire.

But the most shattering moment of all came three days after the race finished when the rider who came back from the brink, took the final yellow jersey in the time trial at Montceau-les-Mines, and received all the honors as the new Tour champion in Paris was declared positive at an antidoping control. The story of this rider, and the sensational developments that could lead to his title being stripped away, is told in the final chapter.

Three thrilling weeks of racing had unfortunately been followed by an outrage whose effects won't fully play out until another Tour de France hits the road in July 2007.

2006 TOUR DE FRANCE
Start List

DISCOVERY CHANNEL

1. José Azevedo (P)
2. Viatceslav Ekimov (Rus)
3. **George Hincapie (USA)**
4. Egoi Martinez (Sp)
5. Benjamin Noval Gonzalez (Sp)
6. Pavel Padrnos (Cz)
7. Yaroslav Popovych (Ukr)
8. José Luis Rubiera (Sp)
9. Paolo Savoldelli (I)

TEAM CSC

11. **Bobby Julich (USA)**
12. Giovanni Lombardi (I)
13. Stuart O'Grady (Aus)
14. Carlos Sastre (Sp)
15. Fränk Schleck (Lux)
16. **Christian Vande Velde (USA)**
17. Jens Voigt (G)
18. **David Zabriskie (USA)**

T-MOBILE

21. Andréas Klöden (G)
22. Giuseppe Guerini (I)
23. Sergei Gontchar (Ukr)
24. Matthias Kessler (G)
25. Eddy Mazzoleni (I)
26. Michael Rogers (Aus)
27. Patrik Sinkewitz (G)

AG2R

31. Christophe Moreau (F)
32. Jose Luis Arrieta (Sp)
33. Mikel Astarloza (Sp)
34. Sylvain Calzati (F)
35. Cyril Dessel (F)
36. Samuel Dumoulin (F)
37. Simon Gerrans (Aus)
38. Stephane Goubert (F)

GEROLSTEINER

41. **Levi Leipheimer (USA)**
42. Marcus Fothen (G)
43. David Kopp (G)
44. Sebastian Lang (G)
45. Ronny Scholz (G)
46. Georg Totschnig (A)
47. Fabian Wegmann (G)
48. Peter Wrolich (A)
49. Beat Zberg (Swi)

RABOBANK

51. Denis Menchov (Rus)
52. Michael Boogerd (NI)
53. Bram De Groot (NI)
54. Erik Dekker (NI)
55. Juan Antonio Flecha (Sp)
56. Oscar Freire (Sp)
57. Joost Posthuma (NI)
58. Mickael Rasmussen (Dk)
59. Pieter Weening (NI)

DAVITAMON-LOTTO

61. Cadel Evans (Aus)
62. Mario Aerts (B)
63. Christophe Brandt (B)
64. **Christopher Horner (USA)**
65. Robbie McEwen (Aus)
66. **Fred Rodriguez (USA)**
67. Gert Steegmans (B)
68. Wim Vansevenant (B)
69. Johan Vansummeren (B)

PHONAK

71. **Floyd Landis (USA)**
72. Bert Grabsch (G)
73. Robert Hunter (RSA)
74. Nicolas Jalabert (F)
75. Martin Perdiguero M.angel (Sp)
76. Axel Merckx (B)
77. Koos Moerenhout (NI)
78. Alexandre Moos (Swi)
79. Victor Hugo Peña (Col)

LAMPRE-FONDITAL

81. Damiano Cunego (I)
82. Alessandro Ballan (I)
83. Daniele Bennati (I)
84. Marzio Bruseghin (I)
85. Salvatore Commesso (I)
86. Daniele Righi (I)
87. Paolo Tiralongo (I)
88. Tadej Valjavec (Slo)
89. Patxi Vila Errandonea (Sp)

CAISSE D'EPARGNE-ILLES BALEARS

91. Alejandro Valverde (Sp)
92. David Arroyo (Sp)
93. Florent Brard (F)
94. Isaac Galvez (Sp)
95. Vicente Garcia Acosta (Sp)
96. Vladimir Karpets (Rus)
97. Oscar Pereiro Sio (Sp)
98. Nicolas Portal (F)
99. Xabier Zandio (Sp)

QUICK STEP-INNERGETIC

101. Tom Boonen (B)
102. Wilfried Cretskens (B)
103. Steven De Jongh (Nl)
104. Juan Manuel Garate (Sp)
105. Filippo Pozzato (I)
106. José Rujano (Vz)
107. Bram Tankink (Nl)
108. Matteo Tosatto (I)
109. Cédric Vasseur (F)

CRÉDIT AGRICOLE

111. Pietro Caucchioli (I)
112. Alexandre Botcharov (Rus)
113. Anthony Charteau (F)
114. Julian Dean (NZl)
115. Jimmy Engoulvent (F)
116. Patrice Halgand (F)
117. Sébastien Hinault (F)
118. Thor Hushovd (Nor)
119. Christophe Le Mevel (F)

EUSKALTEL-EUSKADI

121. Iban Mayo (Sp)
122. Iker Camano (Sp)
123. Unai Etxebarria (Vz)
124. Aitor Hernandez (Sp)
125. Inaki Isasi (Sp)
126. Inigo Landaluze (Sp)
127. David Lopez Garcia (Sp)
128. Gorka Verdugo (Sp)
129. Haimar Zubeldia (Sp)

COFIDIS

131. David Moncoutié (F)
132. Stéphane Auge (F)
133. Jimmy Casper (F)
134. Sylvain Chavanel (F)
135. Arnaud Coyot (F)
136. Cristian Moreni (I)
137. Ramiro Ivan Ramiro (Col)
138. Rik Verbrugghe (B)
139. Bradley Wiggins (GB)

SAUNIER DUVAL

141. Gilberto Simoni (I)
142. David Canada (Sp)
143. David De La Fuente (Sp)
144. Jose Angel Marchante Gomez (Sp)
145. Ruben Lobato (Sp)
146. David Millar (GB)
147. Riccardo Ricco (I)
148. Christophe Rinero (F)
149. Francisco Ventoso (Sp)

FRANÇAISE DES JEUX

151. Sandy Casar (F)
152. Carlos Da Cruz (F)
153. Bernhard Eisel (A)
154. Philippe Gilbert (B)
155. Joly Sébastien (F)
156. Gustav Larsson (Swe)
157. Thomas Lövkvist (Swe)
158. Christophe Mengin (F)
159. Benoît Vaugrenard (F)

LIQUIGAS

161. Danilo Di Luca (I)
162. Michael Albasini (Swi)
163. Magnus Bäckstedt (Swe)
164. Patrick Calcagni (Swi)
165. Kjell Carlström (Fin)
166. Stefano Garzelli (I)
167. Matej Mugerli (Slo)
168. Luca Paolini (I)
169. Manuel Quinziato (I)

BOUYGUES TELECOM

171. Thomas Voeckler (F)
172. Walter Beneteau (F)
173. Laurent Brochard (F)
174. Pierrick Fedrigo (F)
175. Anthony Geslin (F)
176. Laurent Lefevre (F)
177. Jérôme Pineau (F)
178. Didier Rous (F)
179. Matthieu Sprick (F)

MILRAM

181. Erik Zabel (G)
182. Mirko Celestino (I)
183. Ralf Grabsch (G)
184. Andriy Grivko (Ukr)
185. Maxim Iglinskiy (Kaz)
186. Christian Knees (G)
187. Fabio Sacchi (I)
188. Björn Schröder (G)
189. Marco Velo (I)

AGRITUBEL

191. Juan Miguel Mercado (Sp)
192. Manuel Calvente (Sp)
193. Cedric Coutouy (F)
194. Moises Duenas Nevado (Sp)
195. Eduardo Gonzalo Ramierez (Sp)
196. Christophe Laurent (F)
197. José Alberto Martinez (Sp)
198. Samuel Plouhinec (F)
199. Benoit Salmon (F)

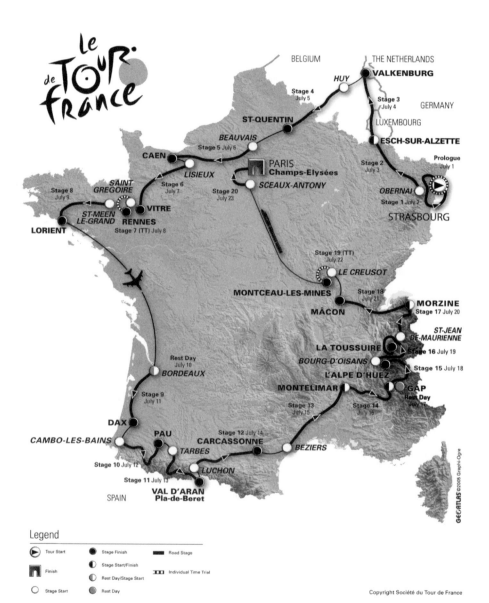

le de TOUR france

BELGIUM

THE NETHERLANDS

HUY **VALKENBURG**

Stage 4
July 5

Stage 3
July 4

GERMANY

ST-QUENTIN

LUXEMBOURG

BEAUVAIS

Stage 5 July 6

ESCH-SUR-ALZETTE

CAEN

LISIEUX

PARIS
Champs-Elysées

Stage 6
July 7

Stage 20
July 23

SCEAUX-ANTONY

Stage 2
July 3

Prologue
July 1

SAINT GREGOIRE

ST-MEEN LE-GRAND

VITRE

OBERNAI

Stage 8
July 9

RENNES

STRASBOURG

Stage 1 July 2

LORIENT

Stage 7 (TT) July 8

Stage 19 (TT)
July 22

LE CREUSOT

MONTCEAU-LES-MINES

Stage 18
July 21

MORZINE

MÂCON

Stage 17 July 20

ST-JEAN DE-MAURIENNE

LA TOUSSUIRE

Stage 16 July 19

BOURG-D'OISANS

Stage 15 July 18

L'ALPE D'HUEZ

Rest Day
July 10

BORDEAUX

MONTELIMAR

GAP

Rest Day
July 17

Stage 9
July 11

Stage 13
July 15

Stage 14
July 16

DAX

PAU

Stage 12 July 14

CAMBO-LES-BAINS

CARCASSONNE

TARBES

BEZIERS

Stage 10 July 12

LUCHON

Stage 11 July 13

SPAIN

VAL D'ARAN
Pla-de-Beret

GEO ATLAS ©2005 Graph-Ogre

Legend

Tour Start	Stage Finish	Road Stage
Finish	Stage Start/Finish	Individual Time Trial
Stage Start	Rest Day/Stage Start	
	Rest Day	

Copyright Société du Tour de France

CHAPTER 1

The Year Starts Out

With Lance Armstrong retired, the new candidates for Tour de France victory enter 2006 with high hopes.

Six months after Lance Armstrong won a seventh consecutive victory at his final Tour de France, the 34-year-old Texan was front and center at the 2006 Discovery Channel team presentation. The American icon dominated the stage when he stepped up to the microphone in a wood-paneled theater at the Museum of Television and Radio in Beverly Hills, California. To a media audience and the 27 members of the Discovery team, Armstrong talked about the Tour de France and his possible successor. As a part owner and an adviser to the team, he told his former teammates to "cherish this role as an underdog."

"We haven't been in that position for a long time, and that's the perfect way to ride the race," Armstrong said. "But on paper it's between Ullrich and Basso and T-Mobile and CSC. Jan [Ullrich] is looking completely different than he's looked in other Januarys in the last seven, eight, nine years. This is a guy who's clearly got new motivation and a new perspective on his sport. The course suits him: a lot of time trials, not particularly hard in the mountains."

As for the U.S. team's aspirations at the Tour, Discovery's team manager Johan Bruyneel said that George Hincapie, Yaroslav Popovych, José Azevedo, and "Chechu" Rubiera were all capable of riding for the overall classification. But Bruyneel knew that finding someone to fill Armstrong's shoes was going to be difficult, if not impossible. No wonder Armstrong advised Bruyneel in late 2005 to sign back their former team rider Floyd Landis. "He's American, he's a great rider, he's not old, gotta have him," Armstrong told Bruyneel. "Unfortunately and I do mean unfortunately," Armstrong said later, "it didn't happen."

LANDIS: READY TO ROLL

A week before the Discovery team presentation, Floyd Landis walked into the noisy bar of the Barceló Pueblo Park hotel in Playa de Palma, Spain, and ordered an espresso. The Phonak team training camp was in full swing, and a hilly training ride had lasted an hour longer than expected. He was tired. "Too tired to think right now," he replied to one question in a lengthy interview.

Weary as he was, the Pennsylvania native was eager to talk about the season ahead, his second as a leader at Phonak. After a stressful first year with the Swiss team that saw him place top ten at the Tour de France, he had earned the respect of teammates and team directors alike.

When he moved to Phonak after functioning as Armstrong's lieutenant at U.S. Postal, Landis was expecting to back up another former teammate, Tyler Hamilton. Then Hamilton and Santiago Perez, Phonak's best riders in 2004, were charged with blood doping and left the team. Whether Phonak could continue at the top level became unclear when the Union Cyclist Internationale (UCI) rejected its ProTour application because of the ethical problems.

After a last-minute appeal, however, Phonak was accepted as a ProTour team in February 2005. Belgian John Lelangue was new team manager, and Spaniard Juan Fernandez was directeur sportif. Landis was team captain. Almost a year into the job, he said he felt more comfortable as the leader "partly because when I came to the team I expected to have another year where I would help Tyler and not have so much focused on me. Then the problems with Tyler started, and we didn't know who should be the leader, me, [Santiago] Botero, or [Oscar] Pereiro, so we went with three.

"I don't mind the pressure, but I just wasn't prepared mentally for what I was getting into. The whole team feels more connected now. We're not wondering if the whole thing is going to dissolve any moment, so from that perspective it's easier for me to take more of a responsibility role."

In 2005 Landis pulled things together and placed third at the Tour de Georgia, eleventh overall at the Dauphiné Libéré, and ninth at the Tour de France. "All things considered, I'm happy with the way the Tour went last year," he said. "Obviously, you go there and want to win the race—everybody would like to win the Tour—but it was the first time I was the leader of a team. It was a learning experience, and there are things that will change, but I can't say it was a disappointment."

On the downside, Landis lost four and a half minutes to Ivan Basso and race champion Armstrong on the mountaintop finish at Pla d'Adet. That was his worst performance. It came in a stage won by his former teammate George Hincapie, ahead of Landis's Phonak colleague Pereiro. "I knew I was having a bad day from the beginning," Landis recalled, "so the last climb was like 'get to the finish, the day's over.' I was cross-eyed the entire last mountain."

Landis observed that "everybody, even the guy who wins, has bad days in the Tour. The objective is that they happen when nobody notices them, on days when you can hide. On a day like [Pla d'Adet] . . . there's no place to hide. I don't know how many climbs there were [in that stage], but it seemed like about 50 to me."

Eliminating (or mitigating) the bad days was one of Landis's goals for 2006. Another goal was building a solid squad to support him at the Tour. "Obviously there has to be some changes from last year. Pereiro left, but as far as the other guys, we'll sit down during the season," Landis said.

Asked whether he could envision winning the Tour, the Phonak team leader said, "Yeah, I'd like to think that. Whether I win the Tour or not, I don't know. I like my chances . . . but in all fairness, I'm not going to make any claims that I can do anything. We'll see what goes."

ULLRICH: RENEWED ENERGY

An hour's drive across the Mediterranean island of Majorca from the Phonak team hotel in Palma lies the sprawling Robinson Club, a gated, cliff-top tourist resort in Calla Serena. This is where the mighty German squad, T-Mobile, held its mid-January team presentation.

Team leader Jan Ullrich looked totally relaxed, despite being Armstrong's pick to succeed him at the Tour. Pressure? What pressure? Even when pinned against a wall for an hour by a phalanx of German reporters, the superstar patiently answered a barrage of questions. Later as twilight settled over the club's palm-lined pool, he posed for repeated photo ops next to a model of the Eiffel Tower as he was asked to smile "one more time."

The youthful-looking Ullrich, complete with longer hair and tight curls covering his forehead, had good reason to smile for the photographers. First, he said, "We have a team which is young, fresh, competitive and has an extremely good team spirit. All the new riders have adapted really fast to the group, and I just expect a lot from 2006."

In a slick presentation at the Robinson Club's theater, where the stadium-style seating was filled by a couple hundred journalists, most of them flown in by charter plane from Germany, Ullrich was introduced in a seven-man stage racer group that included team newcomers Sergei Gontchar of Ukraine, Eddy Mazzoleni of Italy, and Michael Rogers of Australia, along with returning team members Andreas Klöden of Germany, Giuseppe Guerini of Italy, and Oscar Sevilla of Spain. Klöden, who placed second in the 2004 Tour, said his 2006 season would be "dedicated to Jan." As for the big race in July, Klöden said, "I think many have a chance to win . . . Jan, Basso, Vinokourov. The Tour is very open."

As for Ullrich, he said, "My biggest goal is to win the Tour de France, so it's pretty logical to form the team around the season highlight. Eddy and Sergei have proved themselves in major stage races, both in going for the GC (general classification) and helping others do well, while Michael is a huge talent."

Indeed, triple world time trial champion Rogers, 26, who already had three Tours under his belt, looked to build on a slew of victories in weeklong stage races that included the 2004 Tour of Germany. Also tapped for the Tour team was the solid German all-rounder Matthias Kessler. It would be a team of workers, just eight men dedicated to putting Ullrich atop the Tour podium—à la Armstrong.

At the 2005 Tour, T-Mobile tried everything it could to dethrone Armstrong, including a blazing acceleration before the Port de Pailhères climb on the first Pyrenean stage. "Yes," Ullrich said, "we tried everything. We attacked really, really hard, but at a certain moment we realized that it was impossible to beat Lance."

Armstrong's retirement opened the way for Ullrich, who looked certain to prepare for the Tour by racing the Giro d'Italia alongside Rogers. "Jan said to me that he thinks he had his best year when he did the Giro [in 2001]," Rogers revealed.

After lengthy winter training camps in Cape Town, South Africa, Tuscany, Italy, and Majorca, Ullrich realized that his legs needed more base miles than they did when he won the 1997 Tour at age 23. "If I race the Giro, it will basically be for training," he confirmed, "and not to measure myself against Basso."

CSC's Basso had already declared he would win the Giro before facing Ullrich at the Tour, where the German knew he couldn't repeat his poor climbing performances on the first mountain stage at each of the past two Tours. "If I want to win the Tour," he said, "I have to at least follow Basso's wheel in the mountains."

Ullrich was also counting on the support of his personal trainer, Rudy Pevenage, to help him win the 2006 Tour. Pevenage had been sidelined during the previous two years by a spat with then team manager Walter Godefroot. "I've worked hard to get Rudy back on the team," said Ullrich. "He's very important to me. The setup couldn't be better."

BASSO: GIRO-TOUR DOUBLE

While the T-Mobile and Phonak teams enjoyed warm sunshine in Majorca, the 2005 Tour runner-up Ivan Basso and his CSC teammates dodged the rain showers in Tuscany for their intense 12-day preseason training camp. They stayed at the four-star Hotel Caesar in the beach town of Lido di Camaiore. From there they took rugged six-hour rides on the coastal roads, south through Pisa or north through La Spezia, or headed east into the Alpi Apuane hills.

At 28, Basso was starting his third year with CSC after a few erratic seasons with Italian teams that grew impatient with him for lack of results, despite his obvious talent. He became a more confident and consistent rider after linking up with CSC boss Bjarne Riis, the 1996 Tour winner.

Basso's transformation from promising rider to top Tour contender demonstrated Riis's Midas touch. Basso said his transformation couldn't have happened without the Danish team manager's prodding and influence. "Riis is more like a father to me. We talk about everything. When I have an important decision to make, even with matters not with cycling, I always consult with Bjarne. When I arrived on this team, I was another rider. I used to be afraid to try to win. Now I try to win every race. Everybody sees how I move in the group during the race; now I attack more, I do a good time trial. . . . I don't believe in a big change at once. I believe in a lot of work, and [improving] little by little."

Basso's trust in Riis, combined with the Dane's experience in shaping Team CSC into a world-class organization, inspired Basso to attempt to win both the Giro d'Italia and Tour de France in 2006.

"We have different goals this season," Riis confirmed. "Now it's time to win one of the big ones." After taking over the CSC team in 2000, Riis relied on good communication and teamwork to manage the bicycle team. To forge a sense of commitment, he introduced military-style boot camps that bring together riders and staff in Denmark's harsh December weather.

B. S. Christiansen, a former NATO special forces commando who organizes the team camps, said, "Ivan used to pull back; now he confronts his fears to overcome them. He's become a leader." Christiansen cited the most recent team-building camp, which included a freestanding 35-foot pole that riders had to climb before leaping onto a swinging trapeze. Basso balked, but Christiansen urged him to try. Basso took the bait and later returned to climb the pole unassisted despite his chronic acrophobia.

"Bjarne knows how to motivate riders, but above all, he never forgets the humanity," said the team's Italian veteran Giovanni Lombardi. "If someone isn't fitting in, then we all work together to solve it. I've known a lot of teams in my career. On many teams, people race and collect a paycheck. There was no ambiance, no loyalty, no team spirit."

With the CSC riders' strong commitment to each other and their tightly focused training programs, Riis saw no problem in his men racing to win both of the year's top grand tours. "In my team, we have [several] riders doing the Giro and the Tour. Of course, we have one rider to do the *classement*, and that's Ivan, but we have more riders doing both," he said.

"We have a rider like Carlos Sastre who's doing a very important role for Ivan in the Tour; we've seen before he's able to arrive in the first ten in the Tour, then have a big focus and go well in the Vuelta [a España]. We have Jens Voigt, we have Bobby Julich doing the Giro and Tour."

Riis left that thought hanging, but obviously he believed that his strong team riders could help Basso become the first Giro-Tour champion since his compatriot Marco Pantani did the double in 1998.

LEIPHEIMER: FITTER THAN EVER

Before heading south to Majorca and its January training camp, the Gerolsteiner squad gathered for an official team presentation at its sponsor's home base of Gerolstein, deep in the Eiffel region of western Germany. A thick overnight frost coated the pine forests marching across the rolling green hills, where medieval castles crown limestone crags and underground aquifers feed the springs at the Gerolsteiner mineral water plant.

Arriving here from San Francisco was Levi Leipheimer, the German team's American leader. The Montana native made his European breakthrough when he finished third at the 2001 Vuelta a España and had stepped up his game every year since. His results were mixed in three years at Rabobank, with two top tens at the Tour, but he didn't really establish his role as a leader until he moved to Gerolsteiner in 2005.

Leipheimer had an outstanding first season with Gerolsteiner, due to unequivocal team support as well as the assistance of a personal coach, Dr. Massimo Testa. "Max has made a huge difference for me," Leipheimer said, as he chatted over a vegetarian lunch in the bistro of the four-star Hotel Calluna overlooking snow-speckled Gerolstein. "I train so much harder than I used to. Sometimes I can't believe it. I'm just like, 'Wow!' I think back to the way I used to train and think, 'How was I even any good?'

"It's almost like I've had to train myself in order to train harder. Mentally. Once you know you've done something in training, you know you can do it and you know you can recover. Then you get stronger in your head. It's just a positive effect."

The changes in his preparation (he also trained extensively with Armstrong before the 2005 Tour) brought Leipheimer greatly improved results in 2005, including second overall at the Tour de Georgia, third at the Dauphiné Libéré, and sixth at the Tour before his outstanding victory over Ullrich at the Tour of Germany.

"Germany was the highlight," he said. "We're in Germany, we're on a German team, we're up against another German team that's probably the biggest team in the world and Germany's biggest sports hero, Jan Ullrich. I went in really relaxed, not expecting anything and came out really good."

Leipheimer learned an important lesson when he lost the leader's jersey at the Dauphiné; his team was not strong enough to hold a long-distance breakaway in check. A couple of months later in the German tour Leipheimer took the race lead in the Austrian Alps on the "the hardest climb I've ever ridden," the 14km Rettenbachferner, which tops out at 8,800 feet above sea level, higher than any mountaintop finish at the Tour de France. Then his team, including Austrian climber Georg Totschnig, helped the American extend his lead over Ullrich on a cold, rain-drenched summit finish in the Black Forest before Leipheimer held on to the win in a flat 31km time trial.

Asked if that victory had given him good morale for the 2006 Tour, Leipheimer said, "Oh, definitely. I think that for me my expectations always go up a little bit based on the results I've had in the past and what I expect out of myself."

At 32, the American looked set for his best year yet. "I can tell you, comparing this year to last year, [my fitness level] is much higher," he said. "I look at the training, I look at the intervals, at the cadence, at the wattage, everything's there [on the power-meter printout] . . . I enjoy training hard now more than I thought I ever would and more than I ever have. It's weird. I love to go out and ride my bike fast . . . and suffer. I think it's just because you have objectives and goals and you can see the progress. Maybe it comes with age, the focus and patience, because the way I pick my racing schedule now, I [have] big chunks of time just training."

A large chunk of that training time, he said, was spent on a time-trial bike in motor-paced sessions. "Time trialing is going to be important this year," he concluded. "Especially in the Tour."

HINCAPIE: HOPES AND DREAMS

When he stepped onto the veranda of his new home on a crisp January morning, George Hincapie felt like he had made it. From his hilltop perch in Greenville, South Carolina, he could see lavish homes surrounded by meticulous landscaping. Beyond that lay the Blue Ridge Mountains, thickly forested and covered with a spider's web of quiet country roads where Hincapie trains in the winter.

It was 8:30 a.m. and the house was buzzing as Hincapie's wife Melanie welcomed visitors. The couple's 14-month-old daughter Julia was just waking up, and Hincapie's mother-in-law, visiting from France, was asleep in one of the guest rooms. Hincapie's celebrity status in his adopted hometown clicked up a few notches after the 2005 Tour de France. After he won the Tour's marquee stage at Pla d'Adet, the city of Greenville unfurled a huge banner in the revitalized downtown to honor his performance.

"I WAS PRETTY AMAZED AT THE IMPACT MY STAGE WIN HAD. EVEN IF I WOULD HAVE WON PARIS-ROUBAIX, INSTEAD OF GETTING SECOND, IT WOULDN'T HAVE BEEN NEARLY AS BIG AS WINNING THAT STAGE IN THE TOUR."

As he relished his last days at home before the season swung into motion, the quiet, hardworking Hincapie said he was surprised at the reception. "I was pretty amazed at the impact my stage win had," he says. "Even if I would have won Paris-Roubaix, instead of getting second, it wouldn't have been nearly as big as winning that stage in the Tour."

There's a touch of irony in a racer who had dreamed of winning gritty spring classics races since his junior days in the rough-and-tumble New York City racing scene reaching stardom in the high peaks of the Pyrénées. "It's pretty interesting because Paris-Roubaix is such a hard race—probably as hard or harder than any one day at the Tour," he said. "But people get Tour fever in July and a lot more people here in Greenville know what I'm doing and recognize it."

Adding to his celebrity status was rampant speculation that this bruising classics racer could be Discovery Channel's next Tour de France leader. Could the man who put aside all personal ambitions in his previous ten Tours really take the team's reins in July?

"It's tough for us because people probably expect another Lance, which we'll probably never see again in our lifetimes," he said. "So for those people, you don't want to let them down, but for me personally, if I can do a better Tour than last year, that would be my main thing. I won a stage last year and I was fourteenth overall, and I think that if I didn't have to do as much work as I did I could probably do better.

"I've just never been in that position without having to work for Lance," Hincapie added. "But it would be hard for me to just totally forget about the classics. I think if I did that, I'd be kind of lost."

At 32, Hincapie figured he had three, maybe four years left, and while his future at the Tour was an unknown, he remained committed to his goal of winning Paris-Roubaix. "There's definitely still a lot of unfinished business in the classics that I love to do—Roubaix, Tour of Flanders, races that are really suited to my style of riding," he said. "There's a select few guys that do well at the Tour and do well at the classics, so I don't see any reason why I can't do well at both."

Team manager Johan Bruyneel said Hincapie might lead Discovery Channel at the 2006 Tour if the team changed its goal from winning the race to finishing in the top five. In order to do that, Bruyneel added, Hincapie might have to forget about the classics. That seemed unlikely. When Hincapie finished his winter training rides and was welcomed home by his wife and daughter, that feeling of having "made it" returned. But when he hit the road the next day, he'd again be consumed by unfinished business—at the classics and, perhaps, at the Tour de France.

EVANS: ON THE FAST TRACK

Like the high-performance Audi TT that Aussie Cadel Evans loves to ply over the winding mountain roads of his adopted Switzerland, life for the popular cyclist moved to the fast lane in 2005. Besides becoming the leader of the Davitamon-Lotto team, Evans rode strongly in his first Tour de France in July, won a grueling mountaintop stage of the Tour of Germany in August, got married in September, and finished building his house on Australia's southeast coast in December.

Evans's personal highlight was his marriage to Chiara, an Italian pianist. In the eyes of the cycling world, however, eighth place in his debut Tour was the real news. That was clear to Evans after the Tour when, among many others, his former Mapei teammate Franco Ballerini and respected directeur sportif Franco Cribiori told him, "You rode a really good Tour, Cadel!" "That means a lot to me," Evans said during an interview over cups of cappuccino in his wife's hometown of Gallarate in northern Italy.

In his heart, Evans always knew the Tour de France was his race. After all, on his grand tour debut for Mapei in 2002, he wore the Giro d'Italia leader's pink jersey until he cracked on the final mountain stage of a race that he began as a rookie *domestique*. Mapei disbanded and Evans joined T-Mobile, but a series of broken collarbones kept him from riding the 2003 Tour, and team politics prevented him from starting in 2004. It finally took a switch to the Davitamon-Lotto team for the former World Cup mountain bike champion to get his chance at proving his worth as a true Tour rider.

"There were a couple of [early] mountain stages where I wasn't as good as I could have been and there was at least one occasion when I probably didn't get the best out of myself, but all in all I was pretty happy with my first Tour," he said.

Evans was disappointed about his lack of team support at the Tour. "I didn't want to ask a lot from my team because I didn't know what I could deliver," he said. "But now I know what I can deliver, [and] I know what I'm going to ask for."

One thing he asked of his team was to sign American Chris Horner to be his right-hand man at the 2006 Tour. Having Horner's strength and climbing ability to help him could make a huge psychological difference for the Aussie. Despite the lack of help in the 2005 Tour, Evans was impressively consistent over the three weeks. His top-ten finish was overlooked by many, even though he finished only 34 seconds behind sixth-place Levi Leipheimer and 49 seconds ahead of ninth-place Floyd Landis. Like them, Evans had to be seen as a serious podium threat in 2006.

Evans grew in stature at the 2005 Tour and proved that he was ready to play a more demanding leadership role in the future. An opportunity for him to prove himself came on the Croix-Neuve climb just before the stage 18 finish at Mende. This Cat. 2 "wall" was only 3.1km long but had a 10.1 percent average grade and 15 percent pitches on its three switchbacks. It was the steepest and most challenging hill of the three weeks. The group of GC leaders fought a no-holds-barred battle on the steep climb.

Evans said, "I wasn't absolutely flat-out flat out because there was a headwind on the climb and a flat finish. Ullrich was on the rivet and got dropped at one section, and [Michael] Rasmussen and [Alexander] Vinokourov had already been dropped. But because of the headwind I thought, 'If I do something extra here, I might not have it at the end.'" What he did have at the end was an unexpected sprint to beat the only riders still with him: Armstrong, Basso, and Ullrich.

Even more encouraging for Evans was his performance in the final time trial at St. Étienne. After several days of hard racing, he finished seventh in the 65.4km stage, only 12 seconds slower than Basso.

At 29, Evans looked ready to make good on his teenage dream of one day winning the Tour de France. "My intention when I was a mountain biker was to have a short and sweet career," he said. "But now I have different motivation. I want to see how far I can go as a Tour rider."

VINOKOUROV: EVERYTHING FOR THE TOUR

Things changed for Alexander Vinokourov going into the 2006 season. Now he was the boss, not the backup man. In his six years with the T-Mobile and

Telekom teams, the media would rush to interview superstars Jan Ullrich and Erik Zabel and virtually ignore the stoic Vinokourov. Admittedly, it was tough for mainly German-speaking reporters to talk to the quiet rider from Kazakhstan who's fluent in only Russian and French, with a smattering of English.

It wasn't much easier for the Spanish press, but because Vinokourov had become the leader of Spain's top ProTour team, he was the center of attention at Liberty Seguros's late-January team presentation in Madrid.

Vinokourov, the former Red Army officer from Kazakhstan, made his Tour breakthrough in 2003, when his incessant attacks took people by surprise. His aggression earned him second place at L'Alpe d'Huez, a stage win after a solo breakaway into Gap the next day, and an eventual third-place finish in Paris behind Armstrong and Ullrich.

Three years later, with Armstrong out of the way, Vinokourov again expected to be battling his former teammate Ullrich at the Tour. "To get on the podium I'll have to attack," Vinokourov conceded. "But I'll change things for this year. Last year [with T-Mobile] I attacked to destabilize the Discovery team [of Armstrong]."

Despite his sometimes reckless aggression, Vino helped team leader (and friend) Ullrich to make the podium. The Kazakh finished the Tour strongly to place third in the difficult final time trial and win the prestigious stage on the Champs-Élysées, to wind up in fifth overall.

That inspired performance helped take Vinokourov to the Liberty Seguros team. Manager Manolo Sáiz signed up the Kazakh well before his previous team leader, Spaniard Roberto Heras, tested positive for Erythropoietin (EPO) in winning the Vuelta a España and had his title handed to Russian Denis Menchov of the Rabobank team. When Heras was suspended for two years, Liberty fully embraced Vinokourov's bid to win the Tour in 2006.

"I will take all the pressure off Vino," Sáiz said, "so he can focus 100 percent on the Tour de France. And I have eight riders who can help him win the Tour. Liberty Seguros is a team with lots of experience. Vino is capable of winning anything, including the Tour, especially now that Armstrong has opened the door.

To win the Tour you need the great qualities of a champion *and* the experience. Vino has both."

VALVERDE: SPAIN'S BIG HOPE

His stage win over Lance Armstrong at the Courchevel summit in the 2005 Tour de France set the church bells ringing across Spain. That Alejandro Valverde later abandoned the race in tears with an injured knee seemed of little consequence. The Spanish believed they had found their man, someone who would return Tour glory south of the Pyrénées.

"I can't help thinking about the Tour because everyone asks me about it everywhere I go," Valverde said at the Caisse d'Épargne-Illes Balears team presentation in Murcia, the Spaniard's home region. "It's the race I like most and it's the race I want to focus on for the rest of my career.

"I get worried about not living up to the expectations, but if things don't work out this year, I still have a lot of time ahead of me," continued Valverde, who would turn 26 before starting his second Tour. "This is only my fifth year as a pro and many riders don't win the Tour until they're 27 or 28, so I have time to progress."

Despite the accolades, not even his own team manager was sure which road Valverde would take. "We don't know yet what kind of rider Alejandro will become," said Eusebio Unzué. "Perhaps he's better suited for the classics and the shorter stage races. This year will tell us a lot because he still hasn't even finished a Tour yet. It's too early to talk about him winning."

Should Valverde not live up to expectations in 2006, then Caisse d'Épargne could rely on Oscar Pereiro, its new signing from Phonak, to bid for a top placing at the Tour. This eternal aggressor won the 2005 Tour's most combative prize, and he finished in the top ten in both of the past two Tours. In 2005, Pereiro grabbed a well-deserved stage win into Pau two days after losing to George Hincapie at Pla d'Adet.

With Valverde still learning the Tour ropes, Pereiro would be free to attack on the transition stages. Another stage win, and perhaps a run at the King of the

Mountains (KOM) jersey (he was second to Michael Rasmussen in 2005), might satiate this jovial Gallego. But riding for the more talented Valverde was the role that Pereiro most expected to play in 2006.

With five months to go before the start of the 93rd Tour de France in Strasbourg, Basso and Ullrich were the clear favorites to battle for the title vacated by Armstrong. But with even these two men conceding that the dynamics of the race would be different in the absence of one dominant, controlling team, everyone was expecting a more open Tour, one that also might be claimed by Landis, Leipheimer, Hincapie, Evans, Vinokourov, or Valverde. The vacuum left by a superchampion has had a habit of being filled by a Tour that astonished the world. Perhaps the 2006 edition was going to follow that trend.

CHAPTER 2

Lessons from the Past

Tour history indicates that another wild Tour is in the works.

What do Jan Ullrich, Stephen Roche, Bernard Hinault, and Roger Pingeon have in common? They all won the Tour de France—after a five-time Tour champion left the sport. Germany's Ullrich won in 1997, the first year that Spaniard Miguel Induráin wasn't on the Tour start line in more than a decade; Irishman Roche was the 1987 winner, the year after Bernard Hinault retired; Frenchman Hinault scored his first Tour victory in 1978, a couple of months after Belgian Eddy Merckx quit the peloton; and Pingeon took the 1967 Tour following the retirement of fellow Frenchman Jacques Anquetil. So what would happen in 2006 following the exit of seven-time winner Lance Armstrong?

The chances were high for a Tour that would be as suspenseful and unusual as those following the retirement of the four earlier superchampions. As preparations for the Tour ramped up, speculation on likely story lines included:

- One of the race favorites, suffering from heatstroke, loses contact with the other leaders and dies on a mountainside; the autopsy identifies a mixture of amphetamines and alcohol in his stomach (1967).
- The yellow jersey holder after the stage to L'Alpe d'Huez is thrown out of the race because of a doping infringement (1978).
- The Tour has eight different race leaders, and the yellow jersey changes hands eleven times (1987).

- A new champion emerges, but his team twice has to rescue him when all seems lost (1997).

Yes, all of those things happened—and much more. Here's a look at the four Tours that the 2006 race could most resemble, along with a look back 20 years to the historic breakthrough victory of Greg LeMond, the first American (and first non-European) to win the Tour de France.

1967: PINGEON'S COUP, POULIDOR'S DILEMMA

At his final Tour in 1966, Anquetil worked hard to stymie longtime rival Raymond Poulidor and allow his young Ford France teammate Lucien Aimar to win the race. A year later, when the Tour temporarily returned to the format of national teams (similar to soccer's World Cup), Aimar was given the No. 1 race number on the ten-man squad representing France. But in most people's books, the true team leader (and overall race favorite) was No. 8, Poulidor. Poulidor, who had been Anquetil's biggest challenger, was a folk hero because he was the battling underdog who never wore the yellow jersey.

Poulidor started the 1967 Tour by taking second place in the prologue time trial behind specialist José Errandonea of Spain. It soon became clear, however, that neither his French national team nor any of the other 12 squads could control the race. Big breakaways on each of the opening four stages saw the yellow jersey shift from Spain to Belgium (Willy Van Neste) to Italy (Giancarlo Polidori) and back to Belgium (Joseph Spruyt). So when another potentially dangerous break formed in the 172km stage 5a from Roubaix to Jambes in Belgium, Poulidor sent his lieutenant Roger Pingeon to cover the move.

Not only did Pingeon catch the 17-man break, but he dropped them one by one and then powered away solo on the cobbled Mur de Thuin climb to win by 1:24 over the chasers and by 6:22 over the peloton containing all of the race favorites: Poulidor, Felice Gimondi (Italy), Jan Janssen (Netherlands), Tom Simpson (Britain), Herman Vanspringel (Belgium), and Julio Jiménez (Spain). Things got worse for Poulidor when he crashed in stage 8 to the Ballon d'Alsace summit and was forced to ride the final climb on a bike too small for him, costing him minutes and any hope for final victory. After that, Poulidor had no choice but to become a *domestique-deluxe* for Pingeon, who went on to win the Tour by 3:40 over Jiménez.

This was also the race in which British team leader Simpson, who had a history of suffering from heatstroke, collapsed and died while climbing Mont Ventoux in stage 13 in 100 degree weather. Amphetamine pills were found in the pockets of Simpson's race jersey while the autopsy revealed he had ingested liquor during the stage. It was a deadly mixture. His death triggered the first clampdown on drugs in sports, and the organizers began antidoping tests at the Tour the following year.

1978: HINAULT'S BELLIGERENCE, POLLENTIER'S DISGRACE

Eleven years after Simpson's death, despite the drug controls, doping was still a problem in cycling. The issue would be front and center before the end of this 1978 Tour, which began with several contenders in the absence of the retired Eddy Merckx. All of France was hoping that their new national champion, 24-year-old Bernard Hinault, would take over. But a ten-man break in the 243km stage 3, from St. Amand to St. Germain in northern France, gained three minutes on the peloton and put one of Merckx's former lieutenants in the spotlight. Joseph Bruyère was the George Hincapie of his day, and after the first long time trial near Bordeaux in stage 8, which Hinault won by just 24 seconds over Bruyère, the experienced Belgian was in the yellow jersey.

Hinault took back a couple of minutes on Bruyère in the Pyrénées, but as the race headed for the Alps Hinault faltered in stage 14, a 52.5km time trial to the Puy-de-Dôme summit, placing fourth behind Dutchman Joop Zoetemelk, Belgian climber Michel Pollentier, and Bruyère. Going into stage 16, from St. Étienne to L'Alpe d'Huez, Bruyère was still the overall leader with a one-minute lead on Zoetemelk and almost two minutes on Hinault. Bruyère cracked on the Alpe's infamous 21-turn climb and lost 11 minutes, but he was replaced in the yellow jersey by another Belgian, Pollentier, who had gained three minutes on an earlier climb and held on up the Alpe to win the stage and take the yellow jersey over Zoetemelk and Hinault.

Pollentier, who won the previous year's Giro d'Italia, was considered a candidate for final victory. But a few hours after the stage finish, there came a shocking announcement from race directors Jacques Goddet and Félix Lévitan: Pollentier was caught trying to cheat the doping control and was disqualified from the Tour.

It was later revealed that at the previous day's medical control, young Frenchman Antoine Gutierrez was caught using a rubber bulb of clean urine hidden in his armpit, from which a tube was taped across his body and under his crotch. It was a novel way to pee in the tester's sample jar. Gutierrez didn't start the Alpe d'Huez stage and officials kept quiet about the incident. It was rumored that others had already gotten away with this ruse. After the stage to L'Alpe d'Huez, the UCI medical inspector was on the lookout for other cheats, and he caught Pollentier with a rubber bulb apparatus too. Ironically, Pollentier's real urine sample was later tested and shown to be clear of any banned drugs. He'd cheated for nothing and lost his chance to win the Tour.

IRONICALLY, POLLENTIER'S REAL URINE SAMPLE WAS LATER TESTED AND SHOWN TO BE CLEAR OF ANY BANNED DRUGS. HE'D CHEATED FOR NOTHING AND LOST HIS CHANCE TO WIN THE TOUR.

A belligerent Hinault—who had led a riders' strike in stage 12 to protest a series of long transfers and multiple stages—went on to win the final 72km time trial, beating race leader Zoetemelk by four minutes and winning his first Tour by the same margin.

1987: ROCHE-DELGADO DUEL
AFTER BERNARD'S ERROR

After the 1986 Tour was dominated by the French team La Vie Claire, with Greg LeMond winning the race from teammate Hinault, the Frenchman retired and the American was expected to repeat his victory in 1987. But that spring, LeMond almost died in a hunting accident, and he wouldn't return to the Tour until 1989. As a result, the leadership of LeMond's team (now sponsored by Toshiba) was taken over by a young Frenchman, Jean-François Bernard, who was given the No. 1 race number. Other contenders at the 1987 Tour included Irishman Stephen Roche, Spanish climber Pedro Delgado, and Frenchman Charly Mottet.

In the Tour's first long time trial—a tough 87.5km from Saumur to Futuroscope—Roche won the stage and Mottet took over the yellow jersey. When the race reached the foot of Mont Ventoux a week later, Mottet was still in yellow, followed at 1:11 by Bernard, with Roche in third at 1:26. It seemed that the 36.5km time trial from Carpentras to the Ventoux summit would settle the issue. On a ferociously hot day, Bernard rode like a man possessed, winning the stage by 1:39 over Colombian climbing ace Lucho Herrera, with Delgado in third (at 1:51), Roche fifth (at 2:19), and Mottet ninth (at 3:58).

In the overall standings, Bernard had a 2:34 lead over runner-up Roche, with Mottet another 13 seconds back in third. It looked like the race was sewn up. But two hours into the next day's 185km stage to Villard-de-Lans, Mottet's Système U team made a preplanned mass attack in the feed zone that Roche and Delgado were astute enough to follow. Bernard was at the back of the peloton due to an untimely puncture, and he and his team chased fruitlessly for the next 100km, conceding four minutes to Delgado and Roche, who jumped away from the breakaway group on the last of a half dozen climbs in the Vercors region.

Roche and Delgado fought an exciting duel in the Alps in three stages that were almost identical to those that awaited the riders in the 2006 Tour. On L'Alpe d'Huez, Roche conceded 44 seconds (and the yellow jersey) to the Spaniard. At the mountaintop finish in La Plagne, Roche fought back from a minute's deficit at the foot of the climb to finish only four seconds back (and needed oxygen to revive). Roche attacked on the descent of the Joux-Plane into Morzine to take back 18 seconds on Delgado. The Tour was finally settled in the 38km time trial at Dijon, where Roche came in second to Bernard, but a minute ahead of Delgado. The final podium was Roche on top, Delgado second at 40 seconds, and Bernard third, at 2:13.

1997: TOUGH WIN FOR ULLRICH

In his final Tour, in 1996, Miguel Induráin faded in the mountains and lost the Tour to an inspired Dane named Bjarne Riis, whose young Telekom teammate Jan Ullrich, in his Tour debut, came in second. Riis was hoping for a repeat win in 1997, but many saw Ullrich, 23, as the real leader of the powerful German squad. Their main opposition was thought to be former Tour runner-up Tony Rominger, but the Swiss crashed out in stage 3. When the mountains arrived in stage 9, it became clear that Ullrich was climbing better than Riis and that their chief opposition lay in the Festina team of Richard Virenque (a year before the French team was busted for organized doping) and Italian climber Marco Pantani.

The second stage in the Pyrénées ended on the Arcalis mountaintop in Andorra. The result was a win for Ullrich, 1:08 ahead of the chasing Pantani and Virenque, with Riis in fifth at 3:23. That put Ullrich in the yellow jersey, and three days later he confirmed his dominance by winning a hilly 55km time trial at St. Étienne, three minutes ahead of runners-up Virenque and Riis.

With almost a six-minute overall lead on second-place Virenque, it looked as though the Tour was over even before entering the Alps. Pantani would win two of the three alpine stages (at L'Alpe d'Huez and Morzine) to move him up to third on general classification. It was the middle stage, though—over the Glandon and Madeleine passes with a mountaintop finish at Courchevel—that tested Ullrich the most. Virenque's Festina team made a premeditated mass attack on the first climb, and launched Virenque on a break over the summit with his teammates Laurent Dufaux, Pascal Hervé, and Laurent Brochard. Ullrich couldn't stay with them on the descent, and by the start of the second climb he was two minutes behind Virenque, who was soon on his own. Meanwhile, Ullrich waited for Riis, who rode relentlessly for his young teammate through the valley and all the way up the Madeleine to close the gap on the Festina leader.

Four days later in the Vosges mountains, Ullrich had another scare when he couldn't hold the tempo set by the Festina riders on the early climbs. Over the Col du Hundsrück, Ullrich, feeling sick, struggled 45 seconds behind a break led by Virenque and three teammates, who were accompanied by dangerous riders like Pantani, Fernando Escartin, Laurent Jalabert, and Michael Boogerd. Two things saved Ullrich: None of the opposing riders would help Virenque and his team, and Telekom's Udo Bölts and Riis worked double time to eventually pull Ullrich back to the front group.

Ullrich confirmed his first (and only) Tour win at the final time trial in Disneyland Paris, where a frustrated Riis—who had hoped to win the stage and finish top five overall—had numerous mechanical problems and ended up tossing his bike in the ditch and losing nine minutes.

Yes, bizarre things can happen at the Tour, even in years when there's a dominating team and clear-cut favorites. That was the case in 1986, when five-time champion Bernard Hinault faced off with his La Vie Claire teammate Greg LeMond. The dramatic race resulted in the first American Tour victory and began the run of ten U.S. victories in twenty years.

1986: DRAMA AND TREACHERY

You can't imagine a more dramatic location for the most historic day in American cycling. At 7,916 feet above sea level, the Col de Granon remains the highest-ever stage finish at the Tour de France. The bleak, bare summit is reached on a one-way, 11km military road that pitches steeply out of the Durance valley and reveals stunning views over the snowbound Pelvoux Massif, whose jagged peaks soar to over 13,000 feet. It was here on July 20, 1986, that Greg LeMond pulled on the Tour's yellow jersey for the first time—and would bring it home to Paris as the first non-European winner of the world's toughest sports event.

Standing in the early-evening sunshine of that remote mountaintop surrounded by media hounds, a joyous LeMond, just 25, proclaimed, "I feel very proud to be the first American to wear the yellow jersey." The scene around him encapsulated the ruggedness of that Tour. Urs Zimmermann, the tall, blond

Swiss champion with whom LeMond had ridden up the final climb, spent long minutes straddled over his bike before he found the breath to speak. American Andy Hampsten, seventh in the stage, was sitting on the gravel shoulder a few yards from Zimmermann in a similar state of sublime exhaustion. Scottish climber Robert Millar was doubled over his handlebars, clinging to a metal barrier, spitting up phlegm before being helped out of his sweat-drenched polka-dot climber's jersey by his *soigneur*. And a French rider, Joël Pelier, who reached the mountaintop half an hour after LeMond, collapsed on the road and was carried to an ambulance with an oxygen mask over his mouth, after forcing his body too far for too long in the thin air.

A more celebrated Frenchman—race leader, defending champion, and five-time Tour winner Bernard Hinault—crossed the line in 13th place, alongside Millar, 3:21 behind LeMond. With a scowl on his sun-blackened face and six hours' worth of sweat staining his yellow jersey, Hinault told a bevy of French reporters, "It was a strained [knee] muscle . . . I raced too hard and put too much pressure on it."

The injury was superficial, but given the extraordinary effort Hinault made to conquer the *maillot jaune*, his pain was much deeper. How come Hinault was wearing the yellow jersey that day? That wasn't supposed to happen.

In Paris 12 months earlier, after winning a fifth Tour by 1:42 over La Vie Claire teammate LeMond, he said to the young American, "In '86, the Tour is for you, Greg. I'll be there to help you." Hinault envisioned he would "have some fun" in his final Tour and pass on his legacy to LeMond. But later, to French journalists, Hinault qualified his promises. He would help LeMond "but only if he shows that he is worthy of the yellow jersey."

This proved to be a double-edged sword. The veteran Frenchman, secretly wanting to be the first man to win six Tours, attacked at every opportunity to see how LeMond would react.

The first of these attacks came in the sixth stage, a mostly flat run through Normandy, where Hinault jumped clear after an intermediate sprint and was joined by ten others, including archrival Stephen Roche and two of the Irishman's

Carrera teammates. Incredibly, Hinault agreed to work with the enemy, and it led to a furious 90-minute pursuit by a ten-man group led by two-time Tour winner Laurent Fignon and his Système U teammate Charly Mottet—with LeMond and Canadian teammate Steve Bauer along for the ride. If Fignon hadn't sparked that chase, Hinault could have ridden away with the yellow jersey.

Hinault did just that a week later when he went on the rampage in a torrid, six-hour stage through the Pyrénées between Bayonne and Pau. Midway through the stage, when Hinault was one of six La Vie Claire riders in a 23-man front group, Frenchman Jean-François Bernard surged for the time bonus at an intermediate sprint. Hinault, his leader, was right on his wheel. Only one rider joined them: Spanish climber Pedro Delgado.

LeMond, when asked what he would have done if he had been on another team, said, "I would have never let him go. That's why I could never understand the attitude of Zimmermann and Millar. How could they let Hinault just walk away like that? I was peeing in my pants that they were just sitting there."

Bernard rode as hard as he could before Delgado and Hinault charged clear to arrive in Pau 4:37 ahead of third-place LeMond, while Roche finished almost 20 minutes back, and Fignon pulled out. Asked what he felt about conceding five minutes to his teammate, LeMond shrugged his shoulders and said, "That's life. I guess I'm going to finish second in the Tour de France again."

Incredibly, Hinault attacked again the next day, solo this time! He left a front group of 17 riders on the descent of stage 13's highest peak, the Col du Tourmalet, and within 40km his lead was almost three minutes. LeMond was again fuming. "If [Hinault] had gone all the way to the finish," the American said, "he would have been eight minutes in the lead. And that would have been it."

But going up the day's next-to-last climb, the Peyresourde, the red-faced race leader visibly wilted. Hinault was passed on the early slopes of the climb to the mountaintop finish of Superbagnères. With Hampsten's help, LeMond won the stage and came within 40 seconds of taking the lead from Hinault.

Hinault's belligerence finally subsided. Three days later, though, as the Tour headed toward the Alps, Hinault was again off the front, "having fun." This time, he attacked on a short climb midway into a fearfully long stage—almost eight hours in the saddle—between Nîmes and Gap. The problem was not so much that Hinault attacked, but he took the dangerous Zimmermann with him.

"I felt like pulling out of the race," said LeMond. "I think that everything Hinault has done in this race has been for himself, not for me." This time, Millar's Panasonic team eventually reeled in Hinault and Zimmermann. "[Greg] came at me very angrily," Hinault said. "I told him to calm himself . . . to steady his nerves."

Nervous or not, LeMond rode brilliantly the next two days, first to take over the lead from Hinault on the Col de Granon, and then to ride with a revived Hinault on an epic two-man breakaway to L'Alpe d'Huez. Despite their stormy relationship, the two rode together for 80km to arrive at the Alpe a massive 5:15 ahead of Zimmermann in third place.

At Hinault's request, the two linked hands as they cruised across the line in what would become the enduring (if fictitious) image of that 1986 Tour. LeMond later confided, "I agreed to [linking hands] because I felt I'd won the Tour and I didn't really care if he won the stage. There had been a lot of tension between us and I felt that it would clear everything up. [But] immediately after the finish [the live TV show host] Jacques Chancel said to Hinault, 'Well, that means you still might attack him?' And Hinault said, 'Possibly. It's not over until the time trial.' The whole pressure started again."

The French media and public still thought that Hinault could pull back his deficit of more than two minutes in the final 58km time trial at St. Étienne. A conspiracy seemed to be brewing, hatched up by the "French" faction of La Vie Claire.

In an interview with the late freelance writer Matthew Mantell in 1995, LeMond's wife, Kathy, revealed, "[Race director] Jacques Goddet came up to Greg the night before the final time trial and said, 'I'll try to protect you in the race tomorrow. I know Hinault has something planned for you; be careful.' And Greg's bike was messed with . . . [it] wasn't working right. That's why he went down." Indeed, a few minutes after LeMond fell heavily on a sharp turn, he was forced to stop. "I thought everything was all right," he said, "but my front brake was hanging on the wheel." Was it sabotage?

Maybe LeMond was overreacting, but clearly Hinault's psychological warfare had worked. The American still came second in the time trial, 25 seconds slower than his boss. He then put time into Hinault in a stage to the Puy de Dôme summit and finished the Tour in Paris the overall winner by 3:10.

It took eight decades before an American started the Tour de France for the first time, but five years after Jonathan Boyer toed the line, the Tour had its first American winner. LeMond was deprived of his chance of becoming a five-time champion by his 1987 hunting accident, but he returned to score two more victories. A decade later, Armstrong became the second U.S. Tour winner and began his incredible seven-chapter series.

Now three more Americans dreamed of standing on the podium in Paris wearing the yellow jersey. This first post-Armstrong Tour was shaping up to be just as shocking, gripping, and thrilling as the memorable races recounted here. They seem to come along once a decade. The Tour seemed to be on the brink of another wild ride.

CHAPTER 3

Doping Nightmare Returns

Police investigations threaten to ensnare the Tour's hopefuls.

When asked to comment on the doping situation in cycling, a former Tour de France winner turned professional team manager said, "This is unacceptable. The riders don't realize that they're headed toward putting the future of their profession in jeopardy."

No, those words didn't come from CSC team boss Bjarne Riis in 2006; they came from Mercier-BP team manager Antonin Magne in 1966. The Frenchman, who won the Tour in 1931 and 1934, was speaking at the Tour de France the day the peloton protested the introduction of doping controls to cycling.

The protest took place shortly after the Bordeaux start of stage 9 in the village of La House. The 122 riders came to a halt, walked slowly with their bikes for a hundred meters, and then stood and voiced their concerns to race organizers about the drug tests carried out by French police the night before. The police, operating under a newly introduced federal law designed to crack down on doping in sports, had visited with several teams in their hotel rooms and had taken urine samples. The first rider tested was French star Raymond Poulidor, the leader of Magne's Mercier team.

Leading the protest the next day was Poulidor's perennial rival, Jacques Anquetil, who was riding his final Tour. All the riders joined with him, some reluctantly. An unnamed rider told the local *Sud-Ouest* newspaper, "We are protesting against the medical controls, which are an intolerable imposition. Why can't they also test the artists, doctors, and students who dope themselves to stay awake at night?"

In the 40 years since the protest at La House, professional cyclists have gradually accepted antidoping controls, but many have tried to keep one step ahead of the testers. With time, the varieties of drugs became more sophisticated: amphetamines in the 1960s and 1970s, steroids in the 1980s, and, perhaps the most frightening, EPO in the 1990s. EPO is a pharmaceutical form of recombinant erythropoietin, a naturally occurring protein produced by the kidney that stimulates the bone marrow to produce red blood cells.

EPO was designed to boost the red blood cell count of those suffering from anemia, particularly cancer patients. But almost as soon as the wonder drug came on the market at the end of the 1980s, athletes began to experiment with it. There were unconfirmed reports of athletes dying in their sleep due to the blood-thickening result of overdosing on EPO. But riders said it increased their power output by as much as 20 percent. Even so, the extent of its use (and the use of other sophisticated drugs) in cycling wasn't fully realized until the Festina team scandal at the 1998 Tour.

That affair, triggered on the Belgium-France border by a seemingly routine police inspection of a team car driven by Festina *soigneur* Willy Voet, showed the extent of cycling's long-rumored drug problem. The police discovered more than 400 vials of EPO, human growth hormone, testosterone, and an assortment of other drugs—destined for the Festina team at the start of the Tour in Dublin, Ireland—launching a slew of arrests, confessions, and lengthy investigations.

The French police brought the scandal to light, in the process almost triggering the demise of the 1998 Tour. After the Festina team director and doctor were jailed and confessed to systematic doping, the Tour organizers threw the whole team out of the race. Festina's nine riders were then asked to report to police for questioning. Their harsh treatment—strip-searched and detained in jail overnight—caused the peloton to stage a sit-down strike. After police detained riders from other teams and a Spanish team doctor, a dramatic rider protest caused one stage to be canceled, while six teams walked out in protest. Only 96 of the 189 starters finished the race.

The French police did more in a single three-week period to reveal the extent of doping in cycling than did years of testing, controls, and public pronouncements from the sport's governing authority, the Union Cycliste Internationale. The investigation into what became known as the Festina Affair would continue for more than a year and marked the beginning of a concerted effort by cycling to clean up the image of the sport. It eventually led to the establishment of an independent drug-testing authority, World Anti-Doping Agency (WADA).

OPERACIÓN PUERTO

As the riders who dreamed of winning the 2006 Tour de France were preparing for the new season at their January training camps, the Unidad Central Operativa (UCO), a special unit of Spain's Guardia Civil police force, started an undercover investigation into an alleged doping ring. The investigation was prompted by a positive doping offense for EPO, exacted on the 2005 Vuelta a España winner Roberto Heras. But that was only the most recent of a series of developments over a two-year period.

First, in March 2004, came a tell-all newspaper story penned by Jesús Manzano, a member of the Spanish team Kelme-Comunidad Valenciana from 2001 to 2003. He claimed that he was forced to engage in blood doping supplemented by a mix of banned drugs, under the team doctor's supervision. The Spanish cycling federation did not act on his claims, but elections that spring brought a socialist government to power in Spain. The new sports minister, Jaime Lissavetsky, said he would clamp down on doping in sport and started work on an antidoping law.

At the same time in France, police were uncovering a drug-trafficking ring centered on the Cofidis team. One of the victims of this operation was Britain's best Tour de France rider of recent years, David Millar. Just before the 2004 Tour, police raided his apartment near Biarritz and discovered empty EPO vials. Millar admitted that he had used EPO on three occasions, saying the drug was supplied by a Spanish *soigneur* who had worked for the Euskaltel-Euskadi team. The Scottish rider was stripped of his 2003 world time trial championship and a stage win at the Vuelta a España, and he was suspended from cycling for two years.

Meanwhile, the Guardia Civil conducted two sting operations. The first, in June 2004, code-named Gamma, included 147 arrests but seized few doping products. The second, a year later, code-named Mamut, saw 70 arrests, and this time millions of doses of doping products, mainly steroids and hormones destined for clandestine sale throughout Europe, were seized from six illegal laboratories in Barcelona. No cyclists were arrested, but the intent of the new Spanish regime was clear: zero tolerance for doping in sport.

With the information gathered from Manzano and similar tip-offs from the UCI, the Guardia Civil focused a new investigation on Eufemiano Fuentes, a sports doctor with a less than stellar reputation. A scion of a wealthy family from Spain's Canary Islands and a reputed daredevil, Fuentes had been linked to doping scandals in cycling, boxing, and track and field events during his controversial career. In the 1980s, he was the official doctor for the Spanish national athletics foundation but was forced out when his wife, hurdler Christina Perez, tested positive in 1987. Dr. Fuentes went on to serve as team doctor for ONCE, which was implicated in the investigations stemming from the Festina Affair at the 1998 Tour. He worked for Manzano's former team, Kelme-Valenciana, from September 2003 to February 2005.

Working undercover, the UCO began tapping phone calls and placed surveillance cameras outside the Madrid offices of Fuentes—now a practicing gynecologist—and José Luis Merino Batres, a hematologist who appeared to be working with Fuentes. Police would later reveal that major athletes from a variety of sports were videotaped entering their respective offices. Something even more shocking was caught on camera that even the police could barely believe they were watching.

On May 23, 2006, a camera on the chic Calle Zurbano in downtown Madrid caught Fuentes and Batres walking into at a bar down the street from their offices. Fuentes was carrying an insulated bag. Moments later, Manolo Sáiz, the rotund team manager of Liberty Seguros-Würth (formerly ONCE), showed up at the same bar with a briefcase in hand. According to police reports, Sáiz was then videotaped carrying out the insulated bag.

As the three men walked down the street toward the private testing laboratory run by Batres, the police swooped in, took them into custody, and *Operación Puerto* was born. The immediate haul looked bad. The briefcase Sáiz carried into the bar was found to contain almost $80,000 in euros and Swiss francs. The insulated bag he left with was said to be filled with doping products.

Police also searched Batres's Madrid clinic and found 200 pouches of blood and plasma, as well as codes to identify the owners of the bags' contents. Neither the codes nor the list of names were immediately released, but the Guardia Civil's Joan Mesquida said, "Major names are likely to become known."

> AS THE THREE MEN WALKED DOWN THE STREET TOWARD THE PRIVATE TESTING LABORATORY RUN BY BATRES, THE POLICE SWOOPED IN, TOOK THEM INTO CUSTODY, AND *OPERACIÓN PUERTO* WAS BORN.

Police searched six other properties, including two apartments owned by Fuentes, where he allegedly worked with athletes. Police said they found banned doping products, including EPO, steroids, human growth hormone, blood transfusion machines, and centrifuges to separate plasma from valued red blood cells. Besides Sáiz, Batres, and Fuentes, two others were taken in for questioning on charges of drug trafficking and endangering public health: the Comunidad Valenciana team's assistant directeur sportif Ignacio Labarta, and ex-mountain bike pro Alberto Leon, who was said to be working for Fuentes as a gofer.

THE FALLOUT

Sáiz was held in jail overnight and was released after apparently collapsing in front of a judge the next day. Labarta and Leon were also released after questioning, but Fuentes and Merino Batres each had to deposit bail money of more than $100,000.

Fuentes didn't seem overly concerned. He told the Spanish daily *El País*, "The blood was for private analysis. It was dirty blood, old blood, to throw away. And most of the medicines are old and worthless. I am not involved in blood doping."

The Fuentes-Batres operation was said to center around autologous blood transfusions, whereby athletes use their own treated blood instead of another person's, a method that was banned after some members of the U.S. national cycling team used it at the 1984 Olympics. According to police sources quoted in the Spanish press, Fuentes and Batres worked in tandem with top athletes to "cleanse and prepare" their blood that would later be transfused ahead of competitions to avoid antidoping tests. Leon was said to work as a mule between clients, who reportedly would pay up to $80,000 to be "treated" by the doctors. The practice of autologous transfusions is favored by dopers in light of antidoping controls that can detect homologous transfusions—the method for which Phonak team riders Tyler Hamilton and Santiago Perez were suspended for two years after the 2004 Vuelta.

Although many things remained unclear after a week of scandalous headlines in Spain, one thing was certain: This was just the beginning. The timing was especially bad for Sáiz. In Italy, his team was entering the difficult final week of the Giro d'Italia, while other riders were preparing for a Tour de France training camp in the Pyrénées.

There were calls to ban Sáiz's Liberty Seguros team and Labarta's Comunidad Valenciana formation from the upcoming Tour de France. Labarta left his team under pressure while the UCI and the World Anti-Doping Agency promised full support of the investigation.

For title sponsor Liberty Seguros, the images of coded bags of blood and Sáiz being hauled away by police were too much to stomach. The parent company, Liberty Mutual of Boston, canceled its ProTour team sponsorship contract, which was believed to be worth $8.5 million annually. "We stayed with the team through the [Roberto] Heras [EPO] case and we reached a new agreement with the team with an emphasis on zero tolerance of doping," said the team's Spanish liaison Fabio Selvig. "We're an insurance company. We have to have people believe us."

The team's secondary sponsor, Würth of Germany, did agree to honor its contract for the time being. Sáiz quickly found a new lead sponsor to take over his team. Team leader and Tour de France contender Alexander Vinokourov hails from Kazakhstan, where a consortium of five of the country's largest companies took over as title sponsor. The team planned to ride the Tour under the name Astaná-Würth; Astaná is the name of the new Kazakh capital.

Spanish police promised a thorough investigation and vowed to uncover the names hidden in the coded messages, even if it meant DNA testing. The media went into overdrive and immediately began leaking names allegedly seen in police videos or heard in recorded phone conversations. As quickly as the names hit the Web, they were followed by denials by riders of any contact with Fuentes or Batres.

The T-Mobile team said it "had nothing to worry about" after its Spanish rider Oscar Sevilla was linked to Fuentes, and Sevilla started the Dauphiné Libéré on June 4 as planned. Phonak, however, took a sterner approach; it benched Colombian star Santiago Botero and Spanish rider José Enrique Gutiérrez until their relationship with Fuentes could be clarified.

One unexpected reaction came from the elusive Italian sports doctor Luigi Cecchini, who broke a decade-long silence after reports in the Italian media linked him to Fuentes. Cecchini, whose client list included Tour contenders Jan Ullrich and Ivan Basso, had refused to speak to the media since the late 1990s after an investigation into his operation by Italian authorities stalled without any findings.

"I am sick of my name being used every time someone talks of doping," Cecchini told the Italian daily *Il Giornale*. "I have never collaborated with Fuentes. This is a public execution that I cannot accept."

It seemed unlikely that the "Puerto Five" would face jail time. Unlike France and Italy, Spain had no antidoping law on the books. Sport minister Lissavetsky's bill, which would mandate two- to six-year jail terms for those implicated in sports doping, wasn't expected to be signed into law until late 2006. Fuentes and Batres faced what appeared to be lesser charges of "endangering the public health." They also might have endangered the existence of the Tour de France.

CHAPTER 4

Countdown to the Tour

Landis and the other favorites look strong heading into July.

The best thing to do is just keep on smiling and pretend you're okay, even if you're not. That goes not just for bad weather, but for anytime you're suffering. Sometimes it helps if you smile, even when it hurts."

That was Floyd Landis talking as he looked out at a thunderstorm from a hotel in Chattanooga, Tennessee, before a mountain stage of the 2006 Tour de Georgia. The following day, the 30-year-old American would employ his own brand of reverse psychology on Brasstown Bald Mountain, his answer to repeated attacks from the defending champion, Tom Danielson of Discovery Channel. Holding strong to the summit, the Phonak team leader sealed his third stage race victory of 2006.

"So far this year has been almost flawless," Landis said of his overall wins at the Tour of California, Paris-Nice and, a few days later, the Tour de Georgia. With the exception of the late-March Critérium International, where he crashed out of the lead group on the first stage and later abandoned, Landis won every race he started. "After the first two wins, I think the spring was a success," he said. "Everything I get now is a bonus."

There's no question that the spring of 2006 saw the emergence of a new and improved Landis. He wasn't just stronger, he was more confident. "I think if I hadn't been in the shape I am in now, or had the results I have now, I probably would have wanted to race more," Landis said of his change of plans to sit out the Giro d'Italia. "But I have all the confidence I need with everything I've done so far, so I'd rather not risk anything at all for the Giro."

Besides new confidence, there were other reasons why Landis had developed into one of the sport's best all-around riders. Already known as a top time trialist—he finished sixth in both time trials at the 2005 Tour—Landis returned to the wind tunnel in February and refined his unusual raised-forearm, praying mantis position. He said his improved time trialing held no secrets.

"It's all about training in that position," Landis said. "For some guys, the time-trial position is not so different than their road position, and the muscles are the same. For me, I sit in a completely different position, so I have to train those muscles. If I don't ride the bike, I don't do well. I have to ride it a couple of times a week, just getting used to the position. I work on all aspects, the climbs, the descents, the flats, so that I feel confident on any type of course."

His practice paid off. Landis won the windy time trial at the Tour of California by 26 seconds over his good friend and Girona, Spain, housemate Dave Zabriskie (CSC), and he won again in Georgia, four seconds ahead of Danielson.

Landis was also showing improved climbing ability. Neither the Tour of California nor Paris-Nice offered summit finishes, but Landis showed his climber's cards on the snow-covered Col de la Croix de Chaubouret at Paris-Nice, where he dropped the main GC contenders, Samuel Sanchez, Fränk Schleck, and José Luis Rubiera, for a minute.

"Just like time trialing, if you want to be a good climber, you've got to work on your climbing," said Landis, who was particularly pleased with his climb up Brasstown, a steep and varying 5km pitch. In 2005 he lost one minute—and the race lead—to Danielson atop the Georgia peak. A year later, the two Americans again squared off for the overall win, and the Discovery Channel rider couldn't shake a determined Landis. "Steep, not so constant climbs were a weakness of mine before," Landis said, "but I've worked on it."

Hard work made the biggest difference in Landis's results, he said, an assertion that his wife Amber Basile seconded. "Over the years he's changed a few things, and obviously it's working this year," she said at the final podium celebration in Georgia. "He's been training a lot. And each race he wins, he can't help but get more confident. He deserves it. He works hard for it."

Talking about the 2006 Tour, Landis shifted back into his game face. Asked if he'd like to be viewed as a favorite, Landis answered tersely. "I don't care," he said. "The outcome is all that matters to me. The goal is to win the Tour. I'm not going there to race for fifth. The only thing that matters is winning."

One of Landis's teammates, Belgian Axel Merckx, backed up his leader. After Landis took the race lead at Paris-Nice, Merckx told Belgian newspaper *Het Laatste Nieuws,* "Floyd can win the Tour. He is really blooming now he's reached 30. He's got all the qualities [to win the Tour]: he's a strong time trialist, a decent climber, and he's not afraid."

Between April's Tour de Georgia and June's Dauphiné Libéré, Landis planned to take a rest, return to training, and ride some of the Tour's critical climbs in the Pyrénées, an hour and a half from his adopted home in Spain. He started the Dauphiné as if he wanted to win that race too, by placing second to Zabriskie in the critical time trial. His newfound confidence went with him to the next day's stage up the mighty Mont Ventoux, said to be the toughest climb in France.

Heading to the base of the mountain, Landis's Phonak team massed at the front of the peloton to close a gap on a nine-man breakaway—and hopefully set up Landis for a counterattack. He seemed ready to pick up where he left off at the Tour de Georgia, but once Landis reached the Ventoux's first steep pitches it became obvious he didn't have the climbing legs he desired.

"We were all riding for Floyd, but then he realized he just wasn't feeling that great. It was his first race back in a while, so he waved us off," said Phonak's Canadian, Ryder Hesjedal.

Landis waved off the rest of the weeklong race too, content to take note of climbs that he would have to ride at the Tour a month later. He was particularly interested in the stage finish at La Toussuire, a climb included in the Tour for the first time. He didn't extend his list of 2006 victories; clearly Landis would have liked to have cut the preamble and started the Tour de France right away.

LEIPHEIMER: RIGHT ON TRACK

When Levi Leipheimer began his 2006 season by decisively winning the uphill prologue at the Tour of California in San Francisco, the Gerolsteiner team leader seemed likely to blaze through the new American event—and perhaps the rest of the season. Newly confident after his successful 2005 campaign and feeling the benefits of a full year under a new coach, Leipheimer was hot. However, it was Landis who took the overall California win and grabbed the springtime headlines by winning Paris-Nice and the Tour de Georgia.

After finishing the California race in sixth, Leipheimer delayed his return to Europe because of a stomach bug. The unplanned rest derailed his plans to test himself at the time trial in Tirreno-Adriatico. Instead, the cold, wet weather did nothing to improve his form and he finished the race as training. Ditto with the following week's Coppi and Bartali Week in Italy, where more bad weather forced Leipheimer to pull out on the second day.

He returned home to Santa Rosa to take a break, initially with the understanding that he would be racing at the Tour de Georgia. "We were invited to Georgia, of course," Leipheimer said, "but we didn't have enough riders to do all the races, one of them being the Rheinland-Pfalz tour [which is in Gerolsteiner's backyard]."

With no April races scheduled, Leipheimer spent the month training under his California-based coach, Dr. Massimo Testa. Riding in three local races, he measured his performance with a power meter aboard his bike. After placing eighth at the Sea Otter Classic circuit race, Leipheimer won the Copperopolis and Wente Vineyards road races, each time making solo breaks to finish minutes ahead of the competition.

"I would really have liked to do Georgia, but it's not going to affect my training for the Tour," Leipheimer said in early May before taking part in Spain's Tour of Catalonia. "I am feeling good, about the same level as last year, and I am looking forward to Catalunya."

He used that race as preparation for the Dauphiné, where he was even stronger than he had been a year earlier. After placing third in the time trial behind

Zabriskie and Landis, Leipheimer took control of the race on Mont Ventoux, after Landis realized his form wasn't as good as he'd hoped.

Leipheimer took over the pacemaking halfway up the 22km climb, where the road pushes clear from the pines onto the lunar-like white limestone expanses of the Ventoux's upper, windswept reaches. In the last 5km to the summit, Leipheimer piled on the pressure, with Rabobank's Denis Menchov and AG2R's Christophe Moreau riding his vapors. Realizing he wasn't going to get any help from his companions, Leipheimer didn't hesitate for a moment. He churned his pedals with deadly, high-cadence effect and simply outspun his rivals.

"I didn't really attack in this race," Leipheimer said. "I didn't have to on the Ventoux. I was the best placed from the time trial and I did a big effort to increase that gap to the others. I wished it was not so windy and it was steeper near the end because I felt like I could have gone alone, but I was only thinking about the yellow jersey."

Even though Menchov sprinted to the stage win from Moreau, Leipheimer duly took the race lead. His Gerolsteiner troops then rose to the occasion in three gripping stages across the Alps to protect his flanks while their American leader calmly marked the key moves to secure a 1:48 winning margin on Moreau.

The Montana native joined elite company, becoming just the fourth U.S. rider to win the Dauphiné after Greg LeMond (1983), Tyler Hamilton (2000), and Lance Armstrong (2002 and 2003). "When I first got into cycling, LeMond was winning the Tour de France and I always heard about the Dauphiné," he said. "It's one of the most beautiful races on the calendar. Any rider would be proud to win it." Armstrong and LeMond, of course, went on to win the Tour. Leipheimer was now planning to join them.

BASSO: ONE DOWN, THE TOUR COMING UP

The emblematic image of the 2006 Giro d'Italia was of a radiant Ivan Basso rolling across the finish line in the grueling 211km stage 20 after fighting his way over the legendary Gavia and Mortirolo passes. Basso fended off attacks by Gilberto Simoni and then joyfully pulled a snapshot of his baby son, Santiago, from the rear pocket of his pink jersey. He hoisted it above his head and showed it to the world.

Basso's celebration in Aprica, 24 hours before the three-week race finished in Milan, confirmed his good-guy reputation as a team player and smiling, polite *capo*. The son of a butcher and a housewife whose life was cut short by cancer, the hardworking Basso made his family and nation proud with a classy win. He seemed the perfect Italian son.

"I don't feel like I did anything spectacular or extraordinary in this Giro," said the CSC team leader. "I was just steady in every stage that counted. I never had a bad day and never gave up any time."

There was talk of a "Basso era" when the world finally got a glimpse of a tougher rider lurking behind the 28-year-old Italian's almond brown eyes and sparkling smile. "I've been working very hard to reach this point and I don't like when they call me an extraterrestrial," Basso said, referring to a remark by Simoni after Basso rode away from him to win the Aprica stage. "People have to remember that I was the only rider to stay with Armstrong in the Tour and I've twice finished on the Tour podium. These results have come with hard work."

Basso did the hard work but it was team manager Riis who polished him into a lethal riding machine that ripped the 2006 Giro to shreds. "Ivan is the winner because he worked hard for it," Riis said. "I've seen the sacrifices he's made. He's become a leader of this team and it's so good to see a new rider come up and take command like this."

"IVAN IS THE WINNER BECAUSE HE WORKED HARD FOR IT," RIIS SAID. "I'VE SEEN THE SACRIFICES HE'S MADE. HE'S BECOME A LEADER OF THIS TEAM AND IT'S SO GOOD TO SEE A NEW RIDER COME UP AND TAKE COMMAND LIKE THIS."

The work to transform Basso began on the bike. Riis supervised his rider's training program and motor-paced him in marathon seven-hour training rides in Tuscany. Using a power meter and intense workout programs, Basso had developed the Armstrong-esque high-cadence pedal stroke that he used with merciless efficiency in the Giro's climbs.

Basso didn't "attack" in this Giro, he simply rode away from everyone else. "Basso has developed climbing skills that are above even the climbing specialists," said Lampre-Fondital team manager Giuseppe Saronni, a former winner of the Giro. "No one could stay with him except Simoni in the final week. Everyone else was left behind."

Riis concurred. "Ivan sometimes is too nice," he said after Basso buried Simoni on the climb to Aprica. "I'm happy today that he wasn't too nice. He demonstrated that he was the strongest in this race. He shouldn't give away a victory."

It was that killer instinct that Basso would need in his attempt to become the first rider to do the Giro-Tour double since his compatriot Marco Pantani in 1998.

ULLRICH: ON THE ASCENDANCY

When the peloton took a hard right turn onto the steepest ramps of the Passo San Pellegrino with 9km to go in stage 19 of the Giro, Jan Ullrich cut under the ropes and slipped into a waiting team car, marking a quiet exit to what he called a three-week training camp. Ullrich and Basso were on two different trajectories in Italy. Basso came to win the Giro. Ullrich came to Italy to win the Tour de France. "I won a stage and I am leaving the race stronger," Ullrich said. "I was losing less time to Basso in each climb, so I know I will be ready for the Tour."

If there was any tension between Ullrich and Basso, it was not overt. In fact, they rarely saw each other during the Giro. The 32-year-old German was oblivious to the contorted faces of the riders trying to stay glued to Basso's back wheel. Instead, the close-cropped Ullrich slipped into an anonymous spot in the pack to ride up the Giro's most demanding climbs with the singular goal of getting stronger.

He lost more than 16 minutes to Basso on the Passo di Lanciano in stage 8, but whittled that difference down to 5:27 up Monte Bondone on stage 16. In Ullrich's mind, that was important progress. "I lost a month [of the season] with my [knee] injury, so I wanted to get stronger. My legs still have a mild imbalance, which creates some back pain, but it's nothing a little massage can't cure," he said. "I had a very good winter training, so I am able to come away from the Giro stronger than ever."

Ullrich got a reassuring confidence boost with his first career Giro stage win when he beat Basso by 28 seconds in the flat 50km Pontedera time trial, proving that despite Basso's improvements against the clock, Ullrich was still superior— even when not at full strength.

Doubts about his readiness for the Tour had plagued Ullrich ever since he became the first German winner in 1997. Despite not starting his season until late April because of the knee injury, Ullrich seemed assured and ready to face the first Tour in the post-Armstrong era. "I see Basso at a Tour level here, but he will have a harder time at the Tour," Ullrich said. "The level is much higher at the Tour than the Giro. Now everyone says Basso is the favorite for the Tour. That's fine with me."

After a short break Ullrich started June's Tour of Switzerland to sharpen his fitness for the Tour. His ascendant form was sharp enough that he matched the climbers in the Swiss Alps and finished them off by winning the final day's time trial to take the overall victory.

Despite his considerable time-trialing skills, Ullrich said that it was tough to win because his rear disc wheel was buffeted by heavy winds in the rainstorm he had to battle as he headed into Bern, the Swiss capital. "I thought if I fall here I risk the Tour," he said. "It wasn't worth risking the Tour de France for the Tour de Suisse."

Time trials would be crucial at the Tour de France, and for that reason Ullrich said that after a few days of rest, he would get behind his coach's motorcycle to re-fine his position. "I will do a week behind the motorbike to become more fluid," he said. "I don't really have much work to do in the mountains as we did 22,000 meters of climbing here, so I will just work on my suppleness.

"I am not tired at all, so there is still every chance to improve," he continued. "A bit of rest will help my body get stronger after this race. The goal here was to get the perfect preparation for the Tour. I feel I can still improve and that the overall win in the Tour de France is possible.

"I also felt ready in 2004," Ullrich added, referring to the last time he won the Tour de Suisse on his way to France. "But I caught a flu. With such a difficult race, if you are sick you are not able to get the performance that you want. As a result, I will pay a lot of attention to my health between now and the Tour. That also means I need to relax my head and stay calm."

EVANS: UNDER THE RADAR

In the accelerating buildup to the Tour de France, the mainstream media focused on heavy hitters Basso and Ullrich as the prerace favorites, while minor play was given to challengers Alexander Vinokourov, Alejandro Valverde, Landis, Hincapie, and Leipheimer. Virtually ignored in all the razzmatazz—except perhaps in Australia—was Davitamon-Lotto's Cadel Evans. Some oddsmakers even put riders like Denis Menchov and Iban Mayo above Evans in the hierarchy.

Like a Stealth bomber, the quiet Aussie had slipped below the radar in the Tour prognostication stakes, despite the excellent progress he'd made since finishing eighth in his debut Tour. Analyzing his race, Evans said he needed to improve his time trialing. "Compared with Armstrong and Basso, I'm losing a lot of time, for sure. Time trialing is so vital in the Tour. So whatever you can gain now can convert into something even bigger in the Tour."

Evans's overall victory at the late-April Tour de Romandie, where he blitzed the final time trial on a hilly course in Lausanne, showed how much he had improved. The lightly built Aussie's time for the 20.4km loop was 26:19, only two seconds outside the course record set by Olympic time trial champion Tyler Hamilton in 2003. Another gauge on Evans's performance was the 62-second margin by which he beat Tour contender Valverde.

His success in Romandie was a huge relief for Evans, since he suffered from severe headaches and loss of vision in one eye at the preceding Belgian classics, Liège-Bastogne-Liège and Flèche Wallonne—races where he had planned to make his early-season peak. The health problem, whatever it was, didn't return.

Romandie was also a collective success for the Davitamon-Lotto team, which took stage wins for sprinter Robbie McEwen and all-rounder Chris Horner. The team accomplished all that while working toward Evans's final victory, demonstrating how Davitamon might operate at the Tour de France: focus on early stage wins by McEwen and then help Evans shoot for the overall in the mountains.

Those tactics were only partially successful at the 2005 Tour, when McEwen took three stage wins and Evans attained his goal of finishing top ten. But the efforts made by the two leaders' teammates in the first half of the race left them weakened later on. "Last year, as soon as the road went up I was on my own," Evans said. "That was not because of the riders, but more so because of the work they had done before we got to the mountains."

Besides Horner, Belgian rider Mario Aerts was assigned to help Evans in the mountains. Aerts and Evans have a good rapport, and in May they trained together for a week, scouting the Pyrenean and Alpine stages of this year's Tour.

Despite limited grand tour experience, Evans said, "My strength is my consistency over a three-week race." His consistency is a solid way of getting another top-ten finish, or even a top five, but would he take major risks for a crack at the yellow jersey? "I don't know," Evans replied. "I took some risks at the [2002] Giro d'Italia to try to win it, and then I had a reputation for a few years for cracking in the big tours. You can go for a sure thing—a fifth or third or something. Or you can try to go for the win, and you might end up 15th overall."

Whether he would choose consistency or risk taking, Evans looked sure to give the oddsmakers some red faces in July.

HINCAPIE: SHOULDER REHAB DELAYS TOUR PREP

When most people rip their collarbone clean off their shoulder, they are treated with surgery and months of slow recovery. Most people, however, aren't George Hincapie, who remained hell-bent on racing the Tour after separating his shoulder in a cobblestone crash at Paris-Roubaix in April.

Hincapie suffered a stage three acromial cromicular separation, meaning all three areas of ligament that connected his right collarbone to his shoulder blade had been completely torn. This caused his shoulder to droop and the outer tip of his collarbone to poke noticeably skyward.

The Discovery Channel rider opted to decline the initial prognosis of surgery in favor of intensive physical therapy so he could immediately begin training for the Tour. "In Europe they said surgery right away," said Hincapie, who flew back to the States after the crash. "But in the U.S. the doctors said that if I wanted to ride the Tour, no surgery. Surgery would have required six to eight weeks of no pressure on the shoulder. That, I didn't have."

Instead, three days after his crash, Hincapie was riding outdoors, his injured arm in a sling. The gamble paid off. In early June, he finished tenth overall at the Dauphiné Libéré, with a solid fourth-place time trial and some impressive climbing form.

Hincapie forced his body to rapidly adapt to its new configuration under the guidance of Dr. Steve Singleton of Stedman Hawkins Clinic, a high-end sports medicine facility, and physical therapist Sean McEnroe of Pivital Therapy. After six years of supporting Lance Armstrong, the lanky American had to alter his training and mental focus in 2006 to ride for himself at the Tour. He could always go under the knife later.

"For this particular injury, there is not a good way of reconnecting ligaments," Dr. Singleton said. "You can't just make an incision and then sew these ligament tears together. That tends to fail because the stresses across the collarbone and this joint are tremendous." So the men decided to tape the joint in place and work to strengthen the surrounding muscles.

For injuries like Hincapie's, McEnroe first secures the arm in a sling to prevent further damage. That done, Hincapie started working out two days after the crash. "The trick was that we had one month to get him ready for training camp in Spain," McEnroe said. "Typically, I would put someone in a sling and tell them not to do a whole lot of movement for a few weeks. With him, we didn't have that. He had to rest hard, then work hard on therapy. We took him out of the sling for two sessions a day. His body heals a lot faster than many would. The improvement he'd make in three days most people wouldn't make in two weeks."

After a month, Hincapie left with a full range of motion and equally strong arms. "Some of the muscles around my shoulder still hurt, but it's getting better,"

Hincapie said. "The only time I really notice the pain is when I lean over on it or lay on it at night."

After the Dauphiné, McEnroe said Hincapie's shoulder was 100 percent. "Obviously he still has a bump there," he said. "It will become what you call a fixed deformity." If he chose, Hincapie could correct the problem with surgery at a later date. In July, however, he had other things he wanted to set straight.

VINOKOUROV: CLIMBING TOWARD JULY

Alexander Vinokourov, the blond Kazakh, was tan from a week of training in Tenerife, a tropical island in the Spanish Canaries. It's where Lance Armstrong did much of his pre-Tour training in recent years, sometimes crossing paths with Vino on the steep roads that climb from sea level to 8,000 feet at the base of Mount Teide, the world's third-largest volcano.

"I've done a lot of training in the mountains this year," said Vinokourov. "I hope it pays off in July." At 150 pounds and 5 feet 10, the former Red Army officer is not a natural-born climber. In May, he headed home to Kazakhstan for more altitude training, this time in the Altay mountains, not far from the border with China.

Vinokourov said that to be fresh for the crucial second half of the 2006 Tour, he'd go into the race with only 20 days of racing in his legs compared with 55 in previous years. Among those 20 days were June's eight-day Dauphiné Libéré and the five-day Vuelta a Castilla y León, which Vinokourov won in late March.

That victory was established by powering a split in the peloton the first day with his teammates; consolidated by placing third in the next day's time trial; clinched by riding away from the leaders' group on the Navacerrada mountain-top finish; and celebrated by winning the final stage into Segovia with a typical late attack on the last climb.

After that win, Vinokourov said, "This has been a good test. I've proved myself in the high mountains . . . and I believe I'm on the right track for the Tour."

Vinokourov seemed to go off track at the Dauphiné Libéré race in June. Apart from a decent showing in the individual time trial, when he placed 17th,

2:40 behind winner Zabriskie, Vinokourov was nowhere to be seen. By the end of the week, the Kazakh star finished in an uncharacteristic 49th place, more than 51 minutes behind winner Leipheimer.

What happened? Had cycling's most fearless rider lost his mojo, or had the doping scandal in Spain involving his Liberty Seguros team manager Manolo Sáiz affected his performance? No, said Vinokourov, he was patiently following a plan he put in place months ago.

"Last year, I peaked too early and didn't have the form I wanted in the Tour," he said. "So I am racing at the Dauphiné only to prepare for July. This is my first race since Liège [in late April]. I will be ready."

While Vinokourov and others on the team were loath to admit it, the allegations and distractions surrounding Sáiz's detention in Spain seemed to be taking their toll. In the wake of Liberty Seguros's decision to end its annual $8.5 million team sponsorship (while subsponsor Würth remained), Vinokourov had to intervene personally to save the squad. Using contacts he had developed with key politicians and business leaders in his home country, he helped secure a new title sponsor for the Spain-based team, Astaná, that would fly the sky blue national colors of Kazakhstan.

"I feel more responsible for this team. I never would have ridden the Tour with any other squad," he said. "This team believes in me and has supported me as I prepare for the Tour.

"Some have asked me if I have lost morale in these times, but I have not," he added. "I am as focused as ever. I have been thinking about the Tour since December. I have maybe this year or next to try to win the Tour. I am 200 percent concentrated on the Tour."

That sounded like the old, aggressive Vino.

VALVERDE: CONFIRMATION

In the first part of the 2006 season, Valverde lived up to his reputation as a winner. He delivered wins in just about every race he started, with a stage of the Tour of Murcia in March and a huge sprint win over Oscar Freire at the Basque

Country tour in April. His amazing run in the Ardennes classics, with wins at the Flèche Wallonne and Liège-Bastogne-Liège, confirmed his arrival among cycling's elite. He continued that form with a stage win and third place overall at the Tour de Romandie to end his first block of racing.

Valverde unplugged for a few weeks before rebuilding for the Dauphiné Libéré, where he confirmed his Romandie showing with further excellent results: ninth in the long time trial, second on the stage to La Toussuire and seventh overall. His strongest teammate was Pereiro, who finished the eight-day race in fourteenth.

Like all the other main contenders, the two Spanish riders seemed ready to rock the Tour.

CHAPTER 5

Le Grand Départ

Big shocks shake the Tour—even before the start.

E verything seemed to be in place for the best Tour de France in years. Strasbourg, where the race was to start, was all spruced up, especially along the cobbled streets by the canals in the ancient heart of the city. Two nights before the prologue time trial, the 21 designated teams lined up aboard boats to be presented to the public. The glitzy presentation, live on European television, was brought forward a day to avoid clashing with the World Cup soccer quarterfinals in Germany. Just as Italy and Germany were among the most popular teams in the world's leading soccer tournament, so Ivan Basso and Jan Ullrich received the biggest cheers at the world's top bike race. And not far behind on the clap-ometer was Alexander Vinokourov, the leader of the newly branded Astaná-Würth team.

As the Tour's top three favorites were smiling and waving to fans near the medieval cathedral of Notre Dame, a few blocks away the top officials of race organizer Amaury Sport Organisation (ASO) and the sport's world governing body, UCI, were studying a faxed summary of the *Operación Puerto* inquiry sent that evening from the Spanish police. Leaked parts of the report said that 58 cyclists were on a blacklist of patients treated by Dr. Eufemiano Fuentes, including Basso and Ullrich, along with several members of Vinokourov's team.

Two weeks earlier, ASO had disinvited the Comunidad Valenciana team, even though the incriminated assistant directeur sportif Ignacio Labarta had been fired. The race organizers didn't want the faintest hint of a doping scandal at the Tour and decided to distance themselves from any teams or riders who were implicated in *Operación Puerto*.

If ASO had had its way, there would be no discussion: Any implicated rider would not be allowed to start. But cycling had become more democratic in recent years, and the managers of the 20 UCI ProTour teams met Friday morning, the day before the start, to discuss their options. First, T-Mobile's Olaf Ludwig said he would retire his two blacklisted riders, Ullrich and Oscar Sevilla. Then CSC's Bjarne Riis confirmed he would send Basso home, while AG2R's Vincent Lavenu suspended his Spanish star, Francisco Mancebo, who placed fourth in the 2005 Tour. A shattered Mancebo immediately quit the sport, while the stunned Basso and Ullrich expressed their innocence before packing their bags and heading home that afternoon.

At their meeting, the team managers debated replacing the "fired" riders, so as not to penalize the AG2R, CSC, and T-Mobile teams. But the French ProTour squads insisted there would be no substitutions. The one remaining question concerned Vinokourov's Astaná team: Three of Vino's teammates were definitely on the blacklist, and two others were mentioned in the police report but not fully implicated. If only three had been sent home, Astaná could stay with the minimum legal number of six starters. But by dinnertime, the new Astaná team management agreed that all riders named in the document would be barred—which meant that even the nonimplicated Vinokourov could not start the race the next day.

The Tour's 93rd edition finally got under way amid conflicting emotions. On the one hand, the riders sent home were only suspected of breaking the UCI ProTour's ethical code; they had not been found guilty. On the other, their reputations of riding clean had been brought into disrepute in the biggest media circus of the year.

As Basso's team manager Riis told the press that Friday afternoon, "We need proof. We have to be careful saying things that are not 100 percent sure. The investigation is going on, but how can I say Ivan has lied to me when I cannot prove it? It's pretty normal that I have to support my riders."

The exclusions confirmed the feelings of impending doom that had festered ever since Madrid's *Operación Puerto* began extending its ghastly tentacles five weeks earlier. The public humiliation of the sport's top stars brought shame to a Tour that had promised to be the most exciting in a decade.

Their exclusion would mean a less competitive prologue, which had already lost some of its luster because of a scheduling conflict and the absence of riders expected to win the Tour opener. Normally a spectacular start to the three-week race in prime time on Saturday night, the prologue would take place in a less dramatic midafternoon slot to allow European fans to watch that evening's World Cup quarterfinal between France and Brazil, a match that promised to consume the French nation as much as the Tour.

As for the prologue itself, the short time trial had been expected to be a duel between two previous Tour prologue winners Brad McGee (Paris, 2003) and Fabian Cancellara (Liège, 2004). But a herniated disc stopped McGee racing at the Tour of Switzerland and he had to pull out of the Tour de France, while the CSC team hadn't included Cancellara in its final selection, preferring an extra climber, Christian Vande Velde.

With the damaging events in the weeks, days, and hours before the 2006 Tour's *Grand Départ,* many doubted whether the race would even take place. This was supposed to be remembered as the first Tour of the post–Lance Armstrong era. The seven-time champ's departure promised a wide-open affair. That theme was touted by Jean-Marie Leblanc, the Tour's longtime race director who was in his last year with the race organization. Leblanc had happily promoted the race's new image, sans Armstrong's iron-fisted rule. The French official went so far as to label Armstrong's win streak "oppressive."

LEBLANC HAD HAPPILY PROMOTED THE RACE'S NEW IMAGE, SANS ARMSTRONG'S IRON-FISTED RULE. THE FRENCH OFFICIAL WENT SO FAR AS TO LABEL ARMSTRONG'S WIN STREAK "OPPRESSIVE."

Leblanc, like the rest of France, was expecting Ullrich or Basso to assume the American's mantle. And then came the *Operación Puerto* guillotine.

It was too early to analyze the long-term implications of the doping scandal, but the Tour had proven before that it's a tough institution to break. This resilient French juggernaut would roll on. The five top finishers from 2005 were gone? Well, then, the race would be just that much more interesting.

Many riders agreed with that sentiment. "It's going to make a better Tour de France," said American Chris Horner, here to support his Davitamon-Lotto teammate Cadel Evans, whose stock rose in the absence of those who were ejected. "That's what everyone wants, isn't it? They want better drama, they want to see guys taking the jersey, losing the jersey, suffering like crazy to keep it. That's what you're going to see now."

Horner spoke for many when he predicted a lack of stone-cold killers making it look easy. "You're not going to see one guy breathing through a straw that's winning the Tour de France," he said. "That guy's going to be sucking on a pipe in order to get air now—one that's attached to an oxygen tank. You'll definitely see more drama."

So, with a heat wave parked over eastern France, the first week got under way.

PROLOGUE SURPRISES

The start clock counted down to zero and Frenchman Cédric Coutouly of the modest French team, Agritubel, rolled off the ramp of the Strasbourg prologue to a momentous sense of relief. In the wake of all that had happened in the previous 24 hours, the entire sport of cycling could finally exhale.

Though the major prerace favorites had been sent home, the sight of Coutouly zipping down the street in his aerodynamic tuck helped take people's minds off the ghosts of the 2006 Tour. The 93rd Tour de France was indeed under way.

Coutouly was the first of 176 starters in the 7.1km prologue, an individual race against the clock. That number reflected the pared-down rosters that resulted from the doping expulsions of the previous day. The mood among the racers was anxious.

One of the teams most shaken by *Operación Puerto*'s shock waves was CSC. Before being suspended by his team, CSC's Basso was tipped to succeed

Armstrong as the next great Tour champion. Now CSC was without its leader. The Denmark-based squad ironically included three Americans but no Danes in its Tour lineup.

While racers took their turns on the Strasbourg prologue course, two of CSC's Americans sought shelter from the blazing sun. Dave Zabriskie and Bobby Julich were riding on trainers shaded by a canopy extending from their team's Tour bus. Separated by nearly a decade of international experience, each contemplated the upcoming three weeks without Basso.

Zabriskie, the 27-year-old Utah native, retreated into his shell, nodding his head to the beat of the music pumping through his earphones as he warmed up. Zabriskie visualized his upcoming ride; big things were expected from the man who won the opening time-trial stage of the 2005 Tour to join Greg LeMond and Armstrong as the only Americans to wear the Tour's fabled yellow jersey.

Zabriskie will always have a fond memory of leading the world's most prestigious bike race, but it's bookmarked by one he'd rather forget. After wearing yellow for three days in 2005, the idiosyncratic American relinquished the lead by crashing a kilometer from the finish line of the stage 4 team time trial. To this day Zabriskie can't explain what happened, but it caused him to lose the yellow jersey, and it also cost Team CSC the stage victory. Team boss Riis had barked out the order for the other riders to leave Zabriskie behind and go for the win, but the chaos of the crash disrupted their flow just enough for Armstrong's Discovery Channel team to beat them by two seconds. Riis didn't mince words regarding his disappointment: "If Dave hadn't crashed, we would have won the stage."

The 2006 Tour wouldn't include a team time trial, and Zabriskie—who has the rare distinction of being a stage winner at all three of cycling's grand tours (Tour de France, Giro d'Italia, and Vuelta a España)—was eagerly anticipating another chance to start the race with a bang.

While Zabriskie warmed up, Julich was cooling down a few feet to his right. The 34-year-old veteran had posted a prologue time of 8:35, which would land him in 29th place, but he had other things on his mind. The veteran of eight previous Tours had seen a lot in his day. Before Armstrong returned from cancer to turn the sport on its ear, Julich was America's top Tour rider. He was on the Cofidis team when he finished third in 1998, the year of the infamous Festina team doping scandal. Like CSC today, Festina had been the world's leading team.

Since then Julich had bounced around a few different formations. While he never again came close to that third-place finish, he later found a home at CSC, which in 2004 resurrected his flagging career. Julich credits Riis and the riders' camaraderie for CSC's success in recent years. Now, less than 24 hours after Basso's ejection, the outspoken American criticized how the UCI and Tour organizers had handled the situation.

"It was an absolute, total shock," said Julich, one of Basso's top support men. "The thing that sucks about this is that they bring this out less than 24 hours before the start of the prologue so people don't have a chance to defend themselves before they're kicked out of the race. It's an absolute joke."

Julich supports the battle against doping, but he said he objected to the timing in this case—and his teammate's lack of opportunity to defend himself against the allegations. "Obviously there's something that needs to be done about the doping in Spain, but Ivan promised each and every one of us [CSC riders] that he had nothing to do with it," Julich said. "But he's out of the race anyway. Tomorrow or the next day, if he proves himself innocent, he's still out of the race. Which is terrible for him, terrible for us, terrible for the race."

Reminded that the cycling community had seen its share of squeaky-clean images sullied by doping convictions, Julich maintained his support, saying it goes deeper than just Ivan Basso. "I'm going to be absolutely devastated if something is proven against Ivan," Julich said. "Because I've been around him and I know he is of the utmost character. And I have so much respect for him, it would just cripple me if I found out that someone of Ivan's character would do something like this, especially when we've worked so hard to build a team and we've always mentioned from day one that this is a team and you're not just playing with your health and your career, but you're playing with the livelihood of 70 other people associated with [Team CSC]. You'd have to be a real frickin' idiot to take that chance."

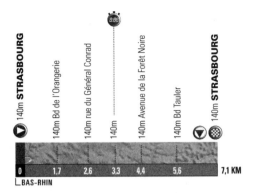

The doping drama would continue in the days, weeks, and months to follow, but for now the race was under way. Despite stifling temperatures that soared into the 90s, fans flocked to the prologue in droves. Most of them seemed unfazed by the scandal, ready to cheer the start of the world's largest annual sports event.

The city of Strasbourg is deeply ingrained in the history of the Tour. Sandwiched between the Rhine River to the east and the Vosges Mountains to the west, this diplomatic center of Europe, which houses the European Parliament and the Council of Europe, has hosted more than 20 stages of the Tour. The list of winners in Strasbourg reads like a who's who of cycling greats: Eddy Merckx in 1971, Bernard Hinault in 1985, and, the last time the Tour finished in Strasbourg, Estonian sprinter Jan Kirsipuu in 2001.

Who would add his name to the list in 2006? After rolling off the start ramp in the Place de Tivoli, riders headed east on a lollipop-shaped route that looped back to the start in front of the Palais de la Musique et des Congrès.

One of the first riders to set an impressive time was Horner. The Davitamon team rider came within one second of early race leader Ralf Grabsch's time of 8:31. "I felt good, but I still wasn't leading," Horner said after his ride. "Someone pipped me by a second. I just kind of messed up in a couple of the corners; I think that's where I lost a couple seconds."

The course was flat and not overly technical, said Horner, who would end up in 19th. However, the westerly wind that barely rippled the French and European Community flags flying from Strasbourg's parliamentary buildings

57

would strengthen later in the afternoon. The first to beat Grabsch's time was fellow German Sebastian Lang, who won his nation's time trial championship a week earlier. The Gerolsteiner rider clocked 4:08 at the 3.7km check, 8:21 by the finish, for an average speed of 51kph.

Lang's time held up for nearly two hours, and it wasn't until the big Norwegian sprinter, Thor Hushovd of Crédit Agricole, came thundering home that Lang's time fell. "I've been really confident the last few weeks, even the last month because I knew the form was there, as well as the experience from the other years," said Hushovd, who won the sprinters' green jersey competition at the 2005 Tour. "I'm quite sure that this is my best form ever."

The top GC riders were still to come, but none could knock off Hushovd, who at the end of the day pulled on the yellow jersey for the second time in his career (he also wore it for a day in 2004). One of the top GC favorites, American Floyd Landis of Phonak, got off to a shaky start when he set off nine or ten seconds late because of a mechanical problem just before he was due to start. Landis had just rolled up to the start house when his team mechanic noticed a problem with the rear tire. "They always check it before the start and there was a cut in it, so we felt it'd be safer to change it rather than risk a crash or something," Landis said. "You don't win the race in the prologue. If I lose the Tour by nine seconds, I guess I can complain then." That wouldn't be the last of Landis's mechanical struggles at this Tour, but overcoming setbacks is not something he complains about. He just sees them as a test. On this occasion, he buckled down to ride as fast as the stage winner—but his late start left him in ninth place. The best of the other favorites was Alejandro Valverde of Caisse d'Épargne-Illes Balears, whose 8:21 put him fifth place.

The next American to take to the course was Gerolsteiner team leader Levi Leipheimer. After finishing 21 seconds slower than Hushovd's time, Leipheimer said he didn't feel great but wasn't about to hit the panic button. "I felt really blocked and didn't go great, but it doesn't worry me," said Leipheimer, who had scored the biggest win of his career three weeks earlier at the Dauphiné Libéré. "I took it really easy after the Dauphiné and I sort of expected that. I didn't want to come in too good. I want to get better as the race goes on," he said.

While Landis and Leipheimer downplayed their struggles, citing bigger fish to fry, Zabriskie was here to win. A victory would go a long way toward easing CSC's disappointment over losing Basso. The lean American started strong, trailing Hushovd's time by just one second at the intermediate time check. But the American faded in the final 2km, giving up four seconds to Hushovd and eventually placing third.

Last to hit the course was George Hincapie. Tipped as one of four possible Discovery Channel riders to fill the shoes of his friend Armstrong at this Tour, Hincapie came agonizingly close to beating Hushovd. Looking incredibly lean as he mashed the big gears, the New York native finished second, losing to Hushovd by just 0.73 seconds.

Was that impressive performance enough to convince Discovery Channel boss Johan Bruyneel that Hincapie would be their man for this Tour? Not just yet. "I think it will not be until after the first two stages in the Pyrénées [stages 10 and 11] that we will know within our team who is stronger than who," said Bruyneel. "Somebody could do a good [stage 7] time trial but fail in the first mountain stage or the opposite. I don't feel the pressure. I don't feel the obligation to win. We had it in the past and it's difficult to deal with. I would definitely prefer that other riders in other teams have to deal with that pressure."

Indeed they would. But for now, before the Tour headed through Germany, Luxembourg, Belgium, and the Netherlands over the following three days, the overall contenders focused on playing it safe. With hilly, classics-type terrain coming up, and chaotic bunch finishes expected, riders like Landis, Hincapie, and Leipheimer would take a backseat to the fast men like Hoshovd and Davitamon's Robbie McEwen.

Commenting on the fact that athletes from other sports had been implicated and identified in *Operación Puerto*, Bruyneel said, "It's about time they named names from other sports. Because as soon as the scandal broke, the only names coming out were cyclists. If there's hard evidence against [the riders] of doing the wrong thing, then of course they need to be punished. But I found it a big shame that names of other sport people—from [soccer], tennis, athletics, whatever, they weren't named at all. All the garbage was getting thrown on cycling. Again."

Hincapie, whose Discovery Channel team was untouched by the scandal, said it was time for him to focus on racing again. "That was definitely an unfortunate situation," he said. "We all want a clean sport, so whatever will push that to happen, then that's a good thing. I know that I've worked hard to be here and I hope that I have a good Tour de France."

PROLOGUE: STRASBOURG

1. Thor Hushovd (N), Crédit Agricole, 7.1km in 8:17 (51.428kph); **2. George Hincapie (USA), Discovery Channel, 8:17; 3. David Zabriskie (USA), CSC, 8:21; 4.** Sebastian Lang (G), Gerolsteiner, 8:21; **5.** Alejandro Valverde (Sp), Caisse d'Épargne-Illes Balears, 8:21; **6.** Stuart O'Grady (Aus), CSC, 8:21; **7.** Michael Rogers (Aus), T-Mobile, 8:23; **8.** Paolo Savoldelli (I), Discovery Channel, 8:25; **9. Floyd Landis (USA), Phonak, 8:26; 10.** Vladimir Karpets (Rus), Caisse d'Épargne-Illes Balears, 8:27.

CHAPTER 6

Battle of the Sprinters

Hushovd, Boonen, and McEwen take center stage.

With pale blue eyes, blond hair, and an icy stare, Thor Hushovd carries himself with the chip-on-his-shoulder stance typical of the world's top sprinters. His first name evokes visions of Norse mythology, and he has the hulking physique to match. Hushovd is beloved among the face-painted, flag-waving Norwegian fans who trek to the Tour each year wearing Viking helmets and toting signs that read "God of Thunder" and "Thor de France."

Hushovd, who has spent his entire seven-year professional career with Crédit Agricole, a French team, isn't a typical sprinter. He is less like Australia's Robbie McEwen and Italy's Alessandro Petacchi—riders designed to collect stage wins at grand tours—and more like Belgium's Tom Boonen, who can power through brutal classics and win sprints at the end of a long, hard race.

On the opening day of the 2006 Tour, Hushovd added another item to his résumé: prologue specialist. On the flat Strasbourg course, Hushovd beat the time-trial specialists, and once again the pundits seemed shocked. Was he surprised to win? Not really, Hushovd said flatly, pointing out that he had finished fifth in the prologue at the 2004 Tour.

Hushovd proudly pulled on the yellow jersey for the second time in his career and said he'd do his best to defend it. But true to character, Hushovd was most looking forward to sprinting against Boonen in the days to come. "This is the first time I will be able to sprint against Boonen this year," he said. "I am very confident."

Throughout the 2006 season, Hushovd had one thing on his mind: beating the best. Although the 28-year-old Norwegian won the green jersey points competition at the 2005 Tour, he came to the 2006 race feeling underrated as one of the world's fastest men. There were a few reasons for that, including the fact that Hushovd's '05 green jersey triumph came without any stage wins.

In the third stage, Hushovd's main rival, McEwen, had been relegated for dangerous sprinting and stripped of his points for that stage—leaving him with an insurmountable handicap in the points competition. That left room for detractors to claim the six-foot, 180-pound Norwegian had won the green jersey by default.

Hushovd's Rodney Dangerfield act continued in 2006. Despite starting the season with the best form of his life, he complained about getting no respect. He was winning races but his success was overshadowed by the eye-popping exploits of the reigning world champion, Boonen. The Belgian superstar was collecting wins by the bucketful at major events such as Paris-Nice, the Tour of Flanders, and the Tour of Switzerland. Hushovd was winning stages at Tirreno-Adriatico in Italy, the Tour of Catalonia in Spain, and the Dauphiné-Libéré in France, but Boonen was making all the headlines.

In April, longing to make a name for himself, Hushovd went head-to-head with Italian super-sprinter Petacchi in the finale of the prestigious Belgian ProTour classic, Ghent-Wevelgem. Hushovd won, and the response was typical. After being asked by reporters in several different languages if he was shocked at beating a star of Petacchi's stature, Hushovd bristled. "I expect to win," he said with a snort. "I already beat Petacchi once this year, and I know I can beat him."

FREAKY FINISH IN STRASBOURG

A few years ago an American sportswriter new to the Tour de France famously asked, "Why do they have all these flat stages? Why not go straight to the mountains? They're more fun, right?" But if there were only mountain stages, half

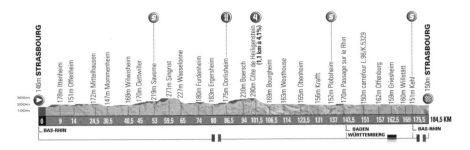

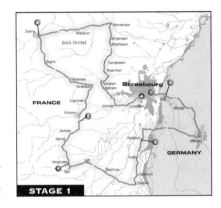

STAGE 1

the field would be eliminated and the race would be boring. What the rookie Tour writer didn't get (at first) is that the flat stages, combined with the climbing stages and the time trials, produce a three-week race that crowns the best all-around rider (and team). In many Tours, the lightly built climbers can be ten or more minutes behind the leaders before they even reach the mountains. So, even in the opening week, any overall contender has to ride strong and smart, and get plenty of help and protection from his teammates.

The 2006 Tour's opening road stage, a mostly flat 184.5km loop that started and finished in Strasbourg, didn't look particularly dangerous. Sure, there would be breakaways on the scenic roads that looped around the Alsatian vineyards famous for their Gewürztraminer, Riesling, and Sylvaner white wines. But with the sprinters' teams having their full complement of nine riders apiece, no breakaway was likely to stay away. Temperatures for the Strasbourg region were again forecast in the high 80s with a fierce sun and moderate winds out of the east, which would make for an even speedier final finish on the day's counterclockwise course.

Before the ceremonial start in steamy Strasbourg, where the 176 riders lined up in front of the Gothic cathedral, there was heightened anticipation of how the stage (and the Tour) would play out. Even before the sport's top stars were ejected, many expected it to be a wide-open affair. With Lance Armstrong and his invincible support crew no longer there to control the peloton, no one knew what to expect.

"Now if you let a ten-minute break get away, there might not be any teams capable of bringing back ten minutes," said American Chris Horner of the Davitamon-Lotto team. "It's not like where Lance could bring back ten minutes on just about anyone other than two guys." Team CSC's Bobby Julich agreed. "Now it's going to be much more open," he said. "I think before, the other teams could have pretty much relied on CSC to control the race. So now [without Ivan Basso], the race just got a lot harder for them."

With just one Cat. 4 climb, the Côte de Heiligenstein, near the 100km mark in the foothills of the Vosges mountains—and speedsters such as Hushovd, Boonen, McEwen, and Germany's Erik Zabel salivating at the thought of a stage win—a thundering herd was expected to arrive back in Strasbourg later in the day.

"THE PERFECT DAY FOR US IS FOR A BREAK OF A FEW GUYS TO GO EARLY... AND THEN HOPEFULLY THE SPRINTERS' TEAMS WILL WORK TO BRING IT BACK AND THERE WILL BE A FIGHT BETWEEN THE SPRINTERS LIKE ME AND ROBBIE AND BOONEN."

Hushovd offered his ideal scenario for keeping his yellow jersey for at least 24 hours. "The perfect day for us is for a break of a few guys to go early," he said. "And then hopefully the sprinters' teams will work to bring it back and there will be a fight between the sprinters like me and Robbie and Boonen."

Shortly after rolling out of town, following the ritual reading of the Tour's code of ethics oath and official ribbon cutting, the race began to unfold as Hushovd had hoped: Frenchman Stéphane Augé of Cofidis initiated a break of seven riders just three kilometers into the race. The break held a 4:30 advantage until the 100km mark, but as the peloton began to head north toward the town of Saverne, the sprinters' teams of Milram (for Zabel), Quick Step-Innergetic (Boonen), and Davitamon-Lotto (McEwen) began taking pulls at the front.

With 43km still to go, riders crossed the Rhine River and looped into Germany for 32km before returning to France back across the river. Germany marked the first of five countries outside of France that the 2006 Tour would visit. The others would be Luxembourg (stages 2 and 3), Belgium (stage 3 and 5), the Netherlands (stage 3), and Spain (stage 11).

In the scenic German towns, where fans lining the roads stood side by side waving French and German flags, the chase heated up. Eventually only Walter Bénéteau, a French rider on the Bouygues Telecom team, remained off the front. The Frenchman managed to cross the border and reenter his home country alone in the lead, but he wouldn't survive much longer.

As the sprinters started to push to the front on their teammates' coattails, the yellow jersey was also in play. With seven-time defending champion Armstrong not there to call the shots, questions abounded about how the Discovery Channel team would fare in this Tour. Fans of America's only ProTour team imagined it would be like the Chicago Bulls without Michael Jordan, the Green Bay Packers without Brett Favre. But none of that seemed to bother the boss. Rather than wring his hands, team manager Johan Bruyneel seemed to welcome something new.

"We're in the same situation now as all the other teams have been in the past," Bruyneel said before the start of the Tour. "I have been observing a lot over the years, so I'm going to be open for everything in this Tour de France. In the past we had a lot of opportunities but we didn't take them because we only had one goal and one obsession and we had to play it safe to bring the yellow jersey to Paris."

Discovery's first opportunity came at the day's final intermediate sprint. And while Bruyneel may be a masterful tactician, this one was out of his hands. He was as surprised as anyone when Discovery's only American rider, George Hincapie, saw an opportunity and seized it.

As the sprinters' teams closed in, and just before they began setting up for the final kilometers, Hincapie exploded out of the main group, surprising Hushovd and the other GC contenders. Hushovd's French teammate Sébastien Hinault managed to get on Hincapie's wheel and come around him to take second in the sprint, but the two-second bonus for third place was all Hincapie needed to seize the overall lead going into the final sprint. It was just the kind of take-charge, on-the-road aggression that Bruyneel had been preaching before the race started. Crafty as it was, Hincapie's move might have remained a footnote to the stage were it not for a bizarre incident at the finish line.

Things were going according to plan heading into Strasbourg, where a bunch sprint developed, to give Hushovd his first chance of sprinting against Boonen and McEwen. The big Norwegian was barreling down the right side of the road close to the barriers, when, 40 meters before the line, a spectator waved an oversize green hand, a promotional handout from Tour sponsor PMU. The Norwegian hit the plastic sign full on but didn't crash. In the chaos of the bunch sprint no one knew initially what had happened, and a ghastly spray of blood splattered the riders around Hushovd, who pulled up and coasted across the line.

Hushovd later reported that he had also hit a camera, and Boonen said he had as well. With those two contenders out of the sprint, an astonished Jimmy Casper angled in to beat McEwen and Zabel, who finished second and third respectively. For Casper, a Frenchman who rides for Cofidis, it was his first Tour stage win in an erratic eight-year pro career. But as he said, "It's really the kind of sprint I like, and it's an honor to beat great champions like Boonen and McEwen."

Moments after the finish, Hushovd's competitors and television viewers around the world were stunned by the chilling image of the Norwegian lying on the pavement with blood soaking his yellow jersey and running down his legs. "I was just behind Boonen and McEwen and I got a small gap between Boonen and the barriers," Hushovd explained later. "Then all the spectators that want to take photos or see what's happening, I hit a few of them. At first it was just pain. But then I saw blood shooting out of my arm."

The green hand sign had opened up a four-inch gash on his right arm, and he was taken to the hospital to be stitched up, unsure if he could start the next day. While Hushovd was loaded into an ambulance, Casper pleaded with organizers to do something about the hazardous sponsor signs. "Those [signs] are dangerous, and it's not the first time this has happened," he said. "I think we should not have them in the last 500 meters."

Tour officials responded by banning PMU from handing out its promotional signs along the final two kilometers of stages likely to end in mass sprints. But it was too late for Hushovd, who received several stitches in his right arm that evening, leaving questions about his ability to sprint, or even ride, in the days to come. Though a top-three finish would have given Hushovd the necessary time bonus to maintain the lead, his ninth-place finish meant that Hincapie, who finished with the main group, was in yellow.

For Hincapie, the race leadership was sweet redemption after his near miss in the prologue. "I was definitely very disappointed to lose by such a close [margin] yesterday," Hincapie said after pulling the *maillot jaune* over his angular, battle-ready torso. "I was really gunning for the prologue and I thought I did a great ride, but I got beat by a great rider. Today it wasn't really the plan to go for any bonus sprints, but when we caught the breakaway I saw an opportunity that I couldn't pass up. I took it, and I think I made a great decision."

While it might not have been the ideal way for Hincapie to take his first yellow jersey, the 33-year-old certainly made a statement at the start of Discovery's post-Armstrong era Tour. Perhaps coincidentally, the last time Hincapie came this close to the yellow jersey was the last time he rode without Armstrong. "In '98 I was two seconds behind [overall leader Bo Hamburger], and that was probably the longest two seconds of my career," Hincapie said. "It was so hard, and I was sprinting against [Stuart] O'Grady back then. But today it wasn't even actually planned to sprint for the bonuses."

Hincapie's instinctual attack for the time bonus made him just the fourth American to wear the yellow jersey after Zabriskie in 2005, Armstrong, and three-time Tour champion Greg LeMond. It also left Discovery Channel with a choice: Defend the jersey or not?

Bruyneel wasn't sure what to say about that. "I've been asked the last ten days the same question: Who's your leader?" Bruyneel said. "We don't have a leader right now. For tomorrow, George will be the leader and we will ride for him."

Hincapie wasn't sure, either. "I'd love to keep it as long as possible, but I just don't know," he said. "I don't have much time, and for me to sprint against Thor

[Hushovd] and Tom Boonen and those guys, that's not really my thing anymore. All I've been training for lately is time trials and climbing, so my sprint has gotten slower for sure."

ON THE ROAD—AT LAST!

It will never be forgotten that the prerace favorites, Jan Ullrich and Ivan Basso, left Strasbourg in public disgrace and private disgust the day before the 93rd Tour de France began. But their departure, and that of the other 11 athletes barred from the race, began to be more distant memories when the remaining Tour riders left their Strasbourg hotels Monday morning and headed west to the stage 2 start in Obernai, a postcard-perfect town set in the vineyards at the foot of the Vosges.

It was a restless night for Hushovd. His yellow-jersey high had come to a sudden, unexpected halt, and instead of celebrating a second day in yellow over a champagne team dinner, Hushovd spent most of the night in the hospital. The Norwegian lost a lot of blood in the freak finish line accident, but the gash in his arm wasn't as bad as initially feared. Doctors gave him medication for the pain, stitched up the wound, and sent the Norwegian back to his team hotel later that night.

But he's not called Thor de France for nothing, and by the next morning he was back in his green-and-white Crédit Agricole team colors, ready to go. Stage 2 presented riders with a more difficult day in the saddle; the 228.5km slog northwest to Luxembourg was the second-longest stage of the Tour. Hushovd joined his teammates at the start in Obernai, swung a leg over his bike at the start, and stated that his objective was merely to finish. Would he be able to sprint today?

"We'll see," Hushovd said. "I'm for sure going to race and I'm going to finish, but I'm afraid I can't sprint. My legs are good, my form is very good, but when I can't pull on the handlebar, that's a problem."

While Hushovd was still feeling a little woozy, Hincapie was soaking up the feeling of wearing the yellow jersey. His BlackBerry had been blowing up the previous night with congratulatory calls and e-mails. Hincapie said he hoped to still be wearing yellow at the end of the day, but his Discovery Channel team would have to play it safe.

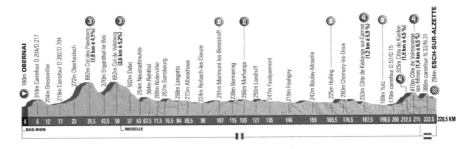

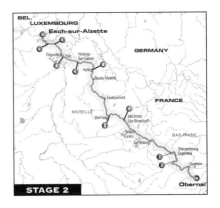

After the previous day's short loop through Germany, the peloton was now headed for a couple more days beyond the French border. Stage 2 would take them to Esch-sur-Alzette, Luxembourg, a mining and steel manufacturing city.

Temperatures were already climbing past 90 degrees when riders departed Obernai just before noon. The route to Luxembourg wasn't flat. It was book-ended by climbs: the Cat. 3 Col des Pandours and Col de Valsberg in the opening 50km on twisting roads through the pine forests of the Vosges, and three more climbs, all Cat. 4s, in the last 41km. But with tight time gaps at the top of the general classification (GC), the sprinters would again be enticed with a shot at snatching the yellow jersey from Hincapie.

In addition to the sprinters' battle, the five categorized climbs promised the first real tussle for the climber's polka-dot jersey. Fabian Wegmann of Gerolsteiner had donned that red-and-white jersey after stage 1 when he claimed the day's only King of the Mountains climb. Wegmann, a blond 26-year-old German, made a name for himself in the States when he won the 2005 San Francisco Grand Prix. He was not afraid to be aggressive, and most expected Wegmann to put up a fight for the KOM lead.

One rider who didn't make it to the start of stage 2 was Italian Danilo Di Luca. The Liquigas rider, who had lit up the 2005 season when he won the UCI

ProTour title, had started the Tour with a prostate infection and became the first rider to quit the 2006 Tour.

Once the long, hot race got under way, Hushovd had to fight through some rough patches, and he made a couple of trips back to the race doctor, who rides in a car behind the peloton. "At first I was tired, probably because of the shock from yesterday," Hushovd said. "I had to take medications after they stitched me [last night], and I think all the medication made me have a stomach ache."

Even so, Hushovd felt that his legs were up to the task of sprinting. When the first intermediate sprint came at the 107km mark in the town of Marimont-les-Benestroff, he decided to go for it. "I knew I was only two seconds behind the yellow jersey, and I wanted to try and get it back," Hushovd said. "That's why I did the sprint during the race. I didn't feel 100 percent, but I think it will just get better and better this week."

The first sprint was a showdown between Hushovd and Belgium's world champion Boonen. The other green jersey favorite, McEwen, held back, saying he preferred to go for the big points at the stage end. Boonen beat Hushovd in that first sprint, taking third place behind two early breakaways, David de la Fuente (Saunier Duval-Prodir) and Aitor Hernandez (Euskaltel-Euskadi), to gain a two-second time bonus and jump up a couple of spots in the GC.

Race leader Hincapie had said that he would love to wear the yellow jersey as long as possible. That view was backed up by team boss Johan Bruyneel, who said, "We have to think that [the yellow jersey] is good for the atmosphere of the team and something to build on."

So, after Hernandez and De la Fuente broke away in the first kilometer, there was a familiar sight for the opening couple of hours: the blue and silver jerseys of Discovery Channel pulling the peloton for its American in the yellow jersey—this year Hincapie and not the retired Armstrong. But once Hushovd showed he was capable of taking back the lead, Discovery stopped riding tempo behind the two Spaniards, who were still off the front when they arrived at the second sprint spot at the 170km mark.

The battle for third-place points was a Boonen-Hushovd rematch. Hushovd won this time, swinging around the left side of Boonen to take the two-second bonus. At that point Hushovd moved ahead of Hincapie to become the virtual GC leader on the road, and it seemed likely the yellow jersey would be decided at the finish line sprint.

Meanwhile, after more than 175km at the front, Hernandez was finally cooked. De la Fuente dropped his breakaway companion, and as the terrain turned hilly the main field began bearing down. De la Fuente dug deep to collect more KOM points, and at the end of the day he would slip past Wegmann with a two-point advantage in the climbers' competition.

With Hernandez absorbed by the main field, second-place points were available to the bunch in the final intermediate sprint, and this time Boonen beat Hushovd.

With 13km to go, Wegmann was off the front alone after attacking on the last KOM hill. But the sprinters' teams, led by Lampre-Fondital and Milram, took charge and swept up the German 7km from the finish.

It was a hilly final approach to Esch-sur-Alzette. On the final climb of the day, not categorized, Germany's Matthias Kessler of T-Mobile launched a solo attack with 6km to go. Kessler went over the top alone and flew down the descent toward the finish. Not wanting to lose a sprint opportunity, Zabel's Milram team led the chase. A crash in the middle of the bunch with about 2km to go held up half the field and temporarily disrupted the chase, but Kessler couldn't hold his lead to the line and was caught with 300 meters to go.

The final kilometer was money time for American Fred Rodriguez, who was McEwen's Davitamon-Lotto lead-out man. Rodriguez charged through the field with McEwen on his wheel, putting the Aussie just where he needed to be. "Fred brought me up to about seventh or eighth position, which is just what I asked him to do," said McEwen. "So he did a good job."

In the mad dash to the line, Hushovd suffered a finish line setback for the second straight day. As he and McEwen were darting for the line, Hushovd brushed up against McEwen and pulled his left foot out of his pedal. With his left leg flailing, Hushovd cranked one-legged the remaining 20 meters and threw up a hand in protest over McEwen's sprint. But finish line judges determined that McEwen had played it clean, and the Aussie was credited with the ninth Tour stage victory of his career.

Afterward, McEwen and Hushovd watched a video replay together, and both agreed with the call. "Robbie, like all other sprinters, sometimes he's dangerous," Hushovd said. "But I saw the sprint on television and he didn't make any mistakes. That's just a sprint and things happen. So I can't blame him today."

Hushovd's initial anger was eased by the fact that his third-place finish allowed him to regain the yellow jersey from Hincapie. It had been an eventful couple of days for the Norwegian, who would carry a five-second lead over Boonen into stage 3. From race leader to the hospital and back to race leader, Hushovd was in for a roller-coaster Tour.

STAGE 1: STRASBOURG TO STRASBOURG

1. Jimmy Casper (F), Cofidis, 184.5km in 4:10 (44.28kph); **2.** Robbie McEwen (Aus), Davitamon-Lotto; **3.** Erik Zabel (G), Milram; **4.** Daniele Bennati (I), Lampre; **5.** Luca Paolini (I), Liquigas-Bianchi; **6.** Isaac Galvez (Sp), Caisse d'Épargne-Illes Balears; **7.** Stuart O'Grady (Aus), CSC; **8.** Bernhard Eisel (A), Française des Jeux; **9.** Thor Hushovd (N), Crédit Agricole; **10.** Oscar Freire (Sp), Rabobank, all s.t.

STAGE 2: OBERNAI TO ESCH-SUR-ALZETTE

1. Robbie McEwen (Aus), Davitamon-Lotto, 228.5km in 5:36:14 (40.775kph); **2.** Tom Boonen (B), Quick Step-Innergetic; **3.** Thor Hushovd (N), Crédit Agricole; **4.** Oscar Freire (Sp), Rabobank; **5.** Daniele Bennati (I), Lampre; **6.** Luca Paolini (I), Liquigas-Bianchi; **7.** Stuart O'Grady (Aus), CSC; **8.** Bernhard Eisel (A), Française des Jeux; **9.** Erik Zabel (G), Milram; **10.** Peter Wrolich (A), Gerolsteiner, all s.t.

GENERAL CLASSIFICATION

1. Thor Hushovd (N), Crédit Agricole

2. Tom Boonen (B), Quick Step-Innergetic, at 0:05

3. Robbie McEwen (Aus), Davitamon-Lotto, at 0:08

4. George Hincapie (USA), Discovery Channel, at 0:10

5. David Zabriskie (USA), CSC, at 0:16

CHAPTER 7

Classic Racing in Classics Country

Kessler and McEwen triumph while Valverde, Dekker, and Rodriguez face disaster.

About four minutes from the finish of stage 3 the leaders were flying up the infamous Cauberg. This steep, narrow hill angles up a limestone butte from streets lined with busy cafés and bars in Valkenburg, a small Dutch town that's an epicenter of Continental cycling. Over the years, Valkenburg has hosted three world championships and countless national championships. Every April it serves as the finish for the UCI ProTour classic, the Amstel Gold Race.

Just as with the Amstel, the climax of this Tour stage brought forth riders who love to attack on short, punchy climbs. The thousands of Dutch fans lining the 800-meter-long Cauberg were cheering for their favorite son, former Amstel Gold Race winner Michael Boogerd, who was setting an infernal pace on the steep grades of the middle part of the hill. He had taken over from Thor Hushovd's pilot fish, New Zealander Julian Dean, who went much too fast into the climb and left behind his Crédit Agricole leader. Perhaps Boogerd, too, was working for his sprinter, Rabobank teammate Oscar Freire. The finish line for this Tour stage was not at the Cauberg summit but 2km farther along the ridge on a straight, flat road that would likely see the leaders regroup for a sprint finish.

Boogerd's effort split the smallish peloton that had emerged from a hectic, crash-laden finale, with Discovery Channel's George Hincapie, Française des

Jeux's Philippe Gilbert, and T-Mobile's Matthias Kessler looking lively in the wake of the fast-moving Dutchman.

"We went over the Cauberg like it was an overpass," said Levi Leipheimer, who was racing hard in the front group. "We flew up that thing."

Once Boogerd finished his pack-splitting operation, the ambitious Gilbert was the first man to attack, but Kessler wouldn't have it. With his mouth agape, the powerful German willed himself off the front of the field. Just as he had done the day before, Kessler was charging to the finish of a Tour de France stage with a couple of kilometers to go.

No one in a select group like the ProTour peloton earns the nickname Pit Bull unless they're tough as nails. And at the Tour there was only one such rider in the pack—Kessler, whose square jaw, flat nose, and cleft chin evoke the face of a middleweight boxer from days gone by.

Kessler is as tough, if not tougher, than any boxer. Riding the 2004 Tour in support of Jan Ullrich, Kessler hit a patch of wood chips descending a mountain pass and slammed headfirst into a cattle fence. Although shaken, the German re-mounted his bike and rode the 60km to the finish of that stage 10 from Limoges to St. Flour, even though it was later revealed that he suffered a concussion, two broken ribs, and a bruised pelvis. Against his wishes, T-Mobile team management took him out of the race the next day.

Kessler returned to the Tour in 2005 to finish 57th in support of Ullrich's podium finish. A crash in stage 16 left him with a concussion and sent teammate Andreas Klöden home with a fractured left wrist. That time, Kessler insisted on staying.

Still only 27, Kessler came into this Tour as a veteran of the sport's grand tours. He had started the Giro d'Italia five times, the Vuelta a España twice, and the Tour three times. A strong all-around rider, he first demonstrated that he is truly a man for April's hilly classics when, at age 22, he finished sixth at the 2002 Liège-Bastogne-Liège. The following year he took fifth at the Amstel Gold Race, and, in 2004, he was third at the Flèche Wallonne and sixth at Amstel Gold.

Kessler turned pro in 2000 and spent two days wearing the leader's jersey in the Tour of Austria. He finished 25th overall at the 2002 Giro d'Italia, and in 2003 he finished an impressive 49th in his maiden Tour while riding in support of third-place finisher Alexander Vinokourov.

The following year, Kessler was re-united with Ullrich, who returned to the T-Mobile squad after a season with Bianchi. The two Germans are good friends. They both have homes on the banks of Lake Constance in Switzerland, where they often train together. In the buildup to the 2006 Tour, Kessler rode the Giro alongside Ullrich, finishing 72nd. But just four days into the 2006 Tour, Kessler's T-Mobile squad was still smarting from the pre-prologue exclusions of Ullrich and teammate Oscar Sevilla. And after his near miss on stage 2, Kessler was determined to bring the squad something to smile about.

NO TIME TO LOSE

When Leipheimer, Gerolsteiner's GC hope, first looked at the course for the 2006 Tour de France, he fingered stage 3 from Esch-sur-Alzette to Valkenburg as the one he would study the most in the first week. Starting in Luxembourg, crossing Belgium, and ending in the Netherlands, the 216.5km stage saved its teeth for the end: six categorized climbs and two sprints in the final two hours of racing.

With ambitious stage stalkers likely to come to the fore, Leipheimer said he was expecting fireworks before the day was over. "I think we have to pay attention," he said before rolling to the start on another hot day at the Tour. "I don't think the sprinters' teams will be so confident today."

Winning a stage of the Tour was the top priority for most of the riders in the peloton, but for the overall contenders *not losing* time was their main goal of this first week. The stage 2 finish into Esch-sur-Alzette showed how easy it was to lose time, when two crashes—one on an uphill, the other in the narrow streets of Esch—delayed more than half the peloton.

The main victim of the first crash, which came 15km from the finish, was Spanish hope José Gomez Marchante, the Saunier Duval rider who won April's Tour of the Basque Country. Marchante was banged up in the multiple crash and eventually crossed the line in 150th place, 2:51 down. Also delayed was one of Tom Boonen's lead-out men, Italian Mateo Tosatto.

The other crash was one that blocked the roadway 2km from the finish. Fortunately for the 80 or so riders involved, a rule change in 2005 meant that they were all given the same time as stage winner Robbie McEwen. The safety zone in which riders can't lose time because of a crash or mechanical incident was extended from 1km to 3km following complaints by riders—notably Tyler Hamilton—caught in a mass fall at the 1km-to-go mark in the stage into Angers in 2004.

It was possible that the stage into Valkenburg could end in a mass sprint, as McEwen expected. His two top rivals for the green (and currently yellow) jersey agreed. Race leader Thor Hushovd—who won his world under-23 time trial title in Valkenburg—said, "[Stage 3] will again be hard. But I can climb the Cauberg okay and keep the yellow jersey."

World champion Boonen was a little hesitant. Talking about stage 2, he said, "This stage was for me six times harder than the Tour of Flanders, with the time bonuses, the hills, and the heat." Talking about the climb just before the stage 3 finish, he added that "the Cauberg should suit me, but if I don't win today then it'll be the next day."

While the sprinters speculated about a finish still five hours away, the diesel-engined riders focused on the opening kilometers. One of these long-distance experts, Jens Voigt of CSC, launched his first attack of the 2006 Tour shortly after leaving Esch-sur-Alzette, a no-nonsense industrial center whose 29,000 inhabitants are known as Eschois. There would be more attacks to come from the reliably aggressive German, who was motivated by the sight of his parents at the start in Esch. Voigt was joined by four others, and the group built a lead of more than six minutes by the time they left Luxembourg and crossed into Belgium.

Things got more interesting as riders ventured into the rolling hills of the Ardennes. Thousands of fans lined the roads through the lush, cycling-mad countryside, many cheering for Boonen. The breakaway riders were 4:35 ahead of the peloton when they topped the second of the day's major climbs, the 3.6km Côte de la Haute Levée, a hill that French greats Jacques Anquetil and Bernard Hinault used as a springboard to make winning solo breaks in legendary editions of Belgium's Liège-Bastogne-Liège classic.

Anquetil and Hinault would have taken charge on these climbs, and so it was good to see Floyd Landis's Phonak riders lifting the peloton's tempo on the Haute Levée. Their efforts helped cut the break-away's lead to under two minutes as **LEIPHEIMER'S FEARS OF DANGER ON THE NARROW, WINDING ROADS WERE REALIZED AS THE FIRST OF SEVERAL DEVASTATING CRASHES ON THE TRICKY COURSE INTO VALKENBURG TOOK OUT TWO KEY TEAM RIDERS.** they headed for the Belgian-Dutch border with 50km to go. Leipheimer's fears of danger on the narrow, winding roads were realized as the first of several devastating crashes on the tricky course into Valkenburg took out two key team riders.

Less than 24 hours after delivering teammate McEwen to victory in stage 2, American Fred Rodriguez hit a deep pothole and crashed heavily onto a Belgian street, suffering a concussion and a shoulder injury. Rodriguez's crash also brought down Dutch veteran Erik Dekker of Rabobank, who ended his final Tour de France—and his distinguished career—with broken teeth and blood pouring from facial cuts and bruises.

After more than 80km in Belgium, the leaders entered the Limburg region of the southeast Netherlands and began taking jabs at each other. One of the breakaways, Frenchman Jérôme Pineau of the Bouygues Telecom team, won four of the first six climbs on the day, which would leapfrog him past David de la Fuente (Saunier Duval) and into the polka-dot jersey by day's end.

Meanwhile, under pressure from the Rabobank team, the peloton's pace ratcheted up a few notches and led to another nasty pileup with 18km to go. The highest-ranked victim was Caisse d'Épargne team leader Alejandro Valverde, who fell and broke his right collarbone. Sadly, the 25-year-old Spaniard's Tour came to a close on the same roads that saw him rise to the top of the sport in April, when Valverde pulled off back-to-back wins at the Flèche Wallonne and Liège-Bastogne-Liège classics. For the second straight year, Valverde, full of potential and shouldering high hopes for Spain, was forced to quit early. In 2005 he abandoned the Tour with knee pain.

Valverde wasn't the only rider whose Tour ended on stage 3. There were other crashes that left a long list of riders requiring medical attention. Included among them were Rodriguez's American teammate Chris Horner, whose Tour was off to a rough start after crashing twice in two days. Horner was riding behind CSC's Stuart O'Grady in a paved gutter when they both fell. "It was a crazy day out there," Horner said. "I was passing in the gutter, and the gutter ran out."

Horner fell in a patch of gravel and grass, and his hand took the brunt of the impact. He ended up losing 8:05 but felt lucky to be able to start the next day. "I thought I busted the pinky," Horner said. "They took me to the hospital and a specialist was going to pin it, but they x-rayed and found out it was just dislocated."

O'Grady was much worse off. He fractured a vertebra in his lower back. The tough Aussie finished 11:35 down, yet he too would go on to start the next day.

HEART-STOPPING FINALE

As the decimated peloton drew close with 15km remaining, Spaniard José Luis Arrieta (AG2R) left Voigt, Pineau, and the other breakaway riders behind with a strong solo attack. He opened a one-minute lead, but unfortunately for Arrieta the main group was closing in fast. As the Spaniard reached Valkenburg, the peloton had him in its sights down the narrow, shop-lined streets. Finally Kessler began to smell a shot at victory.

"At the breakfast table, the talk was about where [Kessler] should attack," said his teammate Andreas Klöden. "We know the final kilometers of the Amstel Gold Race like the back of our hands." A stage win looked unlikely, however, when Kessler was forced to wait and help pace Klöden back to the peloton after the T-Mobile leader went down in the crash that took out Valverde. But Klöden jumped back on his bike uninjured.

Kessler later admitted nearly giving up on the stage win after pacing Klöden up to the field so close to the finish. But after easily following Boogerd, Hincapie, and Gilbert up the first part of the Cauberg's 8.3 percent grade, Kessler felt ready to make his startling move. "I attacked and knew instantly I still had the legs," Kessler said. "Yesterday I had a good feeling, my legs were good. Today was the same, so I had to go again. I gave everything on the last climb. I did it 'Vino style,' not looking around, just burying myself and going for it, and hoping no one would catch me."

The German was ten seconds clear when the grade eased over the Cauberg summit, and the Pit Bull kept on charging.

"This time I attacked closer to home," he said, comparing his ride with his effort the previous day. "The difference was that the last hill yesterday was five kilometers from the finish. That allowed the peloton to reorganize. Today, there were only two kilometers left after the Cauberg, so I knew it would be harder for them to come back."

Kessler's assessment was right. He had five seconds to spare as he turned his head just before the line and then ecstatically celebrated his first Tour stage win. His Aussie teammate Michael Rogers completed a one-two finish for T-Mobile by outsprinting a 47-strong chase group that included most of the race favorites. The 12-second finish line bonus taken by Rogers pushed him into second place overall—just one second behind the new race leader, Boonen.

The world champion felt right at home on the steep climbs near the end of the stage. Boonen is often categorized as a sprinter, but as he has proven in classics such as the Tour of Flanders, he has the power to attack on short hills. When he saw his sprinting rivals Hushovd and McEwen suffering on earlier climbs, Boonen felt that he could do some damage on the Cauberg.

His plan was foiled, however, by a softening front tire. "I had to deal with a slow leak in my tire in the last five kilometers. I had the legs to follow Kessler . . . but I couldn't stand on the pedals as I couldn't put too much weight on the tire," said the 176-pound Belgian. "So I stayed in the saddle and rode defensively."

Boonen was able to contest the sprint for second, but, handicapped by the soft tire, he crossed the line behind Italian rival Daniele Bennati (Lampre-Fondital) and the surprising Rogers. The points Boonen took for fourth place gave him the green jersey by one point over Hushovd and two points over McEwen, who rolled in a half minute back.

It was also enough for Boonen to take the yellow jersey from Hushovd, who got gapped on the last climb and gave up 17 seconds. With the following day's stage starting in Huy, Belgium, where Boonen enjoys godlike status, wearing yellow was the realization of a dream. "It's something that maybe happens once every ten years," he said.

Boonen's finish also gave him the green jersey as leader of the sprinters' competition. The only thing missing was a stage win, but for now the 25-year-old was focused on keeping the yellow jersey as long as possible. How long might that be? "Maybe I'll keep it until Paris," Boonen said with a grin.

MCEWEN'S REVENGE

Huy is no stranger to big-time bike racing. Each spring since 1983, this city has welcomed the finish of the Belgian classic Flèche Wallonne. In 2006, Huy had the rare distinction of hosting stages of the world's two largest stage races, the Tour de France and the Giro d'Italia. At La Flèche, a gritty one-day race held each April, riders must ascend the wall-like Mur de Huy three times; Belgian cyclists dream of winning atop the 1km-long climb with its 18 percent pitches. The riders at the Tour, however, would be spared that punishment on stage 4 from Huy to St. Quentin, back in France. This would be a day for sprinters, not climbers. As a large crowd assembled next to the Meuse River, the infamous Mur sat quietly above, well away from the hubbub.

Most of the spectators in Huy were hoping to glimpse Boonen wearing the yellow jersey. The tall, good-looking rider from Antwerp is so popular in Belgium that he moved to Monaco in 2005 to escape the local spotlight.

Many spectators in Huy proclaimed their loyalty by wearing the blue-and-white caps of Boonen's Quick Step team. Also evident were those of Belgium's other ProTour team, Davitamon-Lotto. Fans knew the best hope for Davitamon was its popular fireplug, McEwen. The compact 34-year-old may be an Aussie, but Belgium has adopted McEwen as one of its own. He speaks the native language and resides in the Belgian town of Brakel with his wife and son. Best of all, McEwen knows how to win bike races.

With a few wispy clouds offering a brief respite from the oppressive heat that marked the Tour's first week, McEwen swung a leg over his Ridley team bike and rolled slowly toward the start. Fans on either side, held back by metal barriers, shouted encouragement. One, wearing a Davitamon team jersey, leaned over the barrier as far as he could and shouted, "You can win today, Robbie!"

Without looking up, McEwen quietly replied, "I know."

McEwen has earned a reputation as a scrapper, an explosive finisher who is comfortable in chaotic finishes. He handles curveballs better than some of his rivals who prefer long, straight finishing stretches and organized team lead-outs, but that doesn't mean McEwen is just winging it. On the contrary, he studies every detail of race finishes. When McEwen flies beneath the little red flag signifying the final kilometer of a race, he knows exactly what he's about to encounter.

When he first scrutinized this 207km stage 4, McEwen's eyes lit up. This stage is mine, he thought. If his team could chase down the inevitable breaks on the rolling terrain, the finish had his name written all over it.

McEwen kept that finish in mind as the field departed Huy, climbed out of the Meuse valley, and set off toward the southwest. An early break of five riders peeled

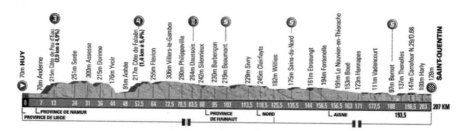

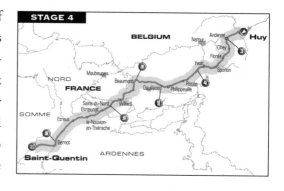

off on the undulating terrain of southern Belgium's Ardennes region and gained five minutes by the 80km mark. Brisk crosswinds made it a tough day for the breakaway group, and by the time they crossed into France with 90km to go, the gap was coming down fast.

The finish to stage 4 suited both McEwen and Boonen. It was almost identical to the stage finish that gave the Belgian his first Tour stage victory at Angers in 2004: gradually uphill after a series of turns in the last 2km. McEwen could not contest that sprint two years ago because he crashed heavily with 1km to go.

As they closed in on St. Quentin, things were playing out just as McEwen had hoped. The breakaway group was fracturing and the sprinters' teams were reeling them in. With everything else going according to plan, McEwen had just one concern—his main lead-out man, Rodriguez, was gone. Without the speedy American, one of several casualties in the treacherous stage 3, McEwen turned to his tall Belgian teammate Gert Steegmans to get the job done. He talked to Steegmans before the start, and then again as they approached the finish.

"I told Steegmans to just keep listening to me and wait until I give you the signal," McEwen said. After the last of the breakaways was caught with less than 2km to go, it was time for the new lead-out man to prove himself. "He almost took off too early and I had him on the reins and told him to wait just a bit longer. I told him just hang back, we're going to wait until 450 meters and from there you can start to come out of the wheels. I told him, imagine that your finish line is at 200 meters to go."

As usual, McEwen knew exactly what to expect in the closing kilometer. "It had about a 3 percent gradient with a very slight corner to the left at 200 meters to go," he said later.

Steegmans did his part, and once he pulled off at the 200-meter mark, McEwen made it look easy. He beat two Spaniards, Isaac Galvez of Caisse d'Épargne and Freire, who were second and third, respectively.

Boonen, who wanted desperately to win a stage so close to home, could only manage fifth in the sprint, a result he called a bitter disappointment. Finishing fourth, just in front of the Belgian, was Crédit Agricole sprinter Hushovd, who also had a disastrous day. Hushovd's Kiwi teammate Dean crashed in the up-hill sprint, and the Norwegian, who wore the green jersey during the stage, was shocked to find out later that officials relegated him from the sprint and stripped him of his fourth-place points because of "irregular sprinting."

It was a devastating blow for the defending champion of the points competition, and he strongly disagreed with the call. "That was just a big mistake by the judge," said Hushovd.

STAGE 3: ESCH-SUR-ALZETTE TO VALKENBURG

1. Matthias Kessler (G), T-Mobile, 216.5km in 4:57:54 (43.605kph); **2.** Michael Rogers (Aus), T-Mobile, at 0:05; **3.** Daniele Bennati (I), Lampre; **4.** Tom Boonen (B), Quick Step-Innergetic; **5.** Erik Zabel (G), Milram; **6.** Luca Paolini (I), Liquigas-Bianchi; **7.** Oscar Freire (Sp), Rabobank; **8.** Eddy Mazzoleni (I), T-Mobile; **9.** Georg Totschnig (A), Gerolsteiner; **10.** Fabian Wegmann (G), Gerolsteiner, all s.t.

STAGE 4: HUY TO ST. QUENTIN

1. Robbie McEwen (Aus), Davitamon-Lotto, 207km in 4:59:50 (41.423kph); **2.** Isaac Galvez (Sp), Caisse d'Épargne-Illes Balears; **3.** Oscar Freire (Sp), Rabobank; **4.** Thor Hushovd (N), Crédit Agricole; **5.** Tom Boonen (B), Quick Step-Innergetic; **6.** David Kopp (G), Gerolsteiner; **7.** Daniele Bennati (I), Lampre-Fondital; **8.** Francisco Ventoso (Sp), Saunier Duval-Prodir; **9.** Michael Albasini (Swi), Liquigas-Bianchi; **10.** Bernhard Eisel (A), Française des Jeux, all s.t.

GENERAL CLASSIFICATION

1. Tom Boonen (B), Quick Step-Innergetic

2. Michael Rogers (Aus), T-Mobile, at 00:01

3. George Hincapie (USA), Discovery Channel, at 00:05

4. Thor Hushovd (Nor), Crédit Agricole, at 00:07

5. Paolo Savoldelli (I), Discovery Channel, at 00:15

CHAPTER 8

Changing Dynamics

Absences put sprinters in the spotlight as the Tour heads west.

Besides prerace favorites Jan Ullrich, Ivan Basso, and Alexander Vinokourov, another rider, Team Milram's keynote sprinter Alessandro Petacchi, was missing from the 2006 Tour, as well as a key event, the team time trial. Petacchi's absence, and particularly that of his lead-out train, was making every sprint finish less predictable. The race organizers' decision to leave out the TTT for geographical and logistical reasons was also having a major impact on the race.

The team time trial, normally held on the Tour's fifth day, always influences the race outcome. It was no coincidence, for instance, that overall winner Lance Armstrong's team had won the TTT the three previous years. As a result, several teams planned their 2006 rosters expecting this group discipline to be included in the Tour. T-Mobile, for example, was somewhat unbalanced because it signed Sergei Gontchar, Michael Rogers, and Eddy Mazzoleni with the TTT in mind. And with no TTT to break up the overall rankings, the sprinters were in the limelight far longer than usual.

Without Petacchi, who was recovering from a fractured kneecap, the dynamics of the field sprints were completely changed. For one thing, the Quick Step-Innergetic teammates of expected sprint dominator Tom Boonen seemed incapable of stepping up their game to replace the Milram lead-out train. And

the longer Boonen went without winning a stage, the more frustrated they became. Also, the weakened T-Mobile and CSC teams had no interest in setting the
peloton's tempo after their respective leaders did not start. This led to a free-for-
all in virtually every stage finale.

Instead of the Tour's scheduled 22 teams and 198 riders, only 20 teams and
176 riders set out from Strasbourg on July 1. This also changed the first week's
racing. By the end of the initial sweep across Luxembourg, the Netherlands
and Belgium, two more team leaders were out of the race. Danilo Di Luca of
Liquigas did not start stage 2 because of a high fever, and Alejandro Valverde
of Caisse d'Épargne-Illes Balears crashed near the end of stage 3, breaking
his collarbone.

"Being only 170 riders after one week is quite strange," said CSC team rider
Christian Vande Velde. "That makes a huge difference, having [fewer] bodies trying to fight for the front. [You're] stressed out a lot [less] when you know you can
get from the back to the front much easier—I'm not saying it's easy to do, but
you know you can do it. Everyone's just relaxed quite a bit more."

Others didn't agree with that assessment, particularly fellow American Levi
Leipheimer, who said before the start of stage 6 in Lisieux, "I've tried to stay as
quiet as possible and relaxed as much as possible, and it hasn't been easy. In my
opinion we haven't had any flat stages. It's been a lot of climbing every day. I don't
know if everyone realizes that, but a lot of up and down and not a lot of time to
relax and just sit in the group. So it's been difficult."

Leipheimer's view was backed by Davitamon's Chris Horner, who was still
in pain from dislocating his left pinkie in stage 3. "There's not a whole lot for
me in these first flat stages," Horner said. "With the exception of the stage that
finished at Valkenburg, which was the only one where you had a chance of any
kind of fun, the rest of the time you're going up these short, little climbs; and, as a
climber, these things just hurt you more than the big climbs because you're climbing with 150 guys next to you and you're [thinking], 'Whoa, man. What's going
on here? How come there's so many guys?' But the climbs are only 1 kilometer,
so what do you expect?"

STORMING INTO NORMANDY

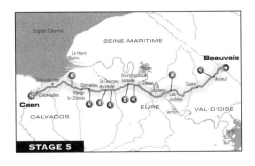

Another effect of omitting the team time trial was that no major time gaps developed in the general classification; in every early break there was someone, timewise, not far from taking the yellow jersey. As a result, the sprinters' teams had a strong incentive to contain the breakaways and give their leaders a chance to take a stage win or the yellow jersey.

In stage 5 several riders near the top of the GC rankings—notably Sebastian Lang of Gerolsteiner, Bram Tankink of Quick Step, and Manuel Quinziato of Liquigas—went with the early eight-man break. Despite several kilometers of flat-out effort (almost 46km were raced in the opening hour on lumpy terrain), the break never took more than 30 seconds' lead. And only when two of those eight, Frenchman Samuel Dumoulin of AG2R and German Björn Schröder of Milram, went on ahead (with the other six dropping back to the field) did the day's long breakaway develop.

After racing through heat wave temperatures on the Tour's opening five days, the peloton was grateful for more temperate conditions on this 225km stage that started in Beauvais, north of Paris, and headed southwest to Caen, just inland from the Normandy beaches. Local forecasts called for temperatures in the low 70s, a 40 percent chance of rain, and moderate west winds in the riders' faces, winds that made the two breakaways' task much harder despite their taking a 12:50 lead after 84km of racing.

Also playing in the sprinters' favor was the course layout. The ups and downs in its middle section through the Seine valley helped cut the leaders' gap to 4:40 by the day's third and last intermediate sprint at Pont-L'Évêque. From there the final 50km were raced on mainly straight, exposed highways that made it easier for the Davitamon, Quick Step, and Crédit Agricole teams to keep closing in on Dumoulin and Schröder. Another sprint finish looked inevitable.

Thor Hushovd's relegation from the sprint the previous day put McEwen back in the green jersey, and the Davitamon rider was now heavily favored to wear it all the way to Paris. McEwen's win in St. Quentin was his tenth Tour stage victory. A nice feather in the cap, he said, but not something he placed much emphasis on. "Every year it's just like starting at zero again," McEwen said. "Because what you've done the year before or two years ago doesn't matter. It doesn't matter how many green jerseys you've got hanging in your closet or how many stages you've won. When you get here you've got to do it again."

> **"EVERY YEAR IT'S JUST LIKE STARTING AT ZERO AGAIN, BECAUSE WHAT YOU'VE DONE THE YEAR BEFORE OR TWO YEARS AGO DOESN'T MATTER. IT DOESN'T MATTER HOW MANY GREEN JERSEYS YOU'VE GOT HANGING IN YOUR CLOSET OR HOW MANY STAGES YOU'VE WON. WHEN YOU GET HERE YOU'VE GOT TO DO IT AGAIN."**

McEwen was all too aware of how quickly a sprinter's fortunes can change. The harsh ruling against Hushovd in stage 4 was something the Aussie had experienced in 2005. "Hushovd has come across what happened to me last year," said McEwen. "He's been disqualified and missed all points. It shows how quickly a green jersey dream can fade away."

At the finish in Caen, McEwen would get a good look at who might pose the top threat at this Tour, with riders like Oscar Freire, Erik Zabel, and Boonen still knocking on the door. A fast, tricky run-in with roundabouts and plenty of turns through the streets of the sprawling city made it hard for a sprinter's lead-out train to succeed. The last 2km were completely flat alongside the horse race course at Caen. It was the sort of finish that favored Rabobank's Freire.

After finishing fourth in stage 2 and third in stage 4, the 30-year-old Spaniard decided he needed a different plan of attack to win stage 5. Instead of reacting to McEwen, he decided to make his move when his rivals least expected it. "After I saw how strong McEwen has been I wanted to be on his wheel [in previous stages] because I haven't felt like I had the strength in my legs," said Freire. "I've been close. I knew if I wanted to win today, I was going to have to make a surprise."

This was the fourth 200-plus-kilometer stage in a row, meaning that riders' legs were getting tired and their concentration strained—exactly the circumstances Freire loves to exploit. And he was very eager to score his first Tour de France stage win since 2002.

Into the finishing stretch, McEwen was tucked in behind his new lead-out man, Gert Steegmans, but Steegmans mistook the 500 meters to go sign for the 300 meters sign and began his effort much too soon. This opened the way for a chaotic drag race down the finishing stretch of Caen's Guillou Boulevard. Now exposed out front and sprinting into a headwind, McEwen was unable to respond to a sudden attack up the right side of the road by Freire approaching the 200-meters-to-go marker. Boonen, coming from the middle, veered toward Freire in the final 100 meters, but he was edged out at the line by a bike length. McEwen could only manage a fifth-place finish.

STAGES OR THE JERSEY?

It was the latest in a series of frustrating near misses for Boonen, but he earned the consolation prize of another day in yellow. "Three days with the yellow jersey, I'm happy with my performance," Boonen said. "It's not bad for the beginning of the Tour."

Perhaps trying to convince himself, Boonen said wearing the yellow jersey made up for not yet winning a stage. "I'm more happy [to wear yellow] because I'm not supposed to wear it," he said. "I'm not the kind of rider to wear yellow in the Tour so I'm very, very proud of what the team and I have realized in the last few days."

Still, Boonen admitted that being the leader was beginning to take a toll on him and his team. "It's been causing a little bit of strain," he said. "But I'm close to the green and I'm wearing the yellow as world champion."

With the important stage 7 individual time trial two days away, Boonen knew his days in yellow were numbered, and he made the most of it while he could. As for Freire, he knew that winning stages ahead of the top sprinters was his ticket to glory.

Springing surprises is Freire's hallmark. Much of his success has been founded on his stunning ability to pull victory from defeat in opportune moments. Riding on a team without a setup train and lacking the personal consistency to regularly be in the mix for the sprints, Freire nonetheless sneaks in and snatches the top prize when his rivals least expect it.

Just ask poor Zabel, who lifted his arms in victory on the Via Roma in 2004 thinking he had just won his fifth Milan-San Remo. Looking from the corner of his eye, the veteran German was helpless to react as he saw Oscar the Cat stab his bike across the line and win by millimeters.

Just ask Ullrich, Frank Vandenbroucke, and Oskar Camenzind, who were part of an all-star eight-man breakaway at the 1999 world road championships in Verona. They were all distraught at watching an unheralded second-year pro ride away with the rainbow jersey after an audacious attack 400 meters from the line.

That was Freire's only win of the season, a shocking result that heralded his arrival on the international scene. Like a good *nieto*, he used his winnings to refit his grandmother's apartment with an elevator.

For a sprinter, Freire's victories are fairly sparse—fewer than 40 wins after seven years in the pro ranks going into the 2006 season. But he has become the new dominator of the world championships. Freire racked up three world victories and a bronze medal in a remarkable six-year run from 1999 to 2004, to equal the all-time record of Alfredo Binda, Rik Van Steenbergen, and Eddy Merckx.

"Oscar has a tremendous ability to win big races," surmised Freire's former teammate Leipheimer, who raced alongside the Spaniard for two seasons at

Rabobank. "And he's so relaxed about how he carries himself. I don't know how he does it, but it works for him."

Despite his pedigree of winning big races, no one ever knows what to expect of the talented Spaniard. Plagued by injuries and setbacks, Freire depends on the element of surprise to maximize the moments when he is feeling 100 percent.

In 2005, for instance, an injury-free Freire reeled off seven wins before the April classics. But a cyst developed on his hip, which made sitting on the saddle acutely painful. Post-spring-classic surgery kept him out of the Tour, but he was expected to come back in time to make a charge at a fourth world title on home roads in Madrid. The recovery didn't go as planned. Freire couldn't train, the cyst became infected, and he had to throw in the towel on the season.

Freire's 2006 campaign started well enough. He won stages at Tirreno-Adriatico, Basque Country, and the Tour of Switzerland before heading to the Tour de France. Without a setup train to challenge Boonen or the top-end speed to come around McEwen, Freire knew he would have to defy convention to win a stage during the first week.

Following the wheels, he was getting knocked down by McEwen; trying to barge Boonen's train, he was losing his position. Finally, coming into Caen at the end of the long stage 5 across Normandy, Freire threw caution to the wind and started an early sprint to catch Boonen and McEwen by surprise.

"This win is for me," Freire said. "It's compensation for all the bad moments that I've gone through, the pain and the injuries."

By the time he charged across the line in Caen, the cat was clearly out of the bag. Freire chalked up his second career Tour stage victory in typical fashion: no train, no setup. Just raw instinct, brilliant tactics, and a trademark surprise.

SPRINTERS AND STRATEGIES

Among the teams that had been restraining breakaways was Phonak, Floyd Landis's team, which had been setting the tempo in the peloton while keeping its leader out of the danger zone. The risks of riding farther back in the pack were demonstrated on the stage into Caen. Fifth-placed Egoi Martinez of Discovery

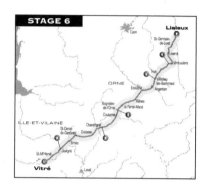

Channel fell with 15km to go and lost a minute, while one of CSC's GC hopes, Fränk Schleck, was involved in a crash 3.5km from the finish—just 500 meters before the crash "safety zone" that begins 3km from the finish line and insulates riders from time losses within its boundaries—and lost more than two minutes.

There would probably be similar incidents in stage 6, which took the Tour peloton 189km across rolling hills from Lisieux to Vitré. Typical of the courses described by Horner and Leipheimer, stage 6 contained just one categorized climb but also featured two dozen significant hills through the open countryside of Normandy. The Cat. 3 climb, the Côte de la Hunière at the Camembert cheese–producing town of Vimoutiers after 26km, triggered a strange bout of infighting.

When an 8km chase by King of the Mountains Jérôme Pineau's Bouygues Telecom team failed to catch all but two riders from an early break on the narrow climb's short 13 percent pitches, the inevitable counterattack happened. It would soon see 17 riders going 1:30 clear of the pack.

This lead group was headed by race leader Boonen and previous yellow jersey Hushovd, along with two other fast finishers, Philippe Gilbert of Française des Jeux and Magnus Bäckstedt of Liquigas. Also there were top team lieutenants in Patrik Sinkewitz of T-Mobile and Axel Merckx of Phonak. Initially McEwen's Davitamon troops led the chase before the teams of GC riders Leipheimer, Denis Menchov, and Carlos Sastre steadily closed the gap.

The chase lasted a good half hour before the move's originators, French rider Anthony Geslin of Bouygues and Florent Brard of Caisse d'Épargne, joined with Bäckstedt to create the day's "tolerated" breakaway 116km from the finish.

Once the break was established, the peloton's tempo was set by the six or so teams that wanted to enable their sprinters to have another chance of winning. The Quick Step team riders had probably worked the hardest in this opening week, and although they had race leader Boonen's yellow jersey, they would rather have seen him win a stage.

The world champion became more anxious with each day that passed without a win. Upon coming in second to Freire at Caen, Boonen admitted that he made a mistake in the last 300 meters; it wasn't the fault of his teammates, he said.

After Boonen's and McEwen's teammates again helped close in on the breakaway, it was the Lampre-Fondital team of Italian hope Daniele Bennati that worked the hardest to catch the leading trio with 3km to go. The finish was demanding: a gradual climb of 164 feet past Vitré's medieval castle with a half dozen tight turns before reaching the 2km, slightly uphill straightaway.

It was a finish that three still active sprinters had contested in the 2000 Tour. That most recent finish at Vitré saw Zabel finish second, McEwen sixth, and Stuart O'Grady eighth. With O'Grady still suffering from his broken vertebra and Zabel, on his 36th birthday, unable to find his former top-end speed, it was McEwen who was most likely to take advantage of his local knowledge. Knowing the layout of the finish, the Davitamon sprinter was able to forewarn his new lead-out man, Steegmans, on where and when to make his effort.

"I told him not to start [the sprint] one meter before the 450-meter sign, to make sure which side opens up, and at 400 meters to just go." McEwen said. "I really had to jump to go with him. And if I had to jump to get on him, I knew nobody else could go. It's like getting on my own personal TGV [express train]— and I'm the only one with a ticket."

While the speedy Steegmans led his Aussie boss up the left side of the road alongside the metal crowd barriers, Boonen, who'd been led out by two teammates, got trapped in the middle of the road. Trying to force a way through,

Boonen banged shoulders with Française des Jeux's Austrian sprinter Bernhard Eisel. As he crossed the line in third place behind McEwen and Bennati, the world champion banged his bars in frustration. Besides running out of road, Boonen was running out of chances at this 2006 Tour.

STAGE 5: BEAUVAIS TO CAEN

1. Oscar Freire (Sp), Rabobank, 225km in 5:18:50 (42.341kph); **2.** Tom Boonen (B), Quick Step-Innergetic; **3.** Iñaki Isasi (Sp), Euskaltel-Euskadi; **4.** David Kopp (G), Gerolsteiner; **5.** Robbie McEwen (Aus), Davitamon-Lotto; **6.** Alessandro Ballan (I), Lampre-Fondital; **7.** Thor Hushovd (N), Crédit Agricole; **8.** Francisco Ventoso (Sp), Saunier Duval; **9.** Erik Zabel (G), Milram; **10.** Bernhard Eisel (A), Française des Jeux, all s.t.

STAGE 6: LISIEUX TO VITRÉ

1. Robbie McEwen (Aus), Davitamon-Lotto, 189km in 4:10:17 (45.308kph); **2.** Daniele Bennati (I), Lampre-Fondital; **3.** Tom Boonen (B), Quick Step-Innergetic; **4.** Bernhard Eisel (A), Française des Jeux; **5.** Thor Hushovd (N), Crédit Agricole; **6.** Oscar Freire (Sp), Rabobank; **7.** Erik Zabel (G), Milram; **8.** Luca Paolini (I), Liquigas; **9.** Gert Steegmans (B), Davitamon-Lotto; **10.** Iñaki Isasi (Sp), Euskaltel-Euskadi, all s.t.

GENERAL CLASSIFICATION

1. Tom Boonen (B), Quick Step-Innergetic

2. Robbie McEwen (Aus), Davitamon-Lotto, at 0:12

3. Michael Rogers (Aus), T-Mobile, at 0:21

4. Oscar Freire (Sp), Rabobank, at 0:25

5. George Hincapie (USA), Discovery Channel, at 0:25

CHAPTER 9

No Decision

Rennes time trial provides more questions than answers.

Less than a minute into his stage 7 time trial, Bobby Julich was moving at a healthy clip of 60kph, or 37mph. He had taken the momentum from a very fast downhill into a wide traffic circle, where barriers funneled the riders to the left around the roundabout's shorter, wrong-way route. As Julich started to straighten up after angling his bike through the swishing left-right-left chicane, his wheels began to slide from under him. He was moving too fast to correct his trajectory and the bike careened into a low granite curb. As his bike clattered to the right, Julich thudded onto the pavement. He didn't get up.

His fall was uncannily similar to the crash the American suffered on a curving left downhill in the Metz time trial at the 1999 Tour, a race that he was favored to win after finishing third overall the previous year. As he did in the same stage seven years earlier, Julich exited the race in an ambulance, this time with a fractured scaphoid.

Julich had anticipated a great ride in this Tour's first long time trial. When his CSC team leader Ivan Basso was sent home before the start and not replaced, Julich became one of several riders on the Danish squad who could raise their personal ambitions. After all, he was the only team member who had previously finished on the Tour's podium. He was also one of CSC's three strongest time trialists, along with Dave Zabriskie and Carlos Sastre. The rider

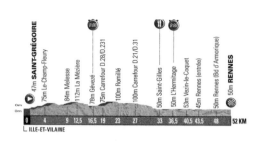

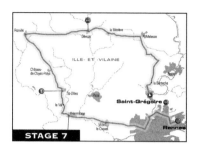

STAGE 7

who did best in this time trial had a good chance of becoming the team leader in the mountains.

Compared with the other leading Americans, Julich was considered a long shot. Going into this 52km time trial, expert race followers agreed that the top tips were the riders who placed first through fourth in the slightly shorter time trial at the previous month's Dauphiné Libéré: Zabriskie, Phonak's Floyd Landis, Gerolsteiner's Levi Leipheimer, and Discovery's George Hincapie. Also expected to do well were Sastre, Rabobank's Denis Menchov, Davitamon's Cadel Evans, and the T-Mobile trio of Andreas Klöden, Michael Rogers, and Sergei Gontchar.

The counterclockwise loop from St. Grégoire, a northern suburb of Rennes, headed north and west along rolling, rural roads before turning south and then east, back to Rennes, the capital of Brittany, and the campus of Beaulieu University. The only other time a Tour time trial had finished here, in 1989, the winner was another American, Greg LeMond, who took the yellow jersey and eventually won the race by eight seconds after a memorable battle with Frenchman Laurent Fignon.

There was less joy for the American challengers at Rennes this year. Leipheimer, the first to climb into the start house, was the 147th rider of the 171 starters. He seemed smooth when he pedaled out from the start spinning a moderate gear at a cadence of 95 revolutions per minute. But it soon became clear that the Gerolsteiner leader was not riding at his best. Leipheimer was moving at only 40kph where he should have been doing 45, and only 50 when the fastest riders would probably be approaching 60.

Perhaps he was making his typical slow start. Before the stage, Leipheimer had said, "I think realistically I'm not really expecting to win, but to limit my losses to some of the better time trialists like Landis or Rogers. That's basically my goal."

Even that goal looked unattainable when he went through the 16.5km split in 21:38, exactly a minute slower than his Gerolsteiner teammate Sebastian Lang and Française des Jeux's Swedish national time trial champ Gustav Larsson, the stage leaders at that point. Leipheimer's progress looked even worse when the next starter, his training partner, Christian Vande Velde of CSC, started to catch him. As Vande Velde had started two minutes behind Leipheimer, this was a bad sign.

"I've trained with Levi since early May," said Vande Velde. "He's really helped me turn myself around this year. You always want to train with someone who's better than you. I've been chasing a little blue speck in the mountains for the last couple of months . . . so to see him ahead of me after 15 kilometers [in the time trial] was really strange. I almost wanted to help him out . . . but there was nothing I could do."

Not only was Leipheimer the only prerace favorite to completely mess up his time trial, finishing 96th on the stage, but he also finished minutes behind four of his German teammates: Lang (3rd), Markus Fothen (7th), Ronny Scholz (43rd), and Fabian Wegmann (60th). It was a stunning defeat for Leipheimer, who had no immediate explanation for his lackluster performance.

"Somebody asked me if I peaked too early," the Santa Rosa, California, resident said, "but even if I was riding badly I wouldn't lose six minutes. I mean, there's definitely a reason, and I just want to get past it."

Vande Velde added, "Afterwards, I asked him if he's okay, what's going on? He said, 'Oh, I'm all right.' His electrolytes were really out of whack and just made him feel pretty bad on the bike."

Leipheimer was reluctant to give any excuses. "It's not going to help me . . . to keep talking about it," he said. "But now, obviously, if I can feel better, I will have to be more aggressive and do something I've never done before in the Tour. That could be exciting."

LANDIS IS BEST AMERICAN

The American "bad news" day continued with Zabriskie, who never got into the elevated rhythm that won him the Dauphiné time trial and the opening stage of the 2005 Tour. He finished 13th, two minutes off the pace he needed to win the stage.

The next U.S. contender to start was Landis, who set out from St. Grégoire four minutes after Gontchar, a former world time-trial champion, whose intermediate times would be an invaluable reference for the Phonak leader. But before Landis even reached the first checkpoint, just as he was leaving the village of La Mezière after 13km, he had a sudden scare.

Photographer Graham Watson, who was on a motorcycle following Landis and his team car, said, "I heard this loud crack and thought that the front of the team car had hit something. But it was Floyd. He hit a raised cobblestone—not really a speed bump, it was more like a decorative [feature]—and he snapped the right-hand part of his aerobars. If both parts had cracked he would have gone down headfirst. But he was able to stop and get a quick bike change."

Earlier in the day, both of Landis's time trial bikes had been checked by the UCI commissaires to make sure the tops of his raised aerobars did not project above the plane of his saddle, to conform with UCI technical regulations. The cracking probably occurred when the sudden jolt from his front wheel hitting the cobblestone was transmitted straight to the carbon-fiber tube, perhaps combined with the stress exerted by Landis pulling on the bars in his upward-arm position.

Before the stage Landis said, "I think it's important not to start off too fast. It's better to approach it a bit conservatively and then go for it during the final 10km. I'm usually successful with that tactic."

But Landis *did* start fast, perhaps not intentionally, and when he raced through the 16.5km checkpoint, he stopped the overhead digital timer at 19:54. That was second fastest, just 17 seconds down on Gontchar—and Landis probably lost those 17 seconds in changing bikes after his bar broke.

But Landis didn't maintain his initial pace. In the remaining distance, he raced more conservatively, as predicted, and steadily lost time to Gontchar. He still ended up in second place, 1:01 behind the Ukraine veteran. But Landis had a comfortable margin over his expected GC rivals, with the California resident now leading Rogers, Klöden, and Evans by almost a minute, and Menchov, Sastre, and Hincapie by almost two minutes.

While Landis was pleased with his ride, Hincapie was among the riders who were expecting much more. He finished 2:42 off the pace set by Gontchar. "I was disappointed with my performance. I thought I'd do better," Hincapie said. "I felt dehydrated and I ran out of fuel. Maybe I ate too soon. It was definitely not a normal performance for me."

Hincapie said he just couldn't find his rhythm on the rolling course, but said all was not lost. Most riders were using Landis as the Tour reference point, and by that measure Hincapie was only 1:30 behind his former teammate on general classification. "We just have to see and hope I can recover," Hincapie continued. "It was just a bad day for the team."

In the wake of the disappointing results, Discovery Channel was forced to reassess its strategy. The team began the time trial with two riders in the top ten, but after the dust settled, Paolo Savoldelli was 13th, 2:10 behind new race leader Gontchar, with Hincapie in 17th at 2:30.

"It doesn't have an explanation," said Discovery team boss Johan Bruyneel. "The team is disappointed, but everything is not

"THANK GOD ULLRICH IS NOT HERE BECAUSE IT WOULD BE ALL LOST IF HE WERE."

lost. We lost some options, but the hope of making a great Tour continues."

Then, commenting on the superior showing by the T-Mobile squad, which placed four riders in the top eight, Bruyneel said, "I am most surprised about T-Mobile—thank God [Jan] Ullrich is not here because it would be all lost if he were."

MENCHOV MENACE

Besides the T-Mobile surprise, Rabobank's quiet leader, Menchov, was one of the looming threats in this wide-open Tour. The lanky Russian is a man who prefers to let his legs do the talking. Inquiries in Strasbourg about his form before the start of the Tour were met with a shrug—an "I don't know" and a halfhearted "we'll see." Menchov was not saying a thing.

It was hard to tell what to expect from Menchov, a 28-year-old in his second year with Rabobank, who finished 11th overall and took the best young rider's white jersey in 2003 but had since struggled at the Tour. The 2005 race was a complete meltdown for the quiet but ambitious Russian, who many believe could be the first from his nation to win cycling's biggest prize. He fell flat after a cold sapped his strength and finished a distant 85th.

After limping through the '05 Tour, Menchov roared into the 2005 Vuelta a España intent on proving he should be counted as a legitimate contender for the three grand tours. He won the 7km prologue in Granada and then scored an even more impressive victory in the challenging 48km time trial at Lloret de Mar. The Russian seemed to have the overall win in the bag after fending off a string of attacks from Roberto Heras of Liberty Seguros up the brutally steep climbing stage to Lagos de Covadonga. But he then got caught out by a Liberty team ambush on a rainy, cold climbing stage to Puerto de Pájares and lost the lead to Heras.

A few days later, in the final time trial, Heras tested positive for EPO. The Spaniard was eventually suspended for two years and runner-up Menchov was given his first grand tour victory. "I would have preferred not to have won like that," Menchov said. "I was content with my second place and what happened later wasn't good for the Vuelta or good for cycling."

The options were clear for Rabobank brass, however, when it came to planning for the 2006 Tour. The two long, flat time trials ruled out any hopes for its Danish climber, Michael Rasmussen, so the team rallied its overall hopes around Menchov's icy persona.

"We discussed it over the winter," Rasmussen said. "With 115 kilometers of flat time trials, it made it quite obvious that Denis, who came fresh off victories in time trials at the Vuelta, was the better option."

"I would like to have a good Tour," Menchov said at the time. "I've had good preparation and the team believes in me. I don't know; we'll have to wait and see how things go."

Discreet is one way to describe Menchov, a quiet, unassuming man with a big mop of hair who would prefer that no one paid any attention to him. He'd just as soon get down to the business of racing his bike and leave the hoopla to others.

Menchov was born in Orel on the wide-open steppes of western Russia, the ancient home of the marauding Cossacks, about 350km south of Moscow. A keen cross-country skier, Menchov has a big engine and finds the bicycle to be a natural ally. Unlike many of his compatriots who drifted to Italy, Menchov found refuge in the Russian amateur team, Lada-Samara, with which he won the 1998 Ronde de l'Isard, a tough climbing stage race in southern France. Menchov's performance was noted by a Banesto team official, Francis Lafargue, who suggested to team boss José Miguel Echávarri that the long-legged Russian was a jewel in the making. The Spanish team signed him as a pro in 2000.

Menchov quickly assimilated into the team's Spanish culture and settled in a small village in the foothills outside of the team's headquarters in Pamplona. Menchov and his wife, Nadia, welcomed two sons, and he soon became fluent in Spanish.

He delivered on his promise by taking home the 2001 Tour de l'Avenir and scoring a victory on Mont Ventoux at the 2002 Dauphiné Libéré. Those results suggested a prominent role for Menchov at future Tours de France. But at the end of 2004 his team—now sponsored by Illes Balears—lost Menchov to Dutch team Rabobank, which gave him a much bigger contract.

After his 2005 Tour was marred by illness, Menchov was ready for a big comeback. The eventual Vuelta victory was a first boost to his confidence, while a repeat of his Ventoux victory at the 2006 Dauphiné was a second. Now, after getting through the first week of the Tour among the leaders, Menchov was ready to let his legs do the talking once and for all. Just the way he likes it.

STAGE 7: ST. GRÉGOIRE TO RENNES TIME TRIAL

1. Sergei Gontchar (Ukr), T-Mobile, 52km in 1:01:43 (50.553kph); **2. Floyd Landis (USA), Phonak, 1:02:44;** 3. Sebastian Lang (G), Gerolsteiner, 1:02:47; 4. Michael Rogers (Aus), T-Mobile, 1:03:07; 5. Gustav Larsson (S), Française des Jeux, 1:03:17; 6. Patrik Sinkewitz (G), T-Mobile, 1:03:22; 7. Marcus Fothen (G), Gerolsteiner, 1:03:25; 8. Andreas Klöden (G), T-Mobile, 1:03:26; 9. Denis Menchov (Rus), Rabobank, 1:03:27; 10. Joost Posthuma (Nl), Rabobank, 1:03:28.

GENERAL CLASSIFICATION

1. Sergei Gontchar (Ukr), T-Mobile
2. **Floyd Landis (USA), Phonak, at 1:00**
3. Michael Rogers (Aus), T-Mobile, at 1:08
4. Patrik Sinkewitz (G), T-Mobile, at 1:45
5. Marcus Fothen (G), Gerolsteiner, at 1:50

CHAPTER 10

The Lorient Express

The peloton concedes another successful breakaway.

After stage 8, the 20 teams would board two charter flights from Lorient for Bordeaux, where the riders would enjoy a full rest day and have time to take stock of what was developing into one of the strangest Tours in living memory. But before those flights, scheduled to leave at 6:15 and 6:30 p.m. local time, riders had a tricky 181km stage across the hills of Brittany to overcome.

A million fans from this cycling-mad region were expected to line the roads on a bright Sunday, particularly on the Cat. 3 Mur-de-Bretagne climb at 75km; during the day's third intermediate sprint line at 142km in Plouay (where George Hincapie won the ProTour classic GP de Plouay in August 2005); and on the slightly curving finishing straight in the port city of Lorient.

It was at Lorient in 1998 that Hincapie first came close to wearing the yellow jersey. In a stage that started on Brittany's north coast at the port of Roscoff, Hincapie worked into a small breakaway that also contained Australia's Stuart O'Grady and Denmark's Bo Hamburger. When they arrived in Lorient a minute or so clear of the pack after two hours of effort, the sprint for the stage win was expected to be between these three men. Hincapie needed to take the first- or second-place time bonus to earn the yellow jersey, but he was surprised by a late attack from German Jens Heppner and Frenchman Xavier Jan, who finished two seconds clear of the others. Hincapie took the third-place bonus that left him in second place overall, two seconds behind the new race leader, Hamburger.

Because Hincapie worked devotedly for Lance Armstrong the following seven years, he never moved any closer to wearing the Tour's fabled *maillot jaune* until he finally took a two-second bonus on the 2006 Tour's opening road stage in Strasbourg.

HINCAPIE'S NEW ROLE

When Hincapie took to the podium and donned the yellow jersey after stage 1, observers agreed it was a good omen for the Discovery Channel team at its first non-Armstrong Tour de France. At 33, Hincapie was only the fourth American, following Greg LeMond, Armstrong, and Dave Zabriskie, to earn cycling's most cherished emblem. That night, in the border town of Strasbourg just west of the Rhine River, Hincapie sipped champagne with his teammates. He received dozens of congratulatory calls, e-mails, and text messages on his BlackBerry PDA.

Although doping-related expulsions of several race favorites left top teams CSC and T-Mobile in a shambles the day before the Tour started, Hincapie and his Discovery Channel teammates seemed to be sitting pretty. The American's impressive form in the Tour's opening days was proof enough that he had recovered from the separated shoulder incurred in an April crash, and many were predicting that Discovery's four-pronged attack, featuring Hincapie, José Azevedo, Paolo Savoldelli, and Yaroslav Popovych, just might work.

"Discovery is now in a really good role because they have four guys I think can win [the Tour]," said American Chris Horner of the Davitamon-Lotto squad.

Minutes before rolling to the start of stage 2 in Obernai, Hincapie smiled and said he was going to enjoy his time in the yellow jersey. He knew it might not last long in these early days, but he hoped to be fighting for it again later, when it really mattered.

As it turned out, though, that morning in Obernai was one of the last times Hincapie had reason to smile during the 2006 Tour. After his failure in the time trial at Rennes, Hincapie could see that his former U.S. Postal Service teammate,

Floyd Landis, was riding much more strongly. Hincapie was starting to wonder if the experiment to transform himself from a one-day classics power to a Tour de France podium contender was perhaps unrealistic.

Hincapie had already ridden ten Tours, starting with the Motorola team in 1996. As a young rider he had dreamed of winning a stage with his excellent sprint. At his third Tour, while riding for the U.S. Postal team, Hincapie came close to the yellow jersey in that stage 3 break from Roscoff to Lorient. He then held second overall and mixed it up with O'Grady in the time bonus and field sprints for a few days before fading from contention in the mountains. The next year, Armstrong began his seven-year winning streak, with Hincapie always by his side.

The first few days of the Tour unfolded masterfully for Hincapie and his teammates. The American was disappointed about missing a prologue win by a fraction of a second to Norwegian Thor Hushovd, but finishing second revealed Hincapie's good form. The following day he made his surprise attack to snatch a time bonus and earn the yellow jersey. Hincapie's crafty move confirmed that the Discovery riders were ready to race without Armstrong.

"It's huge," said team boss Johan Bruyneel of Hincapie's unplanned, take-charge move. "I told the guys this morning, we're going to race this Tour and take every single possibility in front of us. And [George] did it."

It was no surprise when Hincapie lost the yellow jersey to Hushovd the next day (these were the days for the sprinters), but nobody envisioned the struggles that Hincapie and the Discovery Channel riders would face later in the race. Discovery was sailing into uncharted waters when it embarked on its first Tour in eight years without Armstrong steering the ship. For the riders, managers, and even the fans who had become accustomed to watching the American ProTour squad flourish every July, a Tour without Armstrong was an odd thing. And no one felt more unsettled than Hincapie, Armstrong's longtime friend and team-mate who rode shotgun for his Texan team leader.

Until the 2005 Tour, Armstrong's last, Hincapie had a concrete role as first lieutenant, which the hardworking, punch-the-clock New York native relished. The feeling of ushering Armstrong toward the status of Tour legend sated this son of a Colombian immigrant, and the annual clinking of champagne glasses in Paris was deeply satisfying to Hincapie. He had no problems shelving his own personal Tour ambitions for the good of the team.

The world Hincapie knew so well changed on July 15, 2005, when the veteran support rider was given the green light to go it alone on the Tour's most difficult mountain stage. With Armstrong sitting in a comfortable GC position before the colossal mountain stage to Pla d'Adet, Hincapie felt strong and asked Armstrong if he could join an early breakaway. Armstrong responded, "Yeah, man, that's a good idea."

Hincapie joined the break, and by the time the lead group topped the second of six categorized climbs, it had 18 minutes on the field. None of the breakaways posed a threat to Armstrong, and Discovery Channel's assistant sport director, Dirk Demol, told Hincapie, "George, you're not coming back. You can do your own race."

This was unfamiliar territory. "The terrain was something that I had never really raced on," Hincapie said. "I was always working for Lance. I didn't know how I would react."

To the surprise of many, including himself, Hincapie reacted by winning. He outclassed Spaniard Oscar Pereiro, who was riding for Phonak at the time, to win the 2005 Tour's most arduous stage. When he dropped Pereiro with 300 meters to go, Hincapie looked up at the finish line and wondered for a split second why the clock displayed all zeros. "I just couldn't believe it, that I was winning that stage," he said. "All the hard work that I had done for the past 20 years, it was all worth it that one moment I crossed the line."

In the following days, Hincapie's name started being kicked around as a possible successor to Armstrong. Without really trying, he finished 14th overall in the 2005 Tour. He could time trial and he could climb the Tour's most feared cols, but could this 6-foot-3 classics man really be considered a yellow jersey contender?

Why not, said Armstrong. "We always have these dreamers who say they're going to win the Tour, so why couldn't George Hincapie be in that position?" That was less than a full-fledged endorsement, but team boss Bruyneel said, "I'm sure if he could focus on it he could be one of the great [Tour] riders."

Hincapie began focusing on it. When his 2005 season wound down and he went home to Greenville, South Carolina, for winter training, he changed some things. Before heading out for a training day in January, he was asked what goals filled his mind during the long, lonely hours on the road—spring classics or the Tour?

"I definitely have both in my head now, but I've just never been in that position without having to work for Lance," Hincapie said. "I just don't know, it's kind of an unknown thought for me. But it would be hard for me to just totally forget about the classics. I think if I did that, I'd be kind of lost."

Lost would be an accurate description of the Discovery team going into the Tour's final two weeks. Hincapie went into the stage 7 time trial as one of the favorites to take the overall lead, but after starting strongly he finished in 24th place, giving up 2:42 to the day's winner, Sergei Gontchar. Bruyneel called it a disastrous day for the team and seemed defeated before the mountain stages began. "It was not the day George expected, and it was not the day the team expected," Bruyneel said. "The fact is that Lance is not here; we just have to be realistic."

BREAKOUTS IN BRITTANY

Being realistic was not bringing Discovery success at the 2006 Tour. The team seemed to be locked in to its traditional strategy of waiting for the time trials and the mountain stages to assert its superiority. It worked for Armstrong, but Bruyneel should have realized that wiping out in the Rennes time trial meant that his riders would have to try different tactics—perhaps attacking in stages like the one before them.

With no one team dominating this Tour, and with the sprinters' teams having worked overtime through the first week, the race was at a potential breaking point. It was similar to the situation after opening week at the 1960 Tour. That was in a different era, before superchampions scored strings of victories, before Armstrong, Miguel Induráin, Greg LeMond, Bernard Hinault, Eddy Merckx, and Jacques Anquetil combined for almost 30 wins in the 45 years since that 1960 Tour.

Stage 6 of that race went from St. Malo to Lorient for 191km across the Breton peninsula, and took in many of the same roads as this 2006 Tour's 181km stage 7. Back then, the roads were rougher and the bikes were heavier, but, remarkably, that stage in the 1960s was raced at a much faster speed, 44.048kph, than the one in 2006.

Going into it, the leader of the 1960 Tour was Henri Anglade of the French national team. In the preceding 28km time trial, Anglade had finished third, 48 seconds slower than his teammate Roger Rivière, while the Italian team leader, Gastone Nencini, was second, 32 seconds back.

Rivière was not happy playing second fiddle to Anglade. The two had been fierce rivals in their home region. Rivière came from St. Étienne; Anglade lived in Lyon, the neighboring big city. Their rivalry was the catalyst that led Rivière to make a remarkable attack 79km into that stage through Brittany to Lorient.

Amazingly, three other team leaders replied to Rivière's move, and no one else. Italy's Nencini stepped up to the plate along with Jan Adriaenssens of the Belgian national team and Hans Junkermann of Germany. With the Tour's four strongest teams all represented in the break, the peloton did not have the necessary unison to chase down the powerful quartet.

THE INSIDE FAVORITE TO WIN THE 2006 TOUR'S STAGE TO LORIENT WAS CSC'S JENS VOIGT, WHO TOOK THINGS EASY IN THE TIME TRIAL AND FINISHED DEAD LAST . . . A PLANNED TACTIC DESIGNED TO SAVE HIS STRENGTH FOR AN ATTACK IN STAGE 7.

The leaders worked like a four-man team time trial, averaging 45kph and constantly increasing their advantage. Anglade was furious and told his team manager, Marcel Bidot, to stop Rivière from working with the enemy. But Bidot's words fell on deaf ears. By the finish, where Rivière outsprinted the other three on the velodrome in Lorient, the gap had increased to 14:40.

When the disillusioned Anglade spoke to Bidot that evening, he said, "There are only four possible winners of this Tour, the four in the breakaway. In theory, that gives us a one in four chance. In reality, we've already lost because Rivière is sure to make mistakes. I'm even worried about something worse. He will try to follow Nencini on the descents and I'm afraid that one day he won't be able to."

Anglade's words were prophetic. In stage 14, Rivière tried to follow race leader Nencini coming down the twisting Col de Perjuret in the Cévennes. Trying to match the Italian's speed, the Frenchman misread a corner, braked too hard, and collided with a parapet. He shot 60 feet into a ravine and landed in some rocks at the foot of a tree. Rivière's back was broken and he never raced again. Nencini went on to win that Tour, with Anglade coming in eighth.

Among Anglade's fans back in Lyon may have been the Calzati family, recent immigrants from Italy. Their grandson, Sylvain Calzati, was riding the 2006 Tour as a team rider for AG2R's Christophe Moreau. Surely his father had told him Tour tales from the 1960s, including perhaps a story about that four-man breakaway to Lorient.

A BREAKAWAY STICKS

The inside favorite to win the 2006 Tour's stage to Lorient was CSC's Jens Voigt, who took things easy in the time trial and finished dead last, ten minutes slower than new race leader Gontchar. It was a planned tactic, designed to save his strength for an attack in stage 7. On a similar stage through Brittany in 2004, Voigt led a long breakaway over the Mur-de-Bretagne. But his break was caught before the uphill sprint in Quimper won by Norway's Thor Hushovd.

Two years later, when Venezuela's Unai Etxebarria (Euskaltel-Euskadi) was the first to blast away from the bunch at about 18km, Voigt was right on his wheel. Maybe Voigt's ploy was too obvious, but he found good company in Samuel Dumoulin (AG2R), Pieter Weening (Rabobank), Wim Vansevenant (Davitamon-Lotto), Vicente Garcia-Acosta (Caisse d'Épargne-Illes Balears), Ralf Grabsch (Milram), and Cédric Coutouly (Agritubel).

But T-Mobile didn't seem content with the break's makeup and started to chase the group, which never opened a lead greater than 35 seconds. Bouygues Telecom, T-Mobile, Quick Step, and Lampre shut the break down after 45km were covered in the first hour.

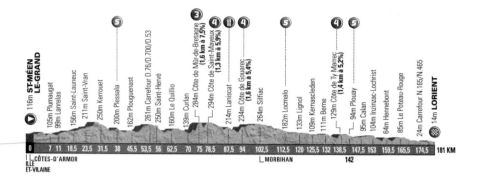

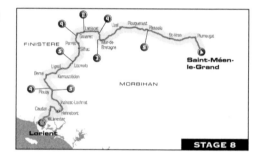

STAGE 8

"I think we are the strongest team at the moment [even though] we're only seven guys," said T-Mobile's Michael Rogers, who was lying third overall, 1:08 down on teammate Gontchar. "From the start of this year, this team has set its sights on this race and prepared well. We've showed the whole team is strong."

T-Mobile showed its strength right after Voigt was brought back and Team CSC unleashed another rider, Zabriskie; the German team sent Matthias Kessler to join the new breakaway. Also there were Calzati, Davitamon's Mario Aerts, Liquigas's Kjell Carlstrom, and Crédit Agricole's Patrick Halgand. The composition of the break suited T-Mobile and away went the six riders, rumbling through the lush, undulating farm country of France's westernmost region.

With the potentially dangerous Zabriskie and Kessler in the break, Floyd Landis's Phonak team rode the middle section of the stage at the front of the bunch to keep the move on a short leash. "We didn't know what T-Mobile's plan would be," said Landis. "But we didn't do that much work. It's a hard stage to ride regardless; it's probably harder in the back than the front. We have to be careful. We don't want to give T-Mobile more options. We're confident. I don't think we're trying to hide anything."

Also happy with the breakaway was green jersey McEwen, who wouldn't have to work his Davitamon teammates. "It's perfect for us," confirmed McEwen's directeur sportif, Hendrik Redant. "It's the perfect situation because we have someone in the break with Mario [Aerts]. We know that Kessler and Zabriskie are also there so the Phonak boys will be quite nervous. It makes life good for us because there's no pressure for us to chase but we should see the other sprint teams start to help in the chase soon."

Zabriskie was the group's best-placed rider, starting the day in tenth overall, at 2:03. (Kessler had the same time but was ranked 11th.) Before long, CSC's American slipped into the virtual *maillot jaune* as the lead grew to 7:30 at 62km. But then Phonak started to set tempo on the front of the peloton.

"We're chasing because of Kessler's presence in the escape," explained Phonak's team manager John Lelangue to French television. "We don't really need to catch the leaders but we need to ensure that the move doesn't get a big lead. We are taking our responsibility but we'll do it pragmatically because I don't want my riders to get too tired."

The lead started to dwindle under pressure from the bunch until Calzati took a solo flier 32km from the finish. "I knew there was a little climb and my plan was to attack there," said Calzati. "I can't explain why, it was just a feeling, but I knew if I could get to the top [of the hill] first, I would be able to get to the finish as I was feeling very fresh."

Halgand began a belated chase with Carlstrom but they never got close to the inspired Frenchman. With 17km to go, Zabriskie, Aerts, and Kessler were swept up, and Calzati bravely fought on to score a huge stage win for his AG2R team, 2:05 ahead of the two chasers. Another ten seconds behind, McEwen outsped Daniele Bennati and Milram's Erik Zabel to take fourth place and another few points in his green jersey quest.

For Calzati, his stage victory was the second race he had won in four years as a professional; the other was winning the overall title at the 2004 Tour de l'Avenir. With the World Cup final between France and Italy commencing later in the day, the French nation was hoping that Calzati's win was a harbinger of success on the soccer field. But when asked which team he was supporting, Calzati, whose bike-racing father is the son of Italian immigrants, said he was going to cheer for Italy.

More important for the 27-year-old stage winner, however, now he would have some Tour tales of his own to share with his family. And as the first rider in this Tour to break the hold of the sprinters, Calzati was the toast of that evening's charter flight to Bordeaux.

STAGE 8: ST. MÉEN-LE-GRAND TO LORIENT

1. Sylvain Calzati (F), AG2R, 181km in 4:13:18 (42.874kph); **2.** Kjell Carlström (Fin), Liquigas, at 2:05; **3.** Patrice Halgand (F), Crédit Agricole, s.t.; **4.** Robbie McEwen (Aus), Davitamon-Lotto, at 2:15; **5.** Daniele Bennati (I), Lampre-Fondital; **6.** Erik Zabel (G), Milram; **7.** Bernhard Eisel (A), Française des Jeux; **8.** Luca Paolini (I), Liquigas; **9.** Tom Boonen (B), Quick Step-Innergetic; **10.** David Kopp (G), Gerolsteiner, all s.t.

GENERAL CLASSIFICATION

1. Sergei Gontchar (Ukr), T-Mobile

2. Floyd Landis (USA), Phonak, at 1:00

3. Michael Rogers (Aus), T-Mobile, at 1:08

4. Patrik Sinkewitz (G), T-Mobile, at 1:45

5. Marcus Fothen (G), Gerolsteiner, at 1:50

CHAPTER 11

Looking for Leaders

Near the halfway point the Tour is still in a state of suspense.

When the Tour de France leader holds a press conference on the rest day, there's nearly always a packed house of reporters, photographers, and TV cameramen in attendance. In the recent past, superstars like Lance Armstrong, Bernard Hinault, and Greg LeMond have occupied the hot seat, answering a barrage of repetitive questions, giving their opinions on pressing topics, and eliciting laughs from the audience with their witty comments. LeMond always spoke candidly, effortlessly switching from French to English. Hinault, who once drove through the pressroom to the podium on a motorcycle, was always provocative, sometimes responding to reporters with a glare. As for Armstrong, his conferences often felt like a war zone, with European journalists pressing him with questions about doping and Armstrong shooting back challenging, hard-hitting replies.

But for this Tour, it wasn't the race leader, Sergei Gontchar, who drew the rest day's biggest crowd. It was Floyd Landis. As a prerace favorite, he was expected to have plenty to say, an expectation heightened by the news that he was suffering a degenerative hip condition that could potentially end his career. That revelation was supposed be the surprise announcement of the day, but it had already been leaked through a couple of Web sites and the *New York Times,* which in a publishing deal would report the full story of Landis's condition in its Sunday magazine the following weekend, the timing prearranged with Landis.

Accordingly, the Phonak press conference attracted a huge crowd. Landis, wearing a tie, long pants, and a borrowed sport jacket two sizes too large in place of his usual sweatpants, T-shirt, and baseball cap, faced a battery of television cameras and a clutch of reporters. Squinting slightly into the hot klieg lights set up by TV technicians, Landis talked calmly about the hip surgery he faced after the conclusion of the Tour, and its implications for his future career.

First of all, said Landis, he was going to finish the race, no matter what. As for the rest, he admitted that the pain in his hip had become so excruciating that he could no longer postpone the operation. The two doctors sitting at his side said the condition—avascular necrosis—reduces blood flow to the upper part of his right femur, which was broken when he crashed on a training ride near his home in Murrieta, California, in January 2003. He had three pins placed inside the femur knob, leaving his right leg one inch shorter than his left. Landis made a remarkable comeback to race the Tour that summer.

He had two more surgeries intended to improve blood flow to the area, the latter in November 2004. The pain worsened through the 2005 season after he joined the Phonak team, and his condition reached new depths following his Tour de Georgia victory in April 2006. The reduced blood flow to the bone left a rotten knob grinding inside the hip socket. "Floyd is in pain with daily activity, living, sleeping, walking. It's like a toothache at night," said Dr. Brent Kay, one of Landis's personal physicians. "It's bone on bone, that's essentially what it is. Normally it's like a smooth ball that rides in the socket. This is like a cauliflower and it grinds down the cartilage. At this stage, it's pretty much worn out."

Landis had kept the condition secret, telling fewer than a dozen people before going public during the Bordeaux rest day "to get the story right. I didn't tell a lot of people," Landis said. "My mom only found out about it last week."

"I found out about it a year ago," said Team CSC's Zabriskie, who shares an apartment with Landis in Spain. "He realizes now it's not going to smooth itself out. He's mentally tough. He felt he could adapt to it."

Landis, who was about to sign a one-year option on his Phonak contract, refused to speculate if his hip problem meant the end of his career. "I don't know how long my time in the peloton goes on. I know it won't go on forever. My hope is it's not over yet," Landis said. "If I had to leave now, I would be disappointed."

Doctors speculated that a full comeback would be possible. Dr. Kay compared Landis's condition to that of former two-sport athlete Bo Jackson, who underwent a similar procedure in 1992 but retired from football and baseball after his hip blew out again. "Bo Jackson ruined that new hip within two years. It's the pounding and jarring that's damaging," said Dr. Kay, who added that surgical methods and prosthesis technology had made big advances in 15 years. "As far as cycling is concerned, it doesn't put much stress on the hip joint."

Landis said that, on the bike, he felt the pain most when he was pushing hard on the pedals in the time trials and on the steepest pitches of mountain climbs. The pain had caused him to change his time trial position by moving his seat forward and raising his handlebars.

Despite the anguish, he vowed to continue to race the Tour with an eye toward overall victory. "Whatever happens, I am focusing on the race itself," Landis said. "Racing is therapy for my hip. It consumes everything I think about. While I am racing, I have the least problems."

So far, he had refused to take medication, said Phonak team doctor Denise Demir, although she confirmed that Landis had received two cortisone injections (approved by the UCI) into the joint area to help reduce the pain and inflammation. "He doesn't want pain medication. Floyd said pain makes him tough," Dr. Demir said. "I couldn't believe that he could ride when I saw images of the hip, or even walk."

Landis has always been known for his grittiness and determination, but to endure the demands of the Tour with a bum hip would set new standards in pain management among the Tour's gallery of suffering heroes. But the question on everyone's lips at the moment was, Why announce the condition now? If Landis had kept this secret for two years, what could he gain by revealing it in the middle of the Tour?

Onlookers were baffled. "I don't know why you would announce it," said Discovery team manager Johan Bruyneel the next day. "If you're the favorite you try to hide your weaknesses and not announce them. I would never do that with Armstrong."

But Landis was having none of it. "What I say to that is, 'I've got a problem and I'm going to beat you anyway,'" he said.

MEANWHILE, YOUR LEADER . . .

Almost forgotten in the hubbub over Landis was the actual Tour leader and his team. In a small conference room in the swank Sofitel Hotel, next to the convention halls in Bordeaux, two riders were sitting before a battery of nine microphones alongside the T-Mobile team manager Olaf Ludwig, who looked sharp in dress pants and a neatly ironed short-sleeve white shirt.

Despite the uncomfortably cool air-conditioning, the riders were wearing casual shorts and team-issue white T-shirts. The German squad's stage 3 winner, the unsmiling Matthias Kessler, was having a bad hair day. Sergei Gontchar was in better shape. He was this Tour's fourth race leader after Norway's Thor Hushovd, America's George Hincapie, and Belgium's Tom Boonen, and the first rider from the Ukraine to lead the Tour. He speaks no German, and he answered questions in Italian through a translator.

The Ukrainian didn't plan on being the yellow jersey at the Tour de France. In the twilight years of his long career, he had signed with T-Mobile in the fall of 2005 as a *domestique,* expecting to serve Jan Ullrich. Now the enigmatic Gontchar was the toast of his team.

"This is an extraordinary moment in my life," said the normally reticent Gontchar, who donned the yellow jersey after winning the stage 7 time trial and then exuberantly grabbed the front of the hallowed garment and tugged it to make sure it was real. The 36-year-old then skipped off the podium like a six-year-old boy who's just been given his first ice cream.

Gontchar again showed that quirky side of his character at the news conference. Smiling impishly and screwing up his eyes, he was most animated when asked about the conflicting spellings of his name: Sergei Gontchar when he notched up 20 wins, including the 2000 world time trial championship, in his first five seasons on a variety of Italian teams; and Serhiy Honchar for the following five seasons, with Fassa Bortolo, De Nardi, and Domina Vacanze.

Is his name spelled with a G or an H? "It's a G," he replied. "When I had my passport renewed a few years ago, it came back with an H instead of a G. I guess the letters are next to each other on the keyboard. It was too much trouble to get a new passport so I changed the spelling on my other documents too," he said pragmatically.

When asked about Gontchar's chances of keeping the lead through the mountains, Ludwig pointed out that the 5-foot-8, 154-pound veteran finished second at the 2004 Giro behind Damiano Cunego. "And the Giro's not flat," he added. In fact, Gontchar had finished top ten at the Giro no less than eight times, and earlier in 2006 he wore the leader's pink jersey before ceding it to the eventual winner, Ivan Basso.

Most of Gontchar's successes have come in time trials, even though his victory at Rennes was his first stage win at the Tour. Gontchar's yellow jersey helped deflect attention from the prerace exclusion of the German squad's leader Ullrich and its Spanish climber Oscar Sevilla, both victims of the *Operación Puerto* doping investigation. Remarkably, T-Mobile retained its collective composure and placed six of its remaining seven riders in the top 14 in the St. Grégoire-Rennes time trial.

> "WHEN I HAD MY PASSPORT RENEWED A FEW YEARS AGO, IT CAME BACK WITH AN H INSTEAD OF A G. I GUESS THE LETTERS ARE NEXT TO EACH OTHER ON THE KEYBOARD. IT WAS TOO MUCH TROUBLE TO GET A NEW PASSPORT SO I CHANGED THE SPELLING ON MY OTHER DOCUMENTS TOO."

But the team's depth still had to be tested in the high mountains. If Gontchar didn't come through, Ludwig said, he also had confidence in Michael Rogers (currently third on GC) and Andreas Klöden (fifth). Regarding the team manager's view on the Tour's likely strongest rider when the Tour entered the Pyrénées, Ludwig said, "For me, it is [Floyd] Landis. He has a very strong team . . . eight riders work for him. I think he is the favorite. [For others], I look to [Denis] Menchov or [Vladimir] Karpets or [Cadel] Evans—but [their teams] have two or three guys going for sprints or attacks, so it's not the same situation as Team Phonak."

OTHER CHALLENGERS

While the Landis press conference barely mentioned the Tour, those in attendance were aware that the Phonak team leader, in second place overall, was regarded as the true overall leader, not Gontchar. But with Rogers, Klöden, and Evans less than a minute down on Landis, and with Menchov, Hincapie, and Carlos Sastre less than two minutes back, the race was wide open.

In yet another press conference, Davitamon's Robbie McEwen said that Evans, his Davitamon-Lotto teammate, was looking like the strongest candidate to succeed Armstrong. "Cadel Evans is going to win the Tour de France 2006," said the deadly serious Aussie sprinter. "It's not a joke." Asked to justify his bold prediction, McEwen added, "He's the only natural GC rider here. The other [contenders] are all time trialists who've turned themselves into GC riders."

McEwen was referring to riders like T-Mobile's Gontchar and Rogers, Phonak's Landis, Rabobank's Menchov, Discovery Channel's Hincapie, and Caisse d'Épargne's Karpets. He went on to say, "Cadel won the Tour de Romandie with a brilliant time trial [in April]. Then I saw him progress at the Tour de Suisse last month. He just got better every day."

Somewhat embarrassed by his teammate's forecast, Evans said, "Robbie exudes confidence; I keep it inside." The former mountain biker then went red in the face and began sweating, which encouraged McEwen to pick up a book and start fanning Evans's face to cool him down. "If that's all I can do for the next ten days," McEwen quipped, "I'll have done my part."

The more pragmatic Evans then analyzed his chances in this very unusual Tour. "Five of those who finished ahead of me last year are not here," he said, referring to Armstrong, Basso, Ullrich, Francisco Mancebo, and Alexander Vinokourov. Evans, who finished eighth in his Tour debut, could have added that the other two who finished above him in 2005, Levi Leipheimer of Gerolsteiner and Michael Rasmussen of Rabobank, were respectively 4:25 and 7:28 behind him after eight stages. Not wanting to exaggerate his chances, Evans then pointed out that of three other likely contenders, Klöden "was not here last year," Sastre "wasn't riding for GC in 2005," and "I don't know much about Menchov."

With the race about to enter Evans's natural terrain, the mountains, he was lying eighth on GC, 1:52 behind Gontchar but only 52 seconds down on Landis.

Earlier in this rest day, Evans showed his seriousness by going for a two-hour training ride, including a long period behind the team car. Explaining his motor-pacing session, Evans said, "My legs blow up the next day if I don't ride hard."

And what did McEwen's rest-day ride consist of? "I went for two and a half hours," he said, "but only an hour of riding. The rest of the time I was on the terrace of a coffee shop with my feet up." Knowing McEwen, that was the perfect preparation for winning another stage of the Tour when it got back on the road the next day.

PHOTO FINISH

The 169.5km stage 9 from Bordeaux to Dax was the flattest of the 2006 Tour, its highest point just 223 feet above sea level. It would be tough for breakaways to stay clear on the long, straight roads that headed south through the pine forests of the Landes region. McEwen, who said, "I'm always tired after the first week, but the rest day always comes on time," was favored to take his fourth stage of the Tour. A short uphill preceded the final straightaway in Dax that was almost identical to the finishes where McEwen won on stage 4 at St. Quentin and stage 6 at Vitré.

Also eager to win was the frustrated Tom Boonen, as were the Spaniards Oscar Freire (Rabobank) and Isaac Galvez (Caisse d'Épargne), who were expecting support from fans arriving by the busload in Dax, which is less than an hour's drive from the Spanish border.

With the prospect of a fast stage, the attacks came early on the road out of Bordeaux. Nothing stuck until Germany's Christian Knees (Milram) shot out just 7km into the stage. He was joined, after a long chase, by the French pair

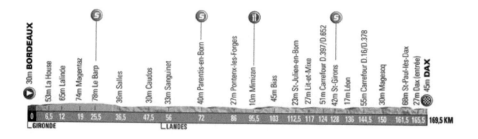

of Stéphane Augé (Cofidis) and Walter Bénéteau (Bouygues Telecom). The peloton gave the trio plenty of rope, as the best placed was Knees, in 45th overall, 5:19 behind Gontchar. The breakaway took a maximum lead of seven minutes before Boonen's Quick Step troops began a steady chase. They found some collaboration from the Lampre, Crédit Agricole, and Liquigas teams.

The three lead riders averaged an impressive 47.214kph, making this the fastest stage of the Tour, but the peloton reeled them in just as they reached the streets of Dax with 4km left. Liquigas and Team CSC sent riders to the front on the short hill before Quick Step drove the pace over the final 1.5km in an attempt to set up Boonen.

The eventual sprint was a wide-open charge along the flat finishing straight. Riders sprang up on both sides of the roads, with Daniele Bennati (Lampre-Fondital) trying his luck on the left. Feeling a slight tailwind, Boonen made a long sprint along the barriers on the right. McEwen was stuck behind Boonen and Erik Zabel, who were hogging the right side of the road, while Freire was moving up fast on their left. "I couldn't get out until the last 100 meters," said McEwen, who finally saw some empty real estate opening up behind Freire. The Aussie angled sharply to his left and then punched for the line with all his power as he challenged to Freire's left.

"I was almost there," McEwen added, "I passed everyone. I was too strong for them." McEwen appeared to just make it as he and Freire threw their bikes at the line at the same time. "I've good and bad memories from finishes like that," said Freire, referring to other photo finishes in his career. "Today I wasn't sure if I had won or not."

The judges eventually gave it to the Spaniard by a tire's width, making the sprint score at the end of the Tour's first ten days: McEwen 3, Freire 2, Boonen 0. It was a spectacular ending to the first half of the Tour, but now the sprinters would give way to the climbers. The Pyrénées were on the horizon.

Perhaps this mysterious Tour would finally start to become clear. Would Landis's hip handicap him? Did Rogers, Klöden, and Gontchar have the strength to dominate in the mountains? Or were Evans, Menchov, Sastre, Hincapie, Leipheimer, or some other challengers going to emerge? Everyone was eager to find out.

STAGE 9: BORDEAUX TO DAX

1. Oscar Freire (Sp), Rabobank, 169.5km in 3:35:24 (47.214kph); **2.** Robbie McEwen (Aus), Davitamon-Lotto; **3.** Erik Zabel (Milram); **4.** Tom Boonen (Quick Step-Innergetic); **5.** Cristian Moreni (I), Cofidis; **6.** Isaac Galvez (Sp), Caisse d'Épargne; **7.** Francisco Ventoso (Sp), Saunier Duval; **8.** Luca Paolini (I), Liquigas; **9.** David Kopp (G), Gerolsteiner; **10.** Thor Hushovd (N), Crédit Agricole, all s.t.

GENERAL CLASSIFICATION

1. Sergei Gontchar (Ukr), T-Mobile
2. Floyd Landis (USA), Phonak, at 1:00
3. Michael Rogers (Aus), T-Mobile, at 1:08
4. Patrik Sinkewitz (G), T-Mobile, at 1:45
5. Marcus Fothen (G), Gerolsteiner, at 1:50

CHAPTER 12

Revelations in the Pyrénées

A big breakaway upstages the noncommittal favorites.

With so many riders in position to take the yellow jersey, everyone knew that tactics and teamwork would be as important as power and performance in the days ahead. But no one knew which team or riders would actually take command. T-Mobile appeared to have the advantage, but even the German squad could make no predictions. Asked if his team would operate in the mountains as Lance Armstrong had—with riders such as George Hincapie, Floyd Landis, and José Azevedo setting a fierce tempo that stopped Armstrong's rivals from attacking—T-Mobile team manager Olaf Ludwig was clear. "No, we don't do the same as Discovery Channel or U.S. Postal," he said. "We are only with seven riders in the Tour and we have a very good situation with [six] riders in the first 15, and so we can wait for the attacks from another team."

As for how the racing might develop on the first of two Pyrenean stages, the 190.5km stage 10, Landis's teammate on the Mercury team in 2000 and 2001, Chris Horner, predicted before the start in hot, humid Cambo-les-Bains, "You take your top 10 or 15 GC favorites, those guys will finish in the group together. It'll probably be a decent-size group, but there's going to be a break that stays off, and then someone in that break that's outside the top 15 favorites is going to be in there who takes the [yellow] jersey."

That's exactly what happened at the 1966 Tour on a course similar to this one—the first mountain stage finishing in Pau. That year, French race favorites Jacques Anquetil and Raymond Poulidor allowed a 23-man group to escape on the Col d'Aubisque with 18 of them, including young French rider Lucien Aimar and Dutch hope Jan Janssen, gaining seven minutes. Anquetil had a reason for allowing such a dangerous group to take so much time—Aimar was a teammate—but Poulidor had no excuses.

His team manager Antonin Magne, a former Tour winner, said, "In all my career, I never let a group of 20 riders get away on a mountain climb. Decidedly, I'll never be able to understand Poulidor." That race, remember, was decades before teams communicated by radio, so any advice Magne had for Poulidor came too late. Poulidor finished that Tour in third place, two minutes behind race champion Aimar and one minute behind runner-up Janssen.

Twenty years later, once again on the opening mountain stage that finished in Pau, events paralleled those described in Chapter 2. Greg LeMond was the rider caught out when his teammates Bernard Hinault and Jean-François Bernard made a surprise attack with the Spanish climber Pedro Delgado. LeMond would have lost the Tour right there if he hadn't made a desperate, late chase after breaking with Colombian climber Luis Herrera on the final climb, the Col de Marie-Blanque.

Could the race favorites get caught out again, another 20 years on?

FREE-FOR-ALL OPENING

With the flat stages behind them, the climbers were champing at the bit to get into a breakaway in this first stage in the high mountains. There were three aborted attempts in the first 7km before a group of local citizens, protesting plans to build a new highway through their region, momentarily stopped the race.

The Cofidis team leader, Sylvain Chavanel, was the first rider to extract himself from the melee, chased by a 17-man group that contained Davitamon's Horner and CSC's Christian Vande Velde. But also in the move was T-Mobile's Patrik Sinkewitz, who was lying fourth on general classification and was listed as a danger man by rival teams. The peloton kept them on a tight, ten-second leash until

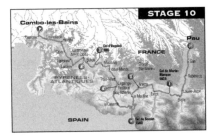

the fast-moving peloton, fully informed of Sinkewitz's presence via their radio earpieces, swallowed them and Chavanel at the 35km point, just before the day's first time-bonus sprint at Larceveau.

It seemed like all 20 teams wanted to get a rider in the day's successful move. And by the time they had covered the 46km in the first, furious hour through the rolling green hills of this French part of the Basque country, 14 teams had a rider in a major 15-man breakaway.

A short, 12 percent pitch on the Cat. 3 Col d'Osquich at 50km condemned the break's two sprinters, Crédit Agricole's Thor Hushovd and Davitamon's Gert Steegmans, while the other 13 were allowed to take a nine-minute lead in the next 35km before they started climbing the day's biggest obstacle, the 15km *hors-catégorie* Col de Soudet. Riding strongest in the breakaway were Frenchmen Cyril Dessel of AG2R, Christophe Rinero of Saunier Duval, and Cédric Vasseur of Quick Step, along with the Italian Cristian Moreni of Cofidis, and the Spaniards Juan Mercado of Agritubel, and Iñigo Landaluze and Iñaki Isasi, both from Euskaltel-Euskadi.

"Today the plan was to try and slip away into an escape group and it eventually came together," Dessel said. "It's true that you have to have good legs to be in the right move but a bit of luck is also useful. That's what happened and I really felt strong today."

125

Mercado then took the initiative on the Col de Soudet, which has an average grade of 7.3 percent. Sections of the road were steeper than the Tour road book indicated, with pitches of 15 percent on the narrow, erratic ascent that featured a number of short downhills. The lanky Mercado won a stage at the 2004 Tour but otherwise had been a bust during two years at Quick Step. Now with the race's only non-ProTour team, Agritubel, Mercado was anxious to make the most of the situation.

INTO THE MIST

With T-Mobile evidently prepared to let Gontchar lose the yellow jersey, none of the other big teams seemed interested in wasting energy the day before an even bigger mountain stage. As a result, the magenta shirts of T-Mobile, led by the remarkable Matthias Kessler, swarmed to the front of the pack on this long ascent into the clouds.

Partway up the climb, CSC's Vande Velde slipped on some gravel, scraped his right leg, and ripped the back of his jersey. "My back and neck is a little tight, that's about it," Vande Velde said after the stage. "I saw some blood come out of my leg and tried to limit my losses."

On the upper stretches of the narrow, twisting climb rowdy Basque fans wearing bright orange T-shirts lined the course, but it wasn't going to be a big day for their favorite, Iban Mayo. The Euskaltel team leader lost contact with the peloton on the first steep slopes and rode the rest of the day in the back group with sprinters like Boonen and McEwen.

"I've had a problem with my throat for several days," Mayo later told Spanish journalists. "I quickly felt today I didn't have the legs, so I held back and conserved energy. I think this will pass in another day or two. We still have the Alps."

Gontchar was also having trouble sticking with the main group, but the yellow jersey eventually recovered and returned to his expected team duties. When he came back to the front, he brought fresh water bottles for his teammates from the team car, and later in the day he was seen pulling the peloton for long stretches on the flatter sections of the course. "Today we lost the yellow jersey, but it's no big thing," said T-Mobile's Ludwig. "[Gontchar] understands it's a big race. Normally [as a race leader] he doesn't work at the front, but he will do this and it's not a problem for him."

First up the final 10 percent slopes to the 5,052-foot Soudet summit was Dessel, who said later, "I knew how steep it was, so I asked my team mechanic to put on a 36×23 gearing for this stage." Mercado crossed five seconds back, while five riders (the two Euskaltel men, plus Moreni, Rinero, and Vasseur) caught them on the 15 percent plunge back through the thick mists.

When, 30km later, Mercado attacked the break up the shorter Cat. 1 Col de Marie-Blanque (whose final 4km average a back-breaking 11 percent), only Dessel could follow him. The Frenchman then scooped up more mountain points and the pair began their bid for the stage win. Almost nine minutes behind, the defending King of the Mountains, Michael Rasmussen of Rabobank, showed his hand by shooting off the front of the peloton coming up the Marie-Blanque to grab some climbing points, but he sank back when the T-Mobile riders re-grouped to ride tempo for the stage's remaining 40km.

Dessel and Mercado rode the final hour like a two-man team time trial to hold off a valiant Landaluze, who came within ten seconds of catching back on, but couldn't close the small gap on the last climbing section 25km from the finish. As the Spaniard fell back, Dessel and Mercado kept up the pressure until they hit the streets of Pau with 5km to go.

Because Dessel had taken the KOM lead and looked sure to move into the yellow jersey, Mercado asked the Frenchman if he could win the stage. "It was a complicated finish because he already had both jerseys yet he still wanted to try to win the stage," said Mercado. So the Spaniard sat on the Frenchman's wheel until the final 250 meters, then sprinted hard to take the stage win.

ANOTHER AIMAR?

The 74-strong main bunch arrived 7:23 behind the two breakaways. And as Dessel had started the stage in 28th overall, only 3:50 back, he became the first Frenchman to wear yellow in this Tour, and only the ninth in the past decade.

"It's huge to get both the King of the Mountains and the *maillot jaune*," said Dessel. "When I started the day, my objective was the climber's jersey. I thought I had the legs to do that. In fact, I was on fire, as rarely happens in your career. With 20km to go and seeing that our lead on the peloton wasn't really coming down, I felt strongly that the yellow jersey was there for the taking."

"IT'S HUGE TO GET BOTH THE KING OF THE MOUNTAINS AND THE *MAILLOT JAUNE*. WHEN I STARTED THE DAY, MY OBJECTIVE WAS THE CLIMBER'S JERSEY. I THOUGHT I HAD THE LEGS TO DO THAT. IN FACT, I WAS ON FIRE, AS RARELY HAPPENS IN YOUR CAREER."

Was Dessel going to be another Lucien Aimar, the little-known Frenchman who snuck into that Pau break in 1966 and went on to win in Paris?

At 31, the new race leader was riding his second Tour. He made his team Tour selections three other times, but a broken collarbone stopped him from starting with Jean Delatour in 2001. A last-minute change of mind by then-Phonak team manager Alvaro Pino left him out of the 2004 Tour, and appendicitis prevented him from competing in 2005. In his only previous Tour in 2002, Dessel crashed three times in the opening week and ended the race in 113th overall.

Dessel was especially down after being left off the Phonak team in 2004. He had been told he would ride the Tour after a strong showing at the Dauphiné Libéré, where he placed second on the third stage into his hometown of St. Étienne, came in 13th on the Mont Ventoux time trial (six seconds faster than Floyd Landis), and worked tirelessly for team leader Tyler Hamilton, notably in helping the American chase back to the leaders after crashing on a mountain descent. However, a week later Dessel's spot on the Tour team was given to another rider. Salt was rubbed into the wound when, a week before the Tour, Dessel narrowly lost the French national road title in a sprint to rival Thomas Voeckler, who went on to wear the yellow jersey for ten days at that 2004 Tour.

The decision to leave Dessel off the team was even more surprising in light of his poster-boy status at Phonak. The Frenchman had been hard of hearing in both ears since birth, and the title sponsor, which manufactures hearing aids, was thrilled to fit him with state-of-the-art products. But his omission from the Tour team sent Dessel looking for another squad, and he moved to AG2R in 2005.

Dessel again looked to be on track to ride the Tour when he started 2005 with a fourth place in the penultimate stage of Paris-Nice in March and placed 13th overall at the Four Days of Dunkirk in April. But ten days before the Tour de France, Dessel had an emergency appendix operation. The Tour would have to wait for another year.

The AG2R team was so impressed with Dessel as a team rider that it hired his personal trainer and best friend, Julien Jurdie, as a directeur sportif for the 2006 season. The two men, who come from the same area of central France, met when they were teenagers and raced together on an amateur cycling team near St. Étienne. When Dessel earned a pro contract in 2000, the less talented Jurdie decided he would stop racing and instead concentrate on becoming a directeur sportif. "We promised each other that we would try to work together one day," Jurdie told the French newspaper, L'Équipe.

The two men acted as best men at each other's weddings, but it was years before they found themselves on the same cycling team. They finally joined forces at AG2R, Dessel on the bike and Jurdie in the team car, and had immediate success. In February 2006, Dessel scored his first major win in seven years as a pro at the Mediterranean Tour stage race. After placing eighth on the steep mountaintop finish at Mont Faron, Dessel won the following stage from St. Laurent du Var to Menton. The stage crossed the infamous Col de la Madone, the climb Lance Armstrong used in training prior to winning his first Tour de France. Up the narrow mountain road, Dessel first chased a breakaway by Swedish hope Thomas Lövkvist and Italian Pietro Caucchioli, and he then aced the descent. After Lövkvist flatted, Dessel went on to win the stage solo and took over the race lead, which he kept to the finish in San Remo, Italy.

After that huge breakthrough, Jurdie told the AG2R team manger Vincent Lavenu that Dessel would be able to ride a great Tour de France if he focused on weeklong stage races rather than starting a lot of one-day races, as most French riders do. "Cyril is not the type of rider who comes back to racing at 60 percent after a three-week break," said Jurdie. "He climbs the hills in the Forez and Pilat ranges and does a lot of motor-paced training, and comes back at 90 percent."

By rationing his race appearances, Dessel continued his strong 2006 season with 18th place overall at Paris-Nice and 25th at the Tour of Catalonia. At June's Dauphiné Libéré, he rode within himself but placed 11th in the stage over the mighty Col d'Izoard to Briançon, a few seconds behind likely Tour favorites George Hincapie, Levi Leipheimer, and Denis Menchov.

Dessel came into the Tour with his reserves fully intact and so impressed Australian teammate Simon Gerrans that he confided in an Aussie journalist, "Just watch Dessel when we get to the mountains."

The confident French rider showed the world his promise on the first Pyrenean stage, but would he be able to defend his yellow and polka-dot jerseys on the second big test, a daunting five-climb stage into Spain?

French legend Raymond Poulidor, the race favorite who was shocked by Aimar in 1966, was asked how he expected Dessel to fare in stage 11. Poulidor said that Dessel would likely pay for his efforts in stage 10, "but if he manages to hang on to the yellow jersey, then he will be the big revelation of this Tour."

STAGE 10: CAMBO-LES-BAINS TO PAU

1. Juan Mercado (Sp), Agritubel, 190.5km in 4:49:10 (39.527kph); **2.** Cyril Dessel (F), AG2R, s.t.; **3.** Iñigo Landaluze (Sp), Euskaltel-Euskadi, at 0:56; **4.** Cristian Moreni (I), Cofidis, at 2:24; **5.** Christophe Rinero (F), Saunier Duval, at 2:25; **6.** Iñaki Isasi (Sp), Euskaltel-Euskadi, at 5:03; **7.** Cédric Vasseur (F), Quick Step, at 5:35; **8.** Daniele Bennati (I), Lampre-Fondital, at 7:23; **9.** Erik Zabel (G), Milram; **10.** Stefano Garzelli (I), Liquigas, both s.t.

GENERAL CLASSIFICATION

1. Cyril Dessel (F), AG2R

2. Juan Mercado (Sp), Agritubel, at 2:24

3. Sergei Gontchar (Ukr), T-Mobile, at 3:45

4. Cristian Moreni (I), Cofidis, at 3:51

5. Floyd Landis (USA), Phonak, at 4:45

CHAPTER 13

Through the Circle of Death

A vicious five-mountain stage ends with Landis in yellow.

Before starting stage 11 in the yellow jersey, Cyril Dessel was not overconfident, saying, "I'm going to fight hard to keep the jersey as long as possible, but once it's gone I'll return to being a team worker for [AG2R team leader] Christophe Moreau." In front of Dessel, Moreau, and the other contenders lay five big climbs in the Pyrénées, four of them in France, before the race headed into Spain's Val d'Aran and the lengthy finishing climb up to the Pla-de-Beret ski station at 6,100 feet above sea level.

When Tour de France riders first crossed these high mountain passes in 1910, they were shocked by the severity of the climbs and the dangers they faced. They named this remote area, inhabited by bears and overflown by golden eagles and vultures, *Le Cercle de la Mort*, the Circle of Death. That first year, when the roads were just two wagon ruts cut by horse-drawn carts, only one rider, Gustave Garrigou, was able to stay on his bike all the way up the highest of the passes, the notorious 6,939-foot Col du Tourmalet.

The eventual stage and race winner, Octave Lapize, while pushing his single-gear bike up the next of the stage's four climbs, seemed distressed and about to quit. He shouted a screed of invective at awaiting officials, and when he pulled alongside Victor Breyer, one of the race organizers, Lapize screamed, "You are murderers! Yes, murderers!" Recalling the incident later, Breyer wrote, "To start a discussion in those conditions, with a man in that state, would have been cruel and stupid. I walked alongside him, respecting the silence, even though he continued with his curses."

Lapize didn't quit the race. He battled through 14 hours and 10 minutes to complete that 326km stage, which started at 3:30 in the morning. Only 12 riders finished within two hours of him. The Circle of Death became synonymous with pain and suffering, but it has remained in the Tour to the present day.

Ninety-six years after that first encounter, on a day of brilliant sunshine, the Tourmalet was the first climb in this Tour's stage 11, which featured 17,473 feet of climbing in 206.5km. In physical terms, that amount of vertical difference represents an energy expenditure of about 8,500 kilojoules—almost four days' worth of meals for people on a normal diet. It's impossible to eat that much before and during a race, so riders have to burn calories from their (minimal) fat reserves merely to get through such a day in the saddle.

When previewing the stage, most observers said that the closing climb to Pla-de-Beret would not cause major changes in the general classification because its average grade was only 5.5 percent. That may not be as steep as other summit finishes in the Pyrénées, like Hautacam, Luz-Ardiden, and Plateau de Beille, but when combined with the four climbs that preceded it—the Tourmalet, Aspin, Peyresourde, and Portillon—the stage looked likely to cause more damage than many expected.

"This will be the most difficult stage ahead of the Alps," said Floyd Landis, who was lying in fifth overall, 4:45 behind new race leader Dessel. "The final climb is not so steep but very long, and the stage is difficult before that, so it's going to split up. I think only a small group will be fighting for the win."

The Phonak rider was confident he would be in that small group; his former teammate, George Hincapie of Discovery Channel, was also optimistic about the day's outcome. Looking leaner than ever, maybe too lean, Hincapie looked out over the big crowds at the start in Tarbes and said, "Hopefully, today, I can stay up there with the first five or ten guys. And if I have a really good day maybe even attack those guys."

Images of the 2006
TOUR DE FRANCE

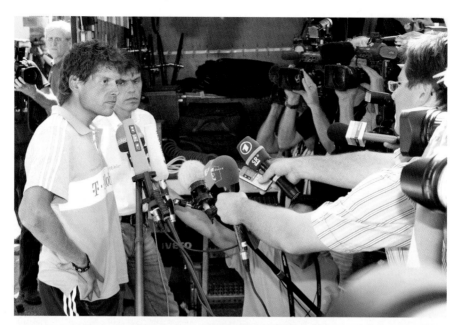

Listed on the Puerto black list, the big favorites were excluded the day before the Strasbourg prologue. Jan Ullrich faced the media outside his hotel, while Ivan Basso heard the bad news after a training ride.

ABOVE Prologue winner Thor Hushovd collapsed after a freak collision with a fan in the stage 1 field sprint.

RIGHT Race doctor Gérard Porte comforted Alejandro Valverde, who was a race favorite before a broken collarbone ended his race on stage 3.

Aggressive Matthias
Kessler gave his
beleaguered T-Mobile
team a huge stage
win at Valkenburg.

ABOVE The day after Sergei Gontchar took the yellow jersey and Bobby Julich wiped out in the stage 7 time trial, CSC's Dave Zabriskie led the Tour's first successful break with Kjell Carlstrom, stage winner Sylvain Calzati (in the blue helmet), Kessler, and Mario Aerts. **BELOW** After a couple of near misses, Oscar Freire timed his sprint perfectly in stage 5, edging out GC leader Tom Boonen (right) and Gerolsteiner's David Kopp (left).

Oscar Freire and Robbie McEwen banged shoulders on stage 9, with Freire taking the photo-finish sprint by millimeters.

ABOVE Levi Leipheimer attacked on the closing climb to Pla de Beret on stage 11 as Denis Menchov and Floyd Landis attempted to bridge.

RIGHT Cyril Dessel rode through the clouds atop stage 10's Col de Soudet on his way to the yellow jersey in Pau.

ABOVE Jens Voigt and Oscar Pereiro headed the break that gained a half-hour on the road to Montélimar.

OPPOSITE RIGHT The peloton descended the Col de la Sentinelle into Gap on stage 14.

RIGHT Despite a decline in TV ratings and lackluster turnouts for some flat stages, the Tour drew a huge and enthusiastic crowd for stage 15's climb over the Col d'Izoard on the way to L'Alpe d'Huez.

ABOVE AND OPPOSITE The day after Phonak's "broken" leader was shepherded to the line at La Toussuire by his teammate Axel Merckx, Floyd Landis rebounded on stage 17. He started his gargantuan 130km breakaway to Morzine by dropping T-Mobile's Andreas Klöden and Michael Rogers on the Col des Saisies.

Far behind Landis, L'Alpe d'Huez stage winner Fränk Schleck and Aussie contender Cadel Evans struggled up the rugged Col de Joux-Plane on stage 17.

In the closing meters of the stage 19 time trial, Oscar Pereiro knew he would lose the yellow jersey and that Floyd Landis would be sharing the Paris podium with Robbie McEwen (in green jersey), Michael Rasmussen (in polka dots), and Damiano Cunego (in white).

A grim-faced Floyd Landis faced a Madrid news conference the day after the world learned that a urine test following his victorious stage 17 ride showed an overly high ratio of testosterone to epitestosterone.

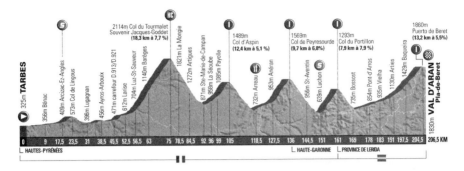

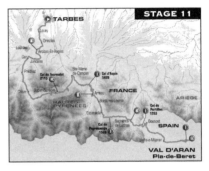

Hincapie seemingly had grounds for optimism because Discovery put seven of its riders into the main group in stage 10, compared with the three Phonak men—Landis, Axel Merckx, and Miguel Martin Perdiguero. Phonak's relative weakness in the mountains also encouraged T-Mobile, which had all but one of its riders in the lead group. Reflecting on the previous stage, T-Mobile's Sergei Gontchar said, "The day was particularly hard as we are only seven [on the team]. We worked without any help. . . . It was a pity that other teams didn't follow our lead. The situation was hard to control."

Stage 11 looked like a much harder task for T-Mobile, even though the yellow jersey had slipped to Dessel's AG2R squad. Should Dessel falter, then the responsibility for controlling the race would again fall to T-Mobile. It looked as if the 2006 Tour would reach its moment of truth on this stage through the Circle of Death.

FOUR-MAN MOVE

Even before reaching the foot of the Tourmalet, the opening 65km offered a succession of short climbs and twisting downhills on mostly narrow back roads. It was the perfect terrain for an early break to gain time before the real climbing began. Indeed, the first significant move came on the first short climb, 19km out of Tarbes, when CSC's Aussie Stuart O'Grady triggered a six-strong break that was chased by a ten-man group containing AG2R's Moreau. No one was going to let Moreau get away, but the resultant chase and catch set up a successful counterattack.

With 168 riders speeding in one long line down a narrow, winding road through the village of Juncalas, gaps opened and two pairs split off the front. When Spaniards Iker Camana of Euskaltel-Euskadi and David de le Fuente of Saunier Duval were joined by Germany's Fabian Wegmann of Gerolsteiner and a third Spaniard, Juan Antonio Flecha of Rabobank, the day's main breakaway had formed. By the foot of the 18.3km Tourmalet the four men were already 8:15 ahead of the pack. That gap was enough to keep them clear over the Tourmalet because after toiling for more than an hour up the grinding 8 percent gradient, the break still had 4:50 in hand.

Behind them, despite the relatively slow tempo set by AG2R, many were having a hard time staying with the peloton. One of the first big names to be cast off was Spanish star Iban Mayo, whose many fans waiting to cheer him in his homeland were going to be disappointed. Mayo was stressed mentally as much as physically on the climb. Little wonder, considering a motorcycle-mounted television crew followed every pedal stroke of his suffering. The Basque waved angrily and later shouted at the crew, only to invite the cameraman to zoom in on his distressed face. Mayo finally abandoned the Tour on the Col de Peyresourde, two climbs later.

Mayo wasn't the only victim of the Circle of Death. American Chris Horner, whose presence later on would have helped his Davitamon team leader Cadel Evans, was struggling because of sickness. Also dropped on the Tourmalet were the talented Venezuelan Tour rookie, José Rujano of Quick Step, and one of Landis's key mountain henchmen, Alexandre Moos.

These weren't the first men to falter on the Tourmalet's spectacular western approach, which heads up a steep valley through the village of Barèges and then crosses an open, grassy mountainside in a series of bold curves. It was on the precipitous 10 percent pitch just before the bleak summit in 1991 that Greg LeMond, when contending for his fourth Tour victory, first experienced the health decline that led to his retirement three years later. Dropped by only a matter of seconds, LeMond, who was a daredevil descender, could not catch back to the Spaniard Miguel Induráin, who was just one of many possible contenders that year. Induráin attacked over the crest of the mountain pass to join solo breakaway Claudio Chiappucci of Italy.

Induráin and Chiappucci continued with their attack over the Aspin and Peyresourde climbs to finish seven minutes ahead of ninth-placed LeMond on the finishing climb at Val Louron. Induráin went on to win that Tour and the following four Tours, while LeMond never transcended his humiliating defeat.

After descending from the Tourmalet on this 2006 stage, the four-man breakaway remained intact over the Col d'Aspin. Then Wegmann accelerated on the longer Peyresourde climb and Fuente counterattacked, leaving Camano and Flecha to be mopped up by the pack. Ahead, Fuente and Wegmann passed through the old spa town of Luchon with a 3:40 advance as they headed to the nastiest climb of the day, the Col de Portillon. It's only 8km long, but its narrowness, switchbacks, bumpy surface, and frequent 10 percent pitches make it a true challenge—especially after riders have spent four hours under a broiling midday sun passing through the Circle of Death.

FINAL SHOWDOWN

As if the Portillon's physical difficulties weren't enough, a sudden, dramatic assault launched by T-Mobile put everyone in the red zone. Setting an infernal pace, T-Mobile's ground troops Giuseppe Guerini and Patrik Sinkewitz fired the first salvo before dropping back. Then Matthias Kessler turned the screw, aided by an impressive-looking Michael Rogers, while Andreas Klöden stayed close to their wheels.

The effect on the race was devastating. Within eight minutes, only 20 riders were left of what had been a peloton about 100 strong. Among the chief casualties were Discovery's Hincapie, Paolo Savoldelli, and Yaroslav Popovych. Hincapie, who would lose more than 20 minutes by the end, later said he was devoid of energy, most likely due to inadequate refueling during the long stage. Other notables who would concede even more time than Hincapie were Savoldelli, Caisse d'Épargne's Oscar Pereiro, Phonak's Martin Perdiguero, CSC's Jens Voigt, and T-Mobile's Gontchar.

Only one of Hincapie's Discovery teammates managed to stay in the front group, Portuguese rider José Azevedo. Among the other top teams with only one man standing were AG2R (Moreau), Davitamon (Evans), Phonak (Landis), Lampre (Damiano Cunego), Caisse d'Épargne (David Arroyo), Euskaltel (Haimar Zubeldia), and Saunier Duval (Gilberto Simoni). The best-placed squads were T-Mobile, Rabobank (Denis Menchov, Michael Boogerd, and Michael Rasmussen), Gerolsteiner (Levi Leipheimer, Markus Fothen, and Georg Totschnig), and CSC (Carlos Sastre and Fränk Schleck).

Kessler eventually dropped back after his huge effort, while Boogerd and Rasmussen moved to the front with Klöden and Rogers. Their elite group crossed the Cat. 1 climb's summit just 1:20 behind Fuente, who scored enough KOM points to take the polka-dot jersey from race leader Dessel, struggling 40 seconds behind the Landis group.

Now in Spain, the leaders headed down the fast descent before turning south on a long, straight highway through the Val d'Aran. On the continually rising valley road, Cunego and Arroyo were the first to catch Fuente, with 28km to go. But they were all swept up after Rabobank's Rasmussen and Boogerd went to the front of the group and rode flat out for team leader Menchov. Their massive pulls, aided by a strong tail wind, condemned Dessel, whose small group was already two minutes down when they reached the town of Vielha. Here, with 23km still to ride, the valley road started to pitch up toward the finish.

Rasmussen pulled hard for most of the next 10km and then peeled off when the grade really kicked in for the final 13km. Then it was Boogerd who kept on the pressure for the surprising Rabobank team for another 5km. When Klöden, so strong and confident on the Portillon, dropped back because of cramps, Menchov accelerated, and Landis then took command to make sure the German wouldn't return. By this time only five were left in front: Landis, Menchov, Evans, Sastre, and Leipheimer.

Leipheimer, confirming his climbing strength, made two sharp attacks, the second one 800 meters from the summit. It was enough to dislodge Evans and Sastre, but Landis and Menchov managed to stay with him. After the KOM point, the last 2km were slightly downhill and led to a right-left chicane 150 meters from the line.

"I really wanted to win," said Leipheimer, happy to have recovered from his time-trial setback. "I knew that I had to be first through the [chicane]—it was hard to see the first corner. In that situation, you don't want to be too late. So I went and it was a little bit too early, and there was a headwind. I should have just moved up alongside Menchov and just pinned him there, and stayed behind Floyd."

Instead, Menchov made it to the corner first and shouted exultantly as he crossed the line a length in front of a gasping Leipheimer. The eight-second bonus taken by Landis for third place was just enough for him to take the yellow jersey because Dessel, who would sprint home in 18th place, finished 4:45 back, the margin by which he led Landis that morning.

FOR FLOYD LANDIS, THE VAL D'ARAN WILL ALWAYS BE THE MOST BEAUTIFUL PLACE IN THE WORLD. HERE, AFTER A GRUELING STAGE 11 OF THE 2006 TOUR DE FRANCE, HE PULLED ON THE *MAILLOT JAUNE* FOR THE FIRST TIME.

LANDIS EXULTANT

After crossing the line, an exhausted Landis poured a bottle of water over his head, toweled himself down, and fell into a bear hug with his coach, Robbie Ventura. On the podium he smiled as never before, perhaps recalling the three Tours when Armstrong was his boss—and when he first began thinking that *he* could win the Tour too.

Locals say that the Val d'Aran is the most beautiful valley in Spain. A patchwork of wildflowers—blue gentian, white cow parsley, yellow safflower—climbs grassy hillsides between picturesque villages of tan-and-gray granite houses with pitched, slate roofs, while jagged mountain peaks rise beyond the fast-flowing creeks and pine forests. For Floyd Landis, the Val d'Aran will always be the most beautiful place in the world. Here, after a grueling stage 11 of the 2006 Tour de France, he pulled on the *maillot jaune* for the first time.

The moment was as emotional as when Greg LeMond became the first American to take the yellow jersey atop the Col de Granon in 1986 and when Armstrong won the prologue in 1999 to start his seven-year reign as Tour champion. For LeMond, taking the yellow jersey was the just outcome in his internecine battle with La Vie Claire teammate Bernard Hinault. For Armstrong, his breakthrough was initially a surprise. Having just recovered from cancer, he shed a few tears in what he described as the most emotional moment in his storied career.

For Landis, it was more complicated. In the year since learning he would need a new hip, he accelerated his long-term goal of winning the Tour. "I should probably have been aware that my career won't go on forever from the beginning," he said at Pla-de-Beret, "but it made me think about it more. And since then I see things a little differently."

The difference, according to friends and pro cyclists he rides with, was intensified training and a laserlike focus on his ambitions. If his hip couldn't be repaired to extend his career, he knew this might be his last chance to wear the yellow jersey, his last chance to win the Tour. Those mixed feelings, along with the normal thrill of moving into the driver's seat of the world's biggest bike race, were spelled out all over his beaming face.

Despite the pressure to perform in what could be his last Tour, Floyd was still Floyd. With his backward baseball cap firmly in place, he was still the guy who knows how to kick back. Paris was ten days away, the yellow jersey was in hand, and life was good. His team manager John Lelangue later recounted that, on the way down to their Val d'Aran hotel, a laid-back Landis asked him if he wanted anything when the car was slowed to a halt by a mob of spectators. "Because I was thirsty," Lelangue said, "[Floyd] traded his jersey with a fan for a six-pack of beer."

Landis was quick to stress that defending the *maillot jaune* at all costs was not something he'd ask of his Phonak boys. "It will be difficult to control and keep it.

We don't have so much time on a lot of guys," he said. "If it's in our interest and we find a common goal with some help along the way, I wouldn't be opposed for other teams to have [the jersey]. The objective is to have it on the last day."

STAGE 11: TARBES TO VAL D'ARAN (PLA-DE-BERET)

1. Denis Menchov (Rus), Rabobank, 206.5km in 6:06:25 (33.813kph); **2. Levi Leipheimer (USA), Gerolsteiner; 3. Floyd Landis (USA), Phonak, both s.t.; 4.** Cadel Evans (Aus), Davitamon-Lotto, at 0:17; **5.** Carlos Sastre (Sp), CSC, s.t.; **6.** Michael Boogerd (Nl), Rabobank, at 1:04; **7.** Haimar Zubeldia (Sp), Euskaltel-Euskadi, at 1:31; **8.** Fränk Schleck (Lux), CSC; **9.** Andreas Klöden (G), T-Mobile, both s.t.; **10.** Christophe Moreau (F), AG2R, at 2:29.

GENERAL CLASSIFICATION

1. Floyd Landis (USA), Phonak

2. Cyril Dessel (F), AG2R, at 0:08

3. Denis Menchov (Rus), Rabobank, at 1:01

4. Cadel Evans (Aus), Davitamon-Lotto, at 1:17

5. Carlos Sastre (Sp), CSC, at 1:52

CHAPTER 14

Dangerous Strategies

Horrible heat and questionable tactics mark three days in the Midi.

On the evening of stage 12, Oscar Pereiro was ready to go to sleep at the Hotel Le Mas Pierrot, a Mexican-style two-story tavern in the Midi region of France, when fireworks boomed and crackled in the night sky over Carcassonne. Upward of 100,000 people watched the spectacular Bastille Day celebration that bathed the city's medieval ramparts in luminous crimson smoke. Many of the same spectators had been lining the town's sun-blasted streets that afternoon when Discovery Channel's Yaroslav Popovych won stage 12 of the Tour de France at the head of a four-man breakaway. Popovych's win saved face for the U.S. team after its wipeout in the Pyrénées, while the 4:45 that the Ukraine rider gained pushed him into tenth overall.

Popovych's success heartened Pereiro, who had been in a break earlier in the day. The 28-year-old Spaniard knew how hard it was to get in the day's successful move. He also knew that he'd try again.

Pereiro, who had finished the past two Tours in tenth overall when he was at Phonak, joined Caisse d'Épargne-Illes Balears over the winter to ride for Alejandro Valverde, Spain's big hope for victory at the Tour. But Valverde crashed out in the first week, and after the stage 7 time trial the team's GC hopes lay with the Russian, Vladimir Karpets, who was sixth overall entering the Pyrénées. But Caisse d'Épargne's high hopes, like Discovery's, seemed to evaporate on stage 11. Karpets

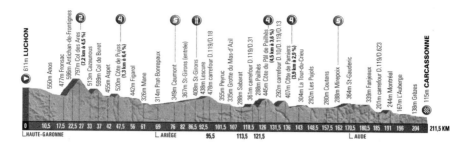

was now languishing in 19th overall, 7:07 behind race leader Floyd Landis, while Pereiro was in 46th, after finishing a disastrous 26:26 back at Pla-de-Beret.

"My legs just couldn't react," said Pereiro on being shocked by the T-Mobile team's sudden acceleration on the Col de Portillon. "And when you lose the morale, it's hard to make the body work as well. I saw my chances for the general classification disappear. I already started to think that I would have to repeat my story from last year, and attack and attack to try to win a stage, and salvage the Tour for my team."

As Pereiro lined up for the start of stage 12 the next morning in Luchon, he realized that he had to get into a long, successful breakaway. That was how he placed second to George Hincapie at Pla d'Adet at the 2005 Tour, won at Pau ahead of Cadel Evans, and placed fourth to Giuseppe Guerini in Le Puy. Hincapie too, after his disastrous stage 11, seemed ready to shift gears and adopt the Discovery team's new aggressive policy. "If things aren't going great for us now, we have to keep working until things can turn around," Hincapie said. "We're the same team as always. Sometimes things don't go as well as you'd like. I worked as hard as I could and I arrived in the best form of my life, but things didn't work out."

In contrast, the mood was jubilant at the Phonak team bus, where Landis poked his head out of the door to find a wall of cameras and microphones waiting for his first appearance as race leader. In response to questions, he chirped, "I didn't sleep in the yellow jersey. Was I supposed to?"

Taking the jersey was the best possible response to earlier criticism that his Phonak team was too weak to support him in the mountains. "Probably some people misjudged the strength of my team, to think that they're all bad," said Landis, who pointed out that he had been able to key off the riding of T-Mobile and Rabobank in the Pyrénées. "They were very confident and did most of the work for us. Probably we can't expect that to happen anymore, but we'll take it."

Phonak was unlikely to get much help from the other teams on the hilly 211km stage, the first of three arduous days across the Midi. The course paralleled the main Pyrenean chain from west to east, and featured constant ups and downs for the opening 140km, including one Cat. 2 and three Cat. 4 climbs.

Pereiro and Hincapie soon went into action on the road out of Luchon. Their uphill attack on the day's first climb, the Cat. 2 Col des Ares, was joined by CSC's Jens Voigt, Lampre's Daniele Bennati, and 11 others. Their lead never topped 1:10; Phonak wanted to contain Hincapie, and it was helped by the teams of sprinters Robbie McEwen and Erik Zabel, who were hoping for a field sprint in Carcassonne.

So determined were the chasers that they achieved an average speed of 46kph for the stage, despite the high temperatures and rolling terrain. With the gap closing, Pereiro decided to drop back to the peloton after 60km, leaving Hincapie, Voigt, and three others out front for another 35km. Shortly after, on winding, up-and-down roads in the limestone hills east of St. Girons, Popovych made a successful counterattack with Lampre's Alessandro Ballan, Rabobank's Oscar Freire, and Crédit Agricole's Christophe Le Mével.

The four men pushed their lead to four minutes, enough of a cushion to dissuade a weary peloton from launching another chase. "This was a really difficult stage to control because the peloton was always nervous during the first two hours," Landis said later. "We then just had to ride to maintain a reasonable gap to those in the escape group. It was an effort that demanded a lot from everyone in my team."

Everyone along the roadside on this national French holiday, July 14, was hoping that Le Mével could pull off the stage win, but he was dropped by the other three with 8km to go. Attention then focused on Freire, who had already won two sprint stages and looked like a shoo-in for the win. The Rabobank rider said he was tired from his efforts in the mountains, but he also seemed to be in cahoots with Popovych when the Discovery rider made a series of accelerations on the flat run-in to Carcassonne. After each attack Freire sat on Ballan's wheel as the Italian closed the gap. Finally, just inside the 3km marker, Popovych went again, and this time he soloed in for the victory.

CALCULATED GAMBLE?

With temperatures forecast to climb into the triple digits in stage 13, everyone was looking for a patch of shade before the noontime start in Béziers, where the clattering sound of cicadas in the plane trees emphasized the heat the riders would have to cope with on this longest stage of the Tour. The 230km between Béziers and Montélimar featured five Cat. 4 climbs and constant undulations across the foothills between the vineyards of Languedoc and the rocky cliffs of the Massif Central. It looked like perfect terrain for a breakaway.

As expected, the racing was intense in the opening kilometers along the Mediterranean coastal plain. After several thrusts, a good-looking move started by Lampre's Salvatore Commesso and Agritubel's Christophe Laurent was joined by CSC's Voigt and Stuart O'Grady, Gerolsteiner's David Kopp, and Milram's Andriy Grivko. They went full gas for 5km before the pack closed in. Voigt, who had been in the previous day's unsuccessful early move, thought, "Oh no, not me again."

But 5km farther on, and with 210km still to race, the big, generous German tried once more, this time with Ukraine's Grivko, Italy's powerfully built Manuel Quinziato of Liquigas, two French riders on Cofidis, Sylvain Chavanel and Arnaud Coyot, and a very determined Pereiro.

Voigt raced ferociously for five more kilometers with his new partners, but they could open up no more than a ten-second gap. Perhaps Voigt and Pereiro were again going to come up short. But there was a reason they were not being allowed to pull away. The French were competing fiercely to be the best team at the Tour, and consequently Française des Jeux and Crédit Agricole didn't like Cofidis

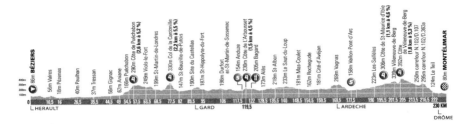

having two men in the break, and they were just chasing and chasing. Understanding the situation, Coyot dropped back to the pack to leave just one Cofidis rider in the break. That was acceptable to the rival teams and the leaders finally started to pull away: 15 seconds . . . 20 seconds . . . 30 seconds.

When the gap reached 50 seconds after 10km of total effort, the peloton decided to pull over for a "nature stop." So when Voigt, Pereiro, and company had put 50km under their wheels in an hour they were ten minutes clear.

Race leader Landis's Phonak team had decided that a break whose best-placed rider, Pereiro, was almost a half hour down on GC was not a true danger. And so the gap steadily widened on the scenic back roads across the chalky scrubland of the Hérault and Gard, reaching 15 minutes after 80km, 20 minutes at 120km, and 25 minutes at 150km.

With 80km still to race in the stage, Phonak decided to increase the tempo a little. Voigt continued to drive the break with Pereiro, who was now realizing that the impossible could happen. He had a chance to take the yellow jersey.

While the peloton suffered in the heat, Voigt and Pereiro continued to drive the break with amazing vigor. The three other riders couldn't stay with them. Grivko made an unwise move on the last hill and then folded, losing six minutes in 25km, while Quinziato and Chavanel, who both made separate attacks in the final 15km, couldn't follow an acceleration by Pereiro 5km out of Montélimar.

"I told Jens [Voigt] earlier I wouldn't sprint if it looked like I was going to take the yellow jersey," Pereiro said. "But when we spoke in the last few kilometers I said we have only 27 minutes, so if I don't go for the sprint I won't have anything [the stage win or the jersey]."

It didn't matter, because Voigt was simply too strong for the Spaniard, while the gap at the line was 29:57 and Pereiro *did* take the jersey.

Asked about Phonak's tactics (there was speculation that the Swiss squad was in collusion with Pereiro's Caisse d'Épargne team), manager John Lelangue denied any such arrangement. "People can think what they want," said Lelangue, "but there's no coalition." T-Mobile's Michael Rogers agreed. "It just goes to show no one can control this race."

Conspiracy theories aside, few observers considered the extraordinary fatigue affecting most riders, and how incredibly tough it is to race in heatwave conditions day after day. On this marathon stage many were stopping off at the medic's car suffering from heatstroke. Quick Step's burly Dutch *domestique* Steven De Jongh said, "I was like unconscious, and I had to go to the doctor twice to get water and tablets."

Others were still trying to recover from their efforts in the Pyrénées. "It's pretty hard to recover on a day like this," said a weary Rogers. "It was so, so hot. Too long." Still others were suffering from injuries or sickness. Davitamon's Chris Horner spoke for dozens of survivors when he said, "It was a slow day, but still particularly hard for me. I got through more bottles than I can remember. I must have a virus or an infection, or the crashes have realigned my legs. . . . The last three days have been incredibly difficult."

But there were two men who flourished on this hot, difficult day: Voigt and Pereiro. "We were desperate for a win, desperate for a real result, something to cheer us up after all the crashes we've had," said stage winner Voigt, whose CSC team started without its leader Ivan Basso. "Only two riders in CSC have not crashed yet, and so after all that bad luck we needed to force some luck back to our side."

As for Pereiro, he said, "I think now that the Tour is much better for my team. This will totally change things . . . and I will fight all I can to keep the jersey."

THE MOVIE STAR

A few weeks before the 2006 Tour de France, Pereiro sat multitasking on a warm spring night on Spain's Costa Dorada following a stage of the Tour of Catalonia. With one leg slung over the arm of a chair, the quick-smiling *Gallego* had one eye glued on a soccer match and another on a handheld video device connecting him with his wife and baby daughter. He was sipping a glass of tonic water and chatting expansively with a reporter about his expectations in the upcoming Tour.

Pereiro was clear about what his responsibilities were going to be. "I will be at the complete disposition of Valverde," he said. "Some people ask me, you've finished in the top ten now two times in the Tour, why not go as a leader? But there's a big difference between finishing in the top ten and winning the race."

Pereiro's status in Spanish cycling skyrocketed following his impressive stage victory into Pau at the 2005 Tour, and it earned him a lucrative contract to ride in support of Valverde at Caisse d'Épargne. Pereiro, in his seventh season as a pro, was very happy with that arrangement. Little did he know that by the third stage of the Tour, Valverde would be out of the race with a broken clavicle and he would be thrust into the role of team leader.

With his quick laugh and swarthy good looks, Pereiro is one of the best-liked characters in pro cycling. His Caisse d'Épargne teammate and French national champion Florent Brard called him the "movie star of the peloton."

Pereiro's intensity on the bike is in sharp contrast to his civility off it. "I have a strong character and I like to joke and have fun, but in the race, I give the maximum, to make the best I can, to try to win," Pereiro said. "This is a sport that is based on suffering, but we don't have to be suffering after the race is over. I like to win. It makes the fans happy, my team happy, and myself."

After his loss to Hincapie on the mountain stage to Pla d'Adet in 2005, however, the world saw the other side of Pereiro's character. The American beat him in a two-up sprint in the Tour's hardest mountain stage after not taking a pull during their long breakaway with eleven other riders. At the line, Pereiro unleashed a string of expletives but made up with Hincapie in the next stage's start village.

"George beat me and, yes, at the time I was very disappointed, but I understood his role on the team was to work for Armstrong. I knew he didn't do any work in the escape and that he'd be the most dangerous rival," Pereiro said.

A year later, after finishing second at the end of another monster breakaway effort, the Spanish rider was less frustrated. "This was an exceptional day," said Pereiro, who was now 1:29 ahead of Landis on general classification after beginning the day 28:31 down. "This morning, I couldn't imagine that I would take the yellow jersey. It's surely the best thing that can happen to a rider at the Tour de France."

"THIS MORNING, I COULDN'T IMAGINE THAT I WOULD TAKE THE YELLOW JERSEY. IT'S SURELY THE BEST THING THAT CAN HAPPEN TO A RIDER AT THE TOUR DE FRANCE."

In addition to making a dramatic difference in the Tour, the breakaway to Montélimar was opening up a whole new chapter in Pereiro's life. The movie star was about to step onto center stage with a flourish.

ANOTHER GRUELING STAGE

Phonak's decision to allow Pereiro to take the race leadership seemed to be an acceptable tactic at the time, since he was on close terms with Landis. "They're all very good friends and I have a good relationship with the team management," said Pereiro, who raced with Phonak for his first four years in the big leagues. But having a Caisse d'Épargne rider in the yellow jersey was not an immediate benefit for Phonak on stage 14 from Montélimar to Gap.

When ten men escaped on the first climb out of the Rhône valley on the 180.5km stage, which twisted its way through the rugged foothills of the Alps just north of Provence, Phonak had to lead the chase. That's because Caisse d'Épargne put David Arroyo in the move. With him were three members of the Lampre team, including Salvatore Commesso, along with Discovery's Hincapie (still a potential danger), T-Mobile's Eddy Mazzoleni, and Rabobank's Michael Boogerd.

The chase lasted for an hour, and then Commesso and Bouygues Telecom's Pierrick Fédrigo made an immediate counterattack, joined by Saunier Duval's David Cañada, Davitamon's Mario Aerts, and T-Mobile's Matthias Kessler. Rik

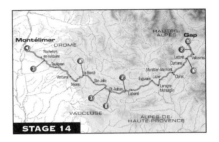

STAGE 14

Verbrugghe of Cofidis made it a sextet when he caught the breakaway at the feed zone after 79km, where the lead was up to 3:35.

Over the day's hardest climb—the 9km, 5 percent Col de Perty that topped out at 4,275 feet elevation halfway though the stage—the speed was so fast that dozens of riders were dropped. In some riders' opinion, this was turning into the Tour's second toughest day yet.

The severity of the stage was emphasized when the leaders came hurtling through an off-camber right turn at the foot of a short downhill, where melting tar and their high speed saw them brake a little too late. Verbrugghe, at the front, went tumbling over a metal guardrail into a ditch, breaking his left leg. Cañada slid into the guardrail and broke his collarbone. Kessler crashed into Cañada and somersaulted over the rail, though he remounted and bravely finished the stage. They don't call him the Pit Bull for nothing.

With just three riders left, the break lost its impetus, but Commesso, riding with his jersey sleeves cut off in the simmering heat, redoubled his efforts. He easily countered an attack by Fédrigo on the closing Cat. 2 Col de la Sentinelle, where Aerts was dropped. The two leaders had just 30 seconds over the top of the climb, which decimated the weary peloton with just 9.5km to go.

Discovery drove the chase on the twisting descent, which was made even trickier by early spatters from a thunderstorm. Popovych was the driver, hoping to set up Hincapie for the stage win. But when it seemed they wouldn't close a 13-second gap in the last 2km, the chase faltered.

Then CSC's Christian Vande Velde, one of the 34 riders in the chase group, had an idea. The American bolted from the group in the last kilometer and, almost colliding with Boogerd, squeezed between the Dutchman and the barriers. "I yelled at him, but I had to hesitate for a second and hit the brakes," Vande Velde recounted. "Luckily, he stayed where he did."

Vande Velde began to close quickly on the two ahead through a series of sharp turns and roundabouts in downtown Gap. "I didn't see [Commesso and Fédrigo] when I attacked," he continued, "and the gap was closing so fast that I thought, 'Oh my God, maybe there is a possibility I can win.' But then they started going."

Commesso accelerated through the last turn with 150 meters to go, which allowed Fédrigo to come from behind and just take the win. Commesso, who had done most of the work and had been in the early break, was in tears, while Vande Velde, third only three seconds back, realized just how close he had come to winning a stage of the Tour de France.

The riders were exhausted from another frantic day in the saddle, but the second rest day at Gap would give them all a needed respite before heading into the Alps.

STAGE 12: LUCHON TO CARCASSONNE

1. Yaroslav Popovych (Ukr), Discovery Channel, 211.5km in 4:34:58 (46.151kph); 2. Alessandro Ballan (I), Lampre-Fondital, at 0:27; 3. Oscar Freire (Sp), Rabobank, at 0:29; 4. Christophe Le Mével (F), Crédit Agricole, at 0:35; 5. Tom Boonen (B), Quick Step, at 4:25; 6. Robbie McEwen (Aus), Davitamon-Lotto; 7. Francisco Ventoso (Sp), Saunier Duval; 8. Erik Zabel (G), Milram; 9. Daniele Bennati (I), Lampre-Fondital; 10. Thor Hushovd (N), Crédit Agricole, all s.t.

STAGE 13: BÉZIERS TO MONTÉLIMAR

1. Jens Voigt (G), CSC, 230km in 5:24:36 (42.513kph); 2. Oscar Pereiro (Sp), Caisse d'Épargne, s.t.; 3. Sylvain Chavanel (F), Cofidis, at 0:40; 4. Manuel Quinziato (I), Liquigas, s.t.; 5. Andriy Grivko (Ukr), Milram, at 6:24; 6. Robbie McEwen (Aus), Davitamon-Lotto, at 29:57; 7. Bernhard Eisel (A), Française des Jeux; 8. Tom Boonen (B), Quick Step; 9. Carlos Da Cruz (F), Française des Jeux; 10. Arnaud Coyot (F), Cofidis, all s.t.

STAGE 14: MONTÉLIMAR TO GAP

1. Pierrick Fédrigo (F), Bouygues Telecom, 180.5km in 4:14:23 (42.573kph); **2.** Salvatore Commesso (I), Lampre-Fondital, s.t.; **3. Christian Vande Velde (USA), CSC, at 0:03; 4.** Christophe Moreau (F), AG2R, at 0:07; **5.** Georg Totschnig (A), Gerolsteiner; **6.** Stefano Garzelli (I), Liquigas; **7.** Michael Boogerd (Nl), Rabobank; **8.** Cristian Moreni (I), Cofidis; **9. George Hincapie (USA), Discovery Channel; 10.** Cadel Evans (Aus), Davitamon-Lotto, all s.t.

GENERAL CLASSIFICATION

1. Oscar Pereiro (Sp), Caisse d'Épargne-Illes Balears

2. Floyd Landis (USA), Phonak, at 1:29

3. Cyril Dessel (F), AG2R, at 1:37

4. Denis Menchov (Rus), Phonak, at 2:30

5. Cadel Evans (Aus), Davitamon-Lotto, at 2:46

CHAPTER 15

Battle on the Alpe

Landis retakes the jersey after CSC sets up Schleck.

T here was a mood of eerie nonchalance before the start of the highly anticipated stage 15 to L'Alpe d'Huez, the first of three days in the high Alps.
The sun was shining again, but a cooling breeze and a relaxing rest day in Gap
seemed to cheer the riders, who were able to chat without being pestered by souvenir hunters. Even so, three of T-Mobile's Germans—Matthias Kessler, Andreas
Klöden, and Patrik Sinkewitz—were too preoccupied to sign in at the presentation
podium. When race speaker Daniel Mangeas split early, the Frenchman's crackling
voice was replaced over the loudspeakers by a lilting U2 track, while French rap
rippled around the white canvas booths in the nearly empty *village de départ*.

At the Discovery Channel team bus a small group of media crews grabbed
quotes from two-time L'Alpe d'Huez winner Lance Armstrong, who'd flown in
with *Brokeback Mountain* star Jake Gyllenhaal, who'd ridden up the Alpe the previous day with the retired champion. Two hundred meters away the CSC riders
drifted out from their red and black bus one by one before mounting their bikes
and cruising to the start.

When Fränk Schleck stepped off the bus, he joined his team's Danish boss,
Bjarne Riis, who was sitting on the curb with his teenage son. Asked later what he
said to his lanky team rider from Luxembourg, Riis said, "[I was telling him] to
stay calm, you know, and don't think too much about his [overall] position and,

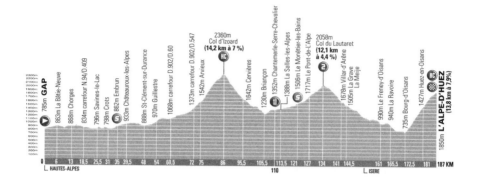

not putting pressure on him, but to do as good as possible. And 'as good as possible' is good enough."

That could have been everyone's mantra—Do your best—in view of the three tough alpine stages they were about to tackle. Three days that contained no less than five *hors-catégorie* climbs, three Cat. 1s, and three Cat. 2s. A foretaste of what might happen in the Alps had come in the finale of stage 14 into Gap, when 100 riders were still together approaching the day's final climb, the 5km, 5 percent Sentinelle. "I didn't think that last climb was so horrible," said Christian Vande Velde, who was one of the last riders out of the CSC bus, "but there were only 35 guys there [at the end], so we must have been going pretty fast."

If a split like that could happen on a little Cat. 2 climb, imagine what could go down on this day's demanding stage over the legendary *hors-catégorie* Col d'Izoard (at 86km) and grinding Col du Lautaret (134km) before the infamous ascent to L'Alpe d'Huez (187km). The day was going to be brutal, and at the start in Gap village, Aussie Simon Gerrans of AG2R spoke for all the riders when he took one look at the race profile card and tossed it. "I threw it out thinking I don't want to look at *that* again," he said.

As if this were like any other stage in a Tour that was averaging 41.802kph, the attacks began as soon as the streets of Gap were left behind. The speed was so fast (50.8km in the first hour despite this being a mountain stage) that the field split in two when the peloton climbed away for the blue, blue waters of the Serre-Ponçon lake less than 30km up the road. The 25 riders in front quickly moved ahead of the rest, and by the time they rolled past the blindingly bright crags of the Queyras canyon at the foot of the Izoard, the gap was 4:25.

Leading the big breakaway were CSC's Jens Voigt, Dave Zabriskie, and Schleck, Lampre's Damiano Cunego and Patxi Vila, and Liquigas's Stefano Garzelli and Michael Albasini. David Arroyo and Vicente Garcia Acosta covered the move for Caisse d'Épargne's race leader Pereiro, while Landis had Phonak teammate Axel Merckx in the move; also included were Discovery's Egoi Martinez and George Hincapie. Later explaining his team's strategy, Hincapie said, "Try and get in the break and try and win the stage. It's pretty simple. We don't have any secrets; just try and get away and do well."

OVER THE IZOARD

Of the 25 leaders, Hincapie, Voigt, Zabriskie, Flecha, Garcia-Acosta, and Rabo-bank's Juan Antonio Flecha had previously won Tour stages, while Schleck was the best-placed rider in the group on overall time, 10:06 behind Pereiro. Because of his relatively high placing, Schleck said he initially drew some criticism for his presence in the breakaway. "It was meant that I stay with Carlos [Sastre] until the end to help him out," Schleck said. "But I got in a breakaway and we had three guys up there. A lot of riders told me to go back because I was too close in overall, but I said no, and I didn't have to pull, either."

When the peloton hit the early slopes of the infamous Izoard, Venezuelan José Rujano of Quick Step, the King of the Mountains from the 2005 Giro d'Italia, broke away solo with little reaction from the field. Ahead, Garzelli soloed clear on the Izoard, a climb included in the 2000 Giro d'Italia that he won. But with such a long way to go on this stage, his move seemed premature.

Behind, seven riders joined Rujano, and they were dangling between the break and the pack, which crossed the summit 6:30 behind Garzelli. The trickiness of the descent was emphasized when two riders in the big chase group had crashes. Discovery's Martinez took several minutes to compose himself before rejoining the main bunch, and Milram's Christian Knees was almost run over by an official's vehicle when he fell in the road.

As Garzelli reached the town of Briançon 105km into the stage, his lead was just 30 seconds over a chase group cut to 15 riders, including Hincapie, Schleck, Voigt, Zabriskie, Merckx, Cunego, Vila, T-Mobile's Eddy Mazzoleni, Cofidis's Sylvain Chavanel, and Saunier Duval's David de la Fuente and Ruben Lobato. Garzelli sat up to wait for the chasers at the feed zone, where Rujano's eight-man chase group was at 3:05, and the peloton at 4:50.

Attacks began again on the gently sloped Lautaret, the first coming from Spain's Vila and Fuente—who was anxious to increase his lead in the King of the Mountains competition. Zabriskie and Voigt led the chase, cresting the climb 30 seconds behind the two Spaniards. The peloton was four minutes back, having caught the Rujano group. Farther back, a distraught Tom Boonen abandoned as rain began to fall. The world champion, who'd failed to win a stage after starting the Tour with high hopes, complained of a sore throat and several other ailments.

On wet roads down the long, 30km descent of the Lautaret, Zabriskie took to the front and drove the group in his trademark aerodynamic tuck. Voigt also contributed to the pace, while teammate Schleck was saving his efforts for the upcoming finish. "It was important that we were represented in the breakaway," Zabriskie said. "But once we had Fränk in the break, I knew we were riding for the win."

The efforts by Zabriskie and Voigt gave the group a healthy advantage on the yellow jersey group as they reached the crowds of spectators jamming the roadside on the daunting opening slopes of L'Alpe d'Huez, a climb that is steeped in Tour history, from Fausto Coppi's inaugural victory in 1952, when the road was still unsurfaced, to Armstrong's time trial win over Jan Ullrich in 2004.

Very little about this Tour de France could be compared with events during the Armstrong years, but one of his favorite tactics was retained on the climb to L'Alpe d'Huez—get a teammate to accelerate like crazy up the opening steep pitch of the 14.2km mountain road and then punch the pace to scatter your rivals. That's exactly what happened in the day's breakaway group, *and* in the pack of race favorites that reached the base of the infamous 21-turn climb 3:19 later.

Up front, former Giro d'Italia champion Cunego used Lampre-Fondital teammate Vila as his greyhound before twice making surges himself that only one of the other 14 breakaway riders could match: Schleck. Unfortunately for Cunego (who was enjoying an outstanding third week after floundering in the first half of his debut Tour), Schleck was craftier. The lean Luxembourger, who made a solo attack to win the 2006 Amstel Gold Race classic in April, surprised Cunego with a similar move 2.4km from the finish line. "My attack wasn't planned," said Schleck, "but when you have an opportunity to win a stage like Alpe d'Huez you have to take it."

Three minutes back down the road, the "Armstrong move" was being played out by T-Mobile. The German squad's man for every situation, "Pit Bull" Kessler, made such a strong surge for his team leader Klöden that only Landis, Evans, and Denis Menchov were able to follow him. Klöden, the only rider still in the race to have finished on the Tour's podium, seemed to be the real candidate for victory.

KLÖDEN'S CHALLENGE

Over the nine-year span of his professional career, Klöden had ridden in Ullrich's shadow. Klöden, 31, turned pro with the Deutsche Telekom team in 1998, six months after Ullrich won the Tour de France at the age of 23. While Ullrich emerged as a star, finishing second on his Tour debut in 1996 before winning it in 1997, Klöden matured at a more gradual pace. He wouldn't ride his first Tour until 2001, when he took a respectable 26th place riding in support of Ullrich, who finished second to Armstrong that year.

In 2003 Klöden again rode in a support role, this time for Alexander Vinokourov, who finished third behind Armstrong and Ullrich. (This was the only season Ullrich raced outside of the Telekom/T-Mobile camp, following a six-month suspension for using the recreational drug Ecstasy.) Klöden didn't make it to Paris, however, as he abandoned in the stage into Gap, the same day Joseba Beloki suffered his race-ending crash and Vinokourov won the stage. Klöden pulled out because he never recovered from the injuries he incurred in the opening stage pileup that also resulted in Tyler Hamilton breaking his collarbone.

The 2004 season brought some of the proudest moments in Klöden's career. He came to the Tour resplendent in the white, orange, red, and yellow jersey of the German national champion. Though he was brought to the Tour to again ride for Ullrich, Klöden outclassed his struggling team leader in the mountains and moved ahead of him on general classification. But the faithful friend and lieutenant asked for Ullrich's consent before pursuing his own interests. After a hard final day in the mountains into Le Grand Bornand, Klöden nearly took his first Tour stage win. After Ullrich chased down U.S. Postal's Landis in the final kilometers, Klöden attacked and looked to have the stage win in his pocket. Unfortunately the German was a victim of Armstrong's "no gifts" policy, and the American outsprinted him to the line. Despite that disappointment, Klöden rode a remarkable final time trial to claim second place in Paris, behind Armstrong and ahead of Italy's Ivan Basso. Ullrich placed fourth, his first time off the podium in seven Tours.

Though he'd bettered Ullrich at the 2004 Tour, Klöden reassumed his *super-domestique* role in 2005. Klöden again narrowly missed winning a stage, this time in a photo finish on stage 8 at Gérardmer, after he and Rabobank's Pieter Weening escaped on the Col de la Schlucht. Three days later, Ullrich was dropped on that Tour's first summit finish at Courchevel, and the stronger Klöden was called back to help limit Ullrich's losses. Later in the race, Klöden broke a bone in his wrist in a crash with teammate Kessler, and he abandoned the following day.

Klöden's 2006 season also started with a crash, in training, that resulted in a dislocated shoulder and put his Tour status in question. But when Klöden returned to competition in May at the Tour of Bavaria, he placed a strong third in the time trial stage. After riding a quiet Tour of Switzerland in support of race winner Ullrich, he was ready for another Tour. Before the start, "Klödi" again swore his allegiance to his close friend Ullrich, saying, "At this year's Tour, we will work for Ullrich without a second thought."

All that changed, however, when Ullrich and teammate Oscar Sevilla were sent home on the eve of the Tour for their alleged involvement in *Operación Puerto*. After Klöden finished a disappointing 24th in the opening prologue, 17 seconds behind winner Thor Hushovd, he said, "After Jan's withdrawal I found it a little hard to motivate myself at first. The tension my teammates and me built up, it suddenly imploded. I noticed that during the prologue, when my head wasn't clear and I didn't have the right legs."

Even without its team captain, T-Mobile looked to be in the driver's seat after the Rennes time trial. It had four men in the top six overall, with Klöden tied for fifth, 1:50 behind teammate Sergei Gontchar. "Placing eighth [in the time trial] is almost perfect," Klöden wrote in his Web diary. "It's a result that gives me courage for the upcoming tough mountain stages. My form is pretty good already, but there's still room for improvement. After all, I don't have that many race kilometers in my legs. So I mainly used the first week to prepare myself for the mountains. I want to be in peak form then."

Klöden had passed the Tour's first test, but he barely passed its second test in the Pyrénées, in the stage to the Pla-de-Beret summit in Spain. The T-Mobile riders were tired after riding in defense of Gontchar's yellow jersey over the previous days, and Klöden cracked on the final climb, finishing ninth in the stage, 1:31 behind stage winner Menchov. Earlier in the day, Klöden had ordered his teammates to ride hard on the Col du Portillon because he was feeling strong.

"I KNEW BEFOREHAND IT WAS GOING TO GET VERY TOUGH, AND I EXPECTED THE TOP RIDERS TO LIFT THE TEMPO. GIVEN THAT I CAME TO FRANCE AS A HELPER, IT WENT WELL."

"I knew beforehand it was going to get very tough, and I expected the top riders to lift the tempo," Klöden said. "Given that I came to France as a helper, it went well. I was suffering from cramps when I lost the wheels, and in this situation I could tell I'm short of race kilometers. When the thighs started to hurt, I even expected to lose some seven minutes. Instead the favorites are still within reach for me now. The tough alpine stages still lie ahead and a lot can happen there."

Before the Alps, Klöden had time to recover from the Spanish setback and build his morale on the three stages in the Midi. "The moderate pace played into my hands," Klöden explained. "I could get more race kilometers in my legs without riding at my limit. Every kilometer after my injury layoff does me good."

FINAL THRUST

Landis may have started the climb to L'Alpe d'Huez worrying about Menchov as a threat to the race lead, but by the time the day had ended he knew that Klöden was the real contender. The German attacked early on, looking to distance himself from the rest of the GC contenders. Only Landis and Cadel Evans were able to respond immediately. AG2R's Christophe Moreau dug deep to bridge, but then blew and lost 2:38 to Landis and Klöden before the top.

Sastre and Levi Leipheimer, maintaining an even-paced pursuit, passed a gasping Menchov after Sastre's teammate Voigt (who had dropped back from the break) gave him a short but incisive pull. It was enough for Sastre and Leipheimer (who said, "I'm a little more tired than those guys, I think") to close on Klöden and Landis, just as they were riding a valiant Evans off of their wheels.

Evans would drop back to ride with yellow jersey Pereiro and fellow Aussie Michael Rogers and concede 1:39 to Landis. "Not good enough today, not good enough. That's all there is to it," said a despondent Evans moments after crossing the line in 16th place.

Meanwhile, the other team leaders, like Sastre, were getting help from teammates who had dropped out of the break. On the middle part of the relentless 8 percent grade, Phonak's Merckx was just ahead of team leader Landis. "I attacked to get to Axel," said the American, who then sat behind his Belgian teammate, with Klöden, Sastre, and Leipheimer in tow.

Then about 5km from the summit, an impressive Klöden suddenly accelerated. Landis followed. "I only had to stay with Klöden, that was my objective," said Landis, who was widely criticized in the European media for "a lack of panache" in not working with his German rival to put struggling race leader Pereiro out of contention.

"It would have been just as well [for me] if Pereiro kept his lead," said Landis after retaking the yellow jersey from the Spaniard by a scant ten seconds. But perhaps Landis was going as hard as he could.

Landis kept his nerve and stayed with Klöden on the Alpe's difficult final slopes. "It was very tough today," Klöden said. "[Kessler] prepared my attack at the beginning of the final climb perfectly. When I saw that Sastre and Evans were struggling, I lifted the tempo again to take some time out of them. Not as much as I hoped at first, but still. Unfortunately I had to do all the work on my own in the chase group, until we reached Mazzoleni."

Klöden crossed the line with the same time as early breakaway survivor, Garzelli, who took third, with Landis in fourth. "Floyd rode a tactical race again and never shared with the lead work," Klöden lamented on his Web diary. "I turned back my head again and again, but there was no help coming from behind, so I just continued to ride at the front. All the more, because Sastre, Evans, and Menchov gained a second wind and started to reduce the gap. Landis is now the man to beat in the coming stages."

With Menchov dropped and Klöden riding aggressively, the Alpe had shown Landis who his biggest threat was. "Klöden was very good," Landis said. "And the time differences are not so big yet. I wouldn't write any of the others off. A bad day could change everything."

Landis couldn't know how right he was.

STAGE 15: GAP TO L'ALPE D'HUEZ

1. Fränk Schleck (Lux), CSC, 187km 4:52:22 (38.376kph); 2. Damiano Cunego (I), Lampre-Fondital, at 0:11; 3. Stefano Garzelli (I), Liquigas, at 1:10; 4. Floyd Landis (USA), Phonak; 5. Andreas Klöden (G), T-Mobile, both s.t.; 6. Ruben Lobato (Sp), Saunier Duval, at 1:14; 7. Sylvain Chavanel (F), Cofidis, at 1:18; 8. Eddy Mazzoleni (I), T-Mobile, at 1:28; 9. Carlos Sastre (Sp), CSC, at 1:35; 10. Levi Leipheimer (USA), Gerolsteiner, at 1:49.

GENERAL CLASSIFICATION

1. Floyd Landis (USA), Phonak

2. Oscar Pereiro (Sp), Caisse d'Épargne-Illes Balears, at 0:10

3. Cyril Dessel (F), AG2R, at 2:02

4. Denis Menchov (Rus), Rabobank, at 2:12

5. Carlos Sastre (Sp), CSC, at 2:17

CHAPTER 16

Bad Days, Good Days

Landis and Rasmussen, a study in contrasts.

E verybody, even the guy who wins, has bad days in the Tour. The objective is that they have them when nobody notices them, on days when you can hide. On a day like that there's no place to hide. I don't know how many climbs there were, but it seemed like there were about fifty."

This was Floyd Landis talking to a reporter at the Phonak team training camp in January 2006. He was remembering his "bad day" at the 2005 Tour de France, the toughest day in the Pyrénées, the day with six major climbs, not fifty, the day that finished atop a mountain called Pla d'Adet, where the stage win went to George Hincapie, and Landis lost four and a half minutes in the final 15km. It was the sort of day that Landis didn't want to repeat in 2006—at least not in stage 16, the toughest of the tough, with more than 17,000 feet of climbing in its 182km.

Everyone has a bad day at the Tour. It happens to the lowliest *domestiques* and the greatest champions. At this Tour, Levi Leipheimer had a bad day at the Rennes time trial, George Hincapie and Oscar Pereiro in the second Pyrenean stage, and, to a lesser extent, Cadel Evans on L'Alpe d'Huez.

The bad days are frequently followed by good days. Leipheimer came back to top strength at Pla-de-Beret and almost won the most difficult stage to date; he was now in ninth place overall. Hincapie, after faltering in the Pyrénées, was the dynamo of a long breakaway the next day. Pereiro was in the same break, and then he turned a half hour deficit into a yellow jersey-winning ride with Jens Voigt in the stage to Montélimar.

In the past, champions like Jacques Anquetil, Eddy Merckx, Greg LeMond, and Miguel Induráin had bad days that compromised their chances of winning the Tour. Lance Armstrong fought through his worst day at the 2003 Tour, when dehydration caused him to lose a vital time trial to Jan Ullrich; Armstrong came back to score his remarkable stage win at Luz-Ardiden a few days later.

So, in this 2006 Tour, was anyone about to have a bad day or a quick turnaround? Those thoughts were in Leipheimer's mind right after he finished the stage at L'Alpe d'Huez, when he was asked to comment on Landis's performance on the famed 21-turn climb. "I could never tell if he was hurting. I don't think he was," he said. "As long as he maintains his advantage on Klöden in the mountains I think he'll win the Tour—as long as the [Phonak] team can control Rabobank. I think you saw that Rabobank had a bad day, and they're going to come out firing tomorrow right from the gun. Rasmussen, Boogerd will be going with everything. You can definitely expect that."

HIGH-FLYING CHICKEN

Michael Rasmussen sprang to media attention at the 2005 Tour when he scored a brilliant solo stage win in the mountain stage to Mulhouse, held a podium spot behind Armstrong until the final time trial, and came away with the polka-dot jersey as the Tour's best climber. But very early during the official presentation in Paris of the 2006 course he knew that his chances for a repeat were remote. "I was sitting there watching them disclose the route and my heart sank with each stage," said Rasmussen. With two long time trials and only three mountaintop finishes, the former world mountain bike champion accepted that he likely had no chance to get within striking distance of the final podium. As a result, he started his third Tour in Strasbourg with different, but still ambitious goals: to help team leader Denis Menchov achieve a high overall placing, to win a big mountain stage himself, and to repeat as King of the Mountains.

The 32-year-old Dane, whose rock-solid confidence belies his nickname of Chicken, completed the first part of his contract in the Pyrénées in the tough climbing stage to Pla-de-Beret. Rasmussen buried himself for Menchov on the long, grinding approach to the final summit to trim the lead group to just a handful of riders before the Russian jumped to the stage win. "When we came to the bottom of the Portillon [that stage], I asked him how he felt and asked if he can win today," Rasmussen recalled. "He said yes and so I took him 25km up the valley and he did the rest himself. That was one of the few days in the Tour I rode with everything I had."

After riding himself to a standstill at Pla-de-Beret and finishing 10 minutes behind Menchov, Rasmussen waited for the Alps where he was determined to win on cycling's most famous mountain: L'Alpe d'Huez. But the Dane's earlier unselfish riding put him in a hole in regard to the polka-dot jersey, which was being worn by Spanish rider David de la Fuente after his long breakaway through the Pyrénées. Fuente then worked himself into the day's big break in stage 15 and increased his lead over Rasmussen, who picked up leftover KOM points when he could.

"I could see that time was beginning to run out for me as we were getting closer [to Paris]," Rasmussen said. "Obviously, I had hoped to take the jersey and win the stage at Alpe d'Huez, but we made a huge tactical error by letting 25 riders go down the road. I was really disappointed."

For a climber like Rasmussen, his entire season comes down to the dramatic mountain stages at the Tour. So throwing away one of his few opportunities to shine was a disaster. Rasmussen was livid that his Rabobank team let unheralded Fränk Schleck steal his glory at L'Alpe d'Huez. Furthermore, Menchov struggled on the Alpe and he was no longer considered a favorite for overall victory after Landis recaptured the yellow jersey.

An angry Rasmussen sat down with Rabobank team boss Erik Breukink after dinner in L'Alpe d'Huez, and said he was going to do it his way in the torturous four-climb stage 16 to La Toussuire. "I told him, 'You can tell me whatever you want; I am going for it tomorrow, from the gun.' We didn't have to argue about that," he said. "Everyone in the peloton knew what I was going to do. There

wasn't a single rider in the peloton that I could surprise by going on the attack."

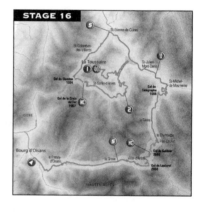

EPIC RIDES

Rasmussen didn't wait long to make his move. Only 6km into the probable six-hour stage, as soon as the course headed up the steep opening slopes of the 43km haul to the 8,681-foot Col du Galibier summit, the rail-thin Rabobank climber tore away from the weary bunch. Only two riders, Frenchman Sandy Casar of Française des Jeux and Slovenian Tadej Valjavec of Lampre, dared to follow him.

For Rasmussen, who'd ridden this entire stage in training in early June, it was the start of a planned 176km escapade over the Tour's highest peak, the Galibier; up its steepest long climb, the Glandon-Croix de Fer combination; down its dodgiest descent, the Mollard; and up its longest mountaintop finish at La Toussuire.

Rasmussen's early move prompted a belated chase from a 13-strong group that included Discovery Channel's José Luis Rubiera and Yaroslav Popovych, Saunier Duval's Gilberto Simoni and José Gomez Marchante, Lampre's Salvatore Commesso, and AG2R's Sylvain Calzati. But they never got closer than two minutes to the leading trio.

At the bare, breezy summit of the Galibier Rasmussen took the $6,000 Souvenir Henri Desgrange Prize, named for the Tour's founding race director. The chasers, led by Calzati, were three minutes back, while the main bunch rolled over 4:40 behind. Several riders crashed on the tricky, high-speed descent, which is almost continuous for 32km, first down the open mountainside of the Galibier before reaching the switchbacks that drop from the Col du Télégraphe into the deep alpine valley of the Maurienne. Among those who tumbled were key team riders for Landis (Miguel Martin Perdiguero) and Cadel Evans (Christophe Brandt). Lampre's Italian sprinter Daniele Bennati was forced to abandon after injuring his left hip and calf, and Cofidis leader Sylvain Chavanel, who slammed into a concrete wall, never returned to the peloton, lost 42 minutes, and dropped from 17th overall to 38th overall.

Meanwhile, on the 20km of gradual downhill in the Maurienne valley, the Rasmussen trio pushed their advantage to seven minutes on a largely regrouped peloton, which was about to absorb the chasers.

If the riders had looked to their left halfway along this *route nationale,* they would have seen the day's final destination, La Toussuire, sitting high on the green mountainside. But for them that destination was still three hours away following a counterclockwise loop over the Glandon, Croix de Fer, and Mollard passes.

Landis's Phonak men pulled the pack at a steady tempo along the valley road, but as soon as the race reached the first steep pitches of the 20km Glandon, it was Carlos Sastre's CSC riders who pushed to the front. Stage 15 winner Schleck set the pace with Christian Vande Velde, as Sastre sat on their wheels, while Landis was partway down the line with only one teammate alongside, Axel Merckx. Pereiro still had three teammates with him, as did Klöden and Dessel.

Race leader Landis wasn't looking too comfortable when the gradient reached 10 percent. "I was struggling," he said later. "I tried to hide it, but I wasn't good."

Up front, Rasmussen had already dropped Casar and Valjavec, and Chicken would keep spinning his spindly legs, even though his shoulders started to rock on the steeper second half of the Glandon. It was here, on a 13 percent pitch just before the hamlet of Léchet, 13km into the climb, that Leipheimer sprang away from the main pack, which had dwindled to just 27 riders. He quickly opened a 150-meter gap and glanced under his right shoulder. No one was giving immediate chase and away he went.

The Gerolsteiner leader, who clinched his victory in the Dauphiné Libéré at La Toussuire a month earlier, made his attack 65km from the stage finish. Leipheimer, who was desperate for a stage win, knew this was a long shot, but he also knew that even if he didn't catch Rasmussen, any time gained over the other leaders might push him up into the small group of podium challengers.

His effort started well. In a half hour of climbing—7km to the Glandon summit plus another 2.5km after joining the top part of the Croix de Fer—Leipheimer gained almost three minutes on the main group, and closed to 5:31 on Rasmussen.

It was a brave effort by Leipheimer, whose long solo chase earned less attention than it deserved. As Rasmussen said, "Many of the favorites were afraid of what was coming. Levi was the only one to try, but he really didn't come close to me." Leipheimer closed to within 3:30 of Rasmussen, but that was with 12km still to climb to the finish in La Toussuire, when more dramatic events were developing in the group behind.

DRAMATIC FINALE

When the Landis group hit the base of La Toussuire, AG2R's Christophe Moreau was one of the first to get dropped. The veteran Frenchman, who finished second overall at the Dauphiné, would later claw back to the leaders and help tow teammate Dessel to the line. Others who were dropped early included T-Mobile's Matthias Kessler and Gerolsteiner's Markus Fothen. Merckx took his final pulls in the opening kilometers of the climb before dropping back and leaving Landis isolated in the front group, which was now down to 16 riders.

Rogers began to push the pace for T-Mobile when, with just under 14km to go, Menchov spurted and sent a jolt through the front group. As the Russian sprang away, Rogers, Pereiro, and Evans were the first to grab his wheel. Landis was much slower to react. Everyone soon found out why.

"He was going behind and I felt that he was suffering," Sastre said about Landis, "and in that moment I didn't think too much and I went. It's like a war out there. You have to attack when you can." So, with 12km still to race, Sastre jumped clear on the right side of the road, prompting T-Mobile's Rogers and Eddy Mazzoleni to take up the chase for Klöden. But Sastre was gaining while Landis was struggling.

Just a day after retaking the leadership of the 2006 Tour de France at L'Alpe d'Huez and looking like he'd hold it all the way to Paris, Landis was having huge problems. The American's sudden reversal from superman to mortal shocked the world. His pedaling became labored. The color left his face. He was out of fuel and riding on willpower alone. "I had to get to the finish line and that was all that was going through my head," he said later. "There was only a certain speed I could go, which wasn't very fast."

The Phonak captain had the look of defeat etched on his face as he realized that his chance of winning the Tour was slipping away from him. Not allowed to take a feed from his car this close to the finish, Landis rode alone in a daze, as rider after rider slipped past his slumped shoulders.

With the race leader gone, the other contenders realized they were now racing for the overall victory. To take the yellow jersey, CSC's Sastre had to make up two minutes on second-place Pereiro, so he was racing as hard as he could go. The valiant Leipheimer finally stalled and was passed by the attacking Sastre, and then by the other leaders in the closing kilometers of this epic day.

At the 5km-to-go point Sastre was 3:00 behind Rasmussen, 30 seconds ahead of Leipheimer, and 45 seconds up on the chase group of Rogers, Mazzoleni, Klöden, Pereiro, Moreau, Dessel, Menchov, Evans, and Crédit Agricole's Pietro Caucchioli. When Sastre was a minute ahead of this group, Klöden attacked to drop everyone except Evans and Pereiro. The trio started to close in on Sastre, who was starting to blow, while Rasmussen was still grinding away in front.

Rasmussen's gargantuan recital—he was alone for the final 75km over three climbs—ended in glory. He crossed the line in La Toussuire with his arms spread wide as if he were flying; or maybe he was just too weary to raise them higher.

Sastre pushed all the way to the line, his unzipped CSC jersey flapping behind him. But his one-minute lead 4km out was cut to just 13 seconds at the finish. Pereiro, who sprinted in for third place ahead of Evans and Klöden, reclaimed the yellow jersey. A spent Menchov crossed in 11th, 3:42 behind Rabobank teammate Rasmussen. But there was still no sign of Landis. His high hopes deflated, his yellow jersey stained black by sweat, Landis took 51 minutes to cover the final 12 kilometers uphill: eight minutes slower than Sastre, Pereiro, and the other podium hunters.

HUMILIATION

His eyes hidden behind dark lenses, Landis crossed the line at the little ski station of La Toussuire knowing he was about to be mobbed by the media. After struggling home on the wheel of Phonak teammate Merckx, his lips trembling, tears welling, and head down, Landis stopped at his *soigneur* to have his face wiped and helmet removed. Asked if he wanted to say anything, Landis simply said no.

AFTER STRUGGLING HOME ON THE WHEEL OF PHONAK TEAMMATE MERCKX, HIS LIPS TREMBLING, TEARS WELLING, AND HEAD DOWN, LANDIS STOPPED AT HIS *SOIGNEUR* TO HAVE HIS FACE WIPED AND HELMET REMOVED. ASKED IF HE WANTED TO SAY ANYTHING, LANDIS SIMPLY SAID NO.

With the Phonak sports doctor Denise Demir striding beside him, Landis pedaled away from the media crush toward a team support car beyond the barriers. At least 20 television crews and assorted reporters chased. Some cameramen and photographers ran backward ahead of him, bumping into one another and shouting at spectators to clear the way. The media pack thinned as Landis picked up the pace, while the doctor, in black polo and sneakers, sprinted to keep up.

Arriving at the team vehicle, a Skoda station wagon with Swiss plates, Phonak's press liaison Georges Luechinger yelled, "Give him two minutes." Luechinger clamped the ex-race leader's special yellow and red BMC to the bike rack as Landis climbed into the front passenger seat. His yellow jersey was soaked from the water he'd poured over his head on the climb. He cracked open a can of Nestea and took a swig. He bent to rip open his Velcro shoe straps and took off the cleats. He peeled off one glove, then the other, and chucked them on the floor. His legs splayed, Landis closed his eyes and leaned back into the car seat as if he'd like to disappear. The Skoda inched clear of the mob.

"That was one of the most humiliating things that's happened to me," Landis said later. "All I felt was humiliation and depression."

Was this the end of his bid to win the Tour? Or could he bounce back?

At that moment, with another tough mountain stage coming up the next day, Landis seemed to have blown his chance of winning what, because of his up-coming hip replacement surgery, could be his final Tour de France. Once more, this crazy Tour had gotten crazier.

Landis's collapse resembled Miguel Induráin's after stage 7 of the 1996 Tour, when the great Spaniard bonked spectacularly, said nothing to the press, and was driven away from the mob in a Mercedes-Benz minivan. That also happened in the Alps, at the summit finish of Les Arcs, a similar climb to La Toussuire's. Induráin lost 3:32 in just 4km in that breakdown and didn't really recover.

The Spanish superstar, who was favored to extend his winning streak to six that year, revived just enough to place 5th in the next day's 30km uphill time trial, but he faded to an 11th place finish at that Tour, his last. As it happened, Landis now occupied 11th overall, just four days away from Paris. History didn't appear to be on the American's side.

As Landis retired to his hotel, Les Chalets Goelia, his sudden collapse was the talk of La Toussuire. Back at the finish area, reporters were grabbing comments from anyone they could find. One man talking was Pereiro's Caisse d'Épargne directeur sportif, Eusebio Unzué, who directed Induráin through his 1991–1995 Tour win streak and now had another rider wearing the yellow jersey. Asked about Pereiro's chances of defending the lead in stage 17, Unzué screwed up his pointed nose, ran his hand through silvery black hair, and said, "Tomorrow is another tough stage, particularly with the last uphill, the Joux-Plane. It's true, if we're not strong tomorrow, we can lose a lot of time to Sastre or Klöden. It could be a difficult finish for Pereiro."

The new race leader was more confident. At his press conference, Pereiro said, "This Tour has been *loco*. No one expected Landis to lose so much time. Today it crossed a very important hurdle. The podium is looking more secure. If we can get through tomorrow, we can dream of winning this Tour de France."

No one was talking about Landis's chances anymore.

STAGE 16: BOURG D'OISANS TO LA TOUSSUIRE

1. Michael Rasmussen (Dk), Rabobank, 182km in 5:36:04 (32.493kph); **2.** Carlos Sastre (Sp), CSC, at 1:41; **3.** Oscar Pereiro (Sp), Caisse d'Épargne-Illes Balears, at 1:54; **4.** Cadel Evans (Aus), Davitamon-Lotto, at 1:56; **5.** Andreas Klöden (G), T-Mobile, s.t.; **6.** Christophe Moreau (F), AG2R, at 2:37; **7.** Pietro Caucchioli (I), Crédit Agricole; **8.** Cyril Dessel (F), AG2R, both s.t.; **9. Levi Leipheimer (USA), Gerolsteiner, at 3:24; 10.** Haimar Zubeldia (Sp), Euskaltel-Euskadi, at 3:42.

GENERAL CLASSIFICATION

1. Oscar Pereiro (Sp), Caisse d'Épargne-Illes Balears

2. Carlos Sastre (Sp), CSC, at 1:50

3. Andreas Klöden (G), T-Mobile, at 2:20

4. Cyril Dessel (F), AG2R, at 2:43

5. Cadel Evans (Aus), Davitamon-Lotto, at 2:56

CHAPTER 17

"I'm the Strongest Guy in This Race"

Floyd Landis makes his comeback ride.

ess than two hours after struggling across the finish line at La Toussuire, Floyd Landis gave a press conference. For a broken race leader to muster the energy to answer a slew of questions from the assembled media so soon after a catastrophe was probably a first in the history of the Tour de France.

Virtually any other rider would have been holed up in his hotel, probably receiving an intravenous drip to replace the fluids and minerals he lost in his struggle up the final climb. After Miguel Induráin crumpled on the mountaintop finish at Les Arcs in 1996, a score of journalists went to his hotel, hoping to see the downed champion. But the only person to speak to them was team manager Eusebio Unzué. Induráin was recovering in his room.

Landis, on the other hand, said he just needed to refuel with his usual post-race nutrition before a massage and a good dinner. And it soon became clear in his get-together with the press that his spirit too was returning rapidly.

As he sat outside Les Chalets Goelia in the late evening sunshine, Landis greeted the gathered reporters in his usual polite, normal-guy manner: "First of all, I want you to now believe me when I say I respect you guys, because this [press conference] is the last thing in the world I want to do. Anyway, what are the questions? I think I can guess, but let's hear it."

What happened today?

"I had a very bad day on the wrong day. My team did a good job in the beginning. I suffered from the beginning and tried to hide it, but at the end I couldn't. I couldn't go. That was the best I could do."

How do you explain it?

"Sometimes you don't feel well, and sometimes it's on the wrong day. Today was not a good day to have a bad day. What can I say?"

Where do you go from here?

"Stage 18, or whatever it is . . . 19?" [Next up was actually stage 17.]

Was there a time on that final climb where you gave up?

"Maybe, mentally, I gave up."

Mentally you gave up because you saw that you were struggling and definitely losing time?

"No, it was the most I could do. I was struggling even on the climbs before that. I tried to hide it, but I wasn't good, and then on the last climb there was only a certain speed I could go, which wasn't very fast."

Did you bonk?

"I don't think it was a problem of not eating enough. I just wasn't good from the beginning, like I said. A lot of times I feel that way and I come around at the end. There was never a flat part for fifteen minutes where I could recover. I think I would have been better off, but that's how it goes."

I'm sure this is a day you would like to forget. How difficult is it for you to come out here and even talk about it?

"Well, ignoring it doesn't change anything, so I thought I'd come out and, at least, smile for you all."

Have you thought about tomorrow at all?

"Yeah, it's another hard day, and things change. As you saw, [Oscar] Pereiro was 30 minutes down, and now he has the lead again. I don't expect to win the Tour at this point; it's not easy to get back eight minutes, but I'll keep fighting. It's not over yet."

What do you think of Pereiro being in the yellow jersey now after you gave him 30 minutes?

"I'm happy for him. He's a friend of mine. That's the way the Tour went. I've said several times that it doesn't matter what the other guys do, I'm focused on what I do, but seeing Oscar in the yellow jersey doesn't disappoint me in any way. He's a good person and he was a good teammate."

How do you deal with this from a mental standpoint?

"I don't know. Drink some beer? That's what I'm thinking about now. I don't know . . . it's not so bad. I never assumed the Tour was won at any point. I said many times that at any time you can have a bad day, and that's why I was trying to race conservatively every day that I did feel good. And, yeah, a bad day came at the wrong time."

If you try to turn this around on a positive note, can you appreciate what you've accomplished here at the Tour already? Or are you just thinking about what might have slipped away from you?

"Yeah, it's a little of both. I am happy about the way it went, and I'm proud of my team for standing behind me the whole time and risking everything on me. That's not easy to do. On the other hand, yeah, I'm disappointed, and I'd be lying if I said I could just forget about it."

Did it have anything to do with your hip?

"No, that was not a factor."

Would you tell us if it was?

"No."

Were you acting yesterday [on L'Alpe d'Huez]?

"No, I felt very good yesterday. If you think back to the Tours of the past, we've seen it happen to many different people. You have a good day and you have a bad day. If you can arrange it so that the bad days are on the easier days, that's the best thing to do, but you can't really predict it. I'd just as soon forget it, but that's the way it is."

Is this the first bad day you've had at this Tour, or have you had others?

"No, up until now I've felt well. I've been consistent. On the easier days, you don't know how bad the day is if you don't feel good. You find out quickly on a day like today. But no, until now I think things went well. Today did not go so well."

Do you have any regrets for not taking some of the opportunities that you may have had that you didn't make more of?

"No, I think I did everything that I could do to be the best I could be at this Tour. I would change today if I could, but I don't know what I would have done differently, so I can't say I regret anything that I did."

Did you feel a lot of pressure to win this Tour?

"No. It was a goal of mine to win, and we said from the beginning that we wanted to win. Pressure from the outside didn't affect me, and I don't think that had anything to do with today."

Do you think, given what happened to you today, is it possible that after tomorrow things could change and the situation could be very different for you?

"Yeah, it could change for a lot of reasons and for a lot of different people. My chances of winning the Tour are very small at this point. But I'll keep fighting because you never know what's going to happen next. But I wouldn't say the odds are good."

Who do you think is going to win the Tour now?

"It looks to me that [Andreas] Klöden has a very good chance, and [Carlos] Sastre was very strong today, but it will be hard for them to get time tomorrow; it's not as difficult a stage as today. And Pereiro was also quite good today. It will come down to the time trial, I imagine. With the top few guys, the gaps aren't so big."

Did you know when you were dropped that the yellow jersey was gone?

"I knew I felt very, very bad. I didn't expect to stay close to the leaders. I did what I could. I kept fighting, but I didn't have much left. I did everything in my power to stay close, but you saw what happened."

Is there anything you can learn from today?

"I'll learn to forget."

Does this change your long-term future, your goals, the way you'll race?

"No. Bicycle racing is a big part of my life, but it doesn't change anything about who I am or what I'll do next. I regret the way it went today, but I don't regret anything I did, because I don't know what I could have done to change it, so I wouldn't say I would change anything now. Thanks, you guys."

READY TO FIGHT BACK

Good to his word, Landis went and had a beer later that evening on the café terrace next to his hotel with his Colorado-based trainer, Alan Lim, and some team personnel. Landis said they didn't stay long because the public was pestering them, but Lim said in his Web log on bicycling.com that "rather than being in a foul mood Floyd was just happy to be acting like a normal person again."

Lim explained that Landis's bad day was likely linked to his exertions of the previous day: "Yesterday [on L'Alpe d'Huez] was a big effort and no matter what you do, sometimes a big effort means the next day isn't going to be so pretty. There's no amount of eating, sleep, magic potion mixing, or aromatherapy that is going to fix that in under eighteen hours, especially after two weeks of racing. Floyd didn't bonk, he wasn't dehydrated, and his hip didn't feel bad. It just wasn't there for him. He felt awful and spent most of the day in damage control."

Another theory for the American rider's bad day came from Lance Armstrong's and Landis's former training consultant, Dr. Michele Ferrari, who had been helping T-Mobile riders Michael Rogers, Patrik Sinkewitz, and Eddy Mazzoleni prepare for this Tour. The sometimes discredited Italian sports doctor postulated on his Web site, 53×12.com, that Landis went hypothermic on the finishing climb to La Toussuire, similar to the condition that led to Tom Simpson's death on Mont Ventoux in 1967. Ferrari added that Landis did not suffer an "energetic breakdown," after which an athlete can't regenerate glycogen stores in twenty-four hours, and he expected Landis to recover quickly.

The truth of that theory was enhanced by Lim's comments that "in time, [Floyd] will understand why an otherwise reasonable average power output of 259 watts [in the stage to La Toussuire] felt like he was being beat by a wrecking ball. If today's terrain had been even a notch lighter, he would've been all right."

Back at the hotel, Landis chatted with his team manager John Lelangue and teammate Axel Merckx, who were old acquaintances. Lelangue is the son of Robert Lelangue, who for many years was the directeur sportif of Eddy Merckx, Axel's father. They talked about strategy and relayed some advice from cycling's superchampion: Don't give up yet, go on the attack! "[Eddy] was one of the few people that believed it was still possible," said Landis later, "because he did some things like that himself."

At the 1971 Tour, for example, after Merckx had two bad days in a row and dropped from first place to being 9:46 off the pace of new race leader Luis Ocaña, Merckx attacked from the very start of the next stage. With two teammates and six other riders, Merckx surprised Ocaña by jumping ahead on a short downhill in the first kilometer. The nine leaders then raced the mostly flat 251km stage at an astonishing average speed of 46.272kph, chased all day by a peloton led by Ocaña's teammates. Merckx gained only two minutes but that was enough to put him up into second place and back in contention. The moral of the story is that a "beaten" champion can quickly turn things around.

Eddy Merckx had a gut feeling that Landis too could turn things around, and that evening he placed a bet with a Belgian bookmaker, at 75-to-1 odds, that Landis would win the Tour.

Back in his room, Landis said later, he had a nip of Jack Daniels to help him sleep. It must have been a good sleep because he woke up the next morning determined to fight back. When Lim went with some scales to check Landis's weight before stage 17, the trainer reported, "He had the music cranked to the max as he paced around his tiny room like a wild animal. . . . His appetite for redemption was so raw, and you could see his thirst for blood as he proclaimed, 'I'm the strongest guy in this race!' And then we just sat there and read each other Jack Handy quotes for the next fifteen minutes. He laughed louder than I think I've heard him laugh all Tour."

One of the quotes from the *Saturday Night Live* character could profitably have been this one: "A good way to threaten somebody is to light a stick of dynamite. Then you call the guy and hold the burning fuse up to the phone. 'Hear that?' you say. 'That's dynamite, baby.'"

Lim also went over some numbers that came out of Landis's power meter during the Tour. He could have pointed out that Landis was at his strongest in the two days before his disaster at La Toussuire. His time up to L'Alpe d'Huez was the sixth fastest time for the legendary mountain course, only 29 seconds slower than Armstrong's best at the end of a long mountain stage, when he put two minutes into all his rivals in 2001. Then there was Landis's remarkable power rating from the Gap rest day, when he "opened it up" on a climb when training near the team hotel and produced 460 watts for ten minutes, higher than any of his numbers from the actual race. "I showed him the numbers," Lim wrote, "and he once again proclaimed, 'I'm the best guy here. Today, I'm going ape shit. Today, I'm going to win.'"

Perhaps, as Handy joked, Landis really was going to "dynamite" himself—and the race.

THE PLAN

It was so audacious that no one expected it to succeed. Not even Landis was totally confident about the plan he hatched overnight with Phonak team manager Lelangue and the Merckx clan. Phonak had shared a hotel at La Toussuire with some other teams, including Pereiro's Caisse d'Épargne riders and Denis Menchov's Rabobank men. By the time they had all descended the 20km to the stage 17 start in St. Jean-de-Maurienne, the news that Landis was going to try something special had already started to spread through the peloton. But only the Phonak team knew exactly what Landis was going to try.

To come back from his humiliating defeat the previous day and get back in contention, Landis *had* to attack. But not even Eddy Merckx did anything quite like the plan he helped concoct: a premeditated attack at the very foot of the first of five climbs in stage 17 in a bid to make up the 8:08 that separated him from race leader Pereiro. "I knew it was a long shot to win the race," Landis said, "but that was my goal."

The layout of the course favored the Phonak plan. The first 50km to Albertville were downhill or flat, so going into the first climb Landis was still accompanied by all eight of his teammates—seven riding in front of him and one riding shotgun—who set a steady tempo. By the time the grade started to increase, about 6km from the base of the Col des Saisies, an early break of 11 riders had gained 11 minutes. It looked like it would be a routine stage.

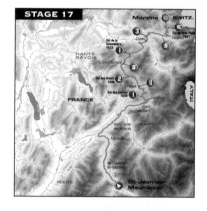

STAGE 17

But the ordinary quickly changed to the extraordinary. Davitamon-Lotto's Chris Horner, riding for his team leader Cadel Evans, had a front-row seat. "The Phonak riders started going on the false flats," Horner said, "and they just brought it up to like 50, 55 kilometers an hour, and then drilled it into the climb."

What Phonak was doing was similar to what a sprinter's lead-out train does in the last kilometers of a flat stage, or how the workers on a classics team gradually accelerate into the first section of cobblestones at Paris-Roubaix.

As each of Landis's teammates finished his surge and peeled off, he left a gap to make it harder for other teams to get on their leader's wheel. The last two Phonak riders to go were Colombian Victor Hugo Peña and Dutchman Koos Moerenhout. Their final accelerations launched Landis on his desperate, dramatic mission. As Landis's first road team manager, John Wordin of Mercury, once said, "With Floyd, it's all or nothing."

When Landis made his first surge, world time-trial champ Michael Rogers tried to pull Klöden up to the American's wheel, while Evans, Menchov, and Sastre clung to the T-Mobile riders' wheels. But they were fighting a losing battle and were quickly 50 meters back.

"Oh, man, he was like a motorbike," said Rogers of the fast-disappearing figure in the green-and-yellow uniform. "I don't think I've ever gone so quick up a mountain. Unbelievable. I've never seen anything like that. When he attacked, he was sitting down, doing 40kph, going up a mountain. It was impressive."

Even riders farther down the line were impressed. "I was cross-eyed," said CSC's Christian Vande Velde. "I went as hard as I possibly could and I barely made it. It was unbelievable how fast he went."

In terms of numbers, Landis rode the first 30 seconds of his break at 544 watts, pushed through the first five minutes at 451 watts, and averaged 431 watts for the opening ten minutes of his break, compared with his 460-watt training spurt three days earlier. Landis was riding within his capabilities, but also in a class of his own. In just 15km of climbing the 7 percent Col des Saisies, Landis gained 3:25 on the decimated peloton and closed to within three minutes of the lead group that had ten minutes in hand at the base of the Cat. 1 climb.

EXECUTION

What was most unbelievable about his attack was that Landis started it 130km from the finish with five mountain passes in front of him. That distance, 130km, just happens to be the distance of Eddy Merckx's greatest-ever solo break, at the 1969 Tour. That day, the Cannibal rode away from the field at the top of the Col du Tourmalet in the Pyrénées, went on to cross the Col d'Aubisque, and finished the stage eight minutes ahead of the runner-up.

The enormity of the task ahead of Landis was emphasized by what happened when 1998 champion Marco Pantani made a similar move at the 2000 Tour. The Italian climber attacked on the Saisies at about the same place as Landis and set out on a solo break over the same mountain climbs to Morzine. Pantani was caught at the foot of the last climb, but his bold effort forced Armstrong's U.S. Postal Service team to chase him for three hours. "Lance was scared," recalled Vande Velde. In the intensity of that long pursuit, Armstrong neglected to refuel, and he bonked on that last climb, the fearsome Col de Joux-Plane, and lost 1:49 to the runner-up, Jan Ullrich.

Six years later, on these same roads, Landis caught and passed all but two of the early breakaway riders and pushed his lead over the 40-strong chase group to eight minutes by the time he started the day's third climb, the Col de la Colombière, 78km from the finish. The riders still with Landis were Patrik Sinkewitz of T-Mobile and Patrice Halgand of Crédit Agricole.

A touch of drama came halfway up the 12km, 5 percent Colombière when Landis suddenly stopped to change bikes. His urgency was clear as he screamed, "Go . . . go . . . go" to his Phonak team mechanic after he got a replacement bike and was being pushed back into the race. Sinkewitz and Halgand appeared to accelerate when they turned around and saw Landis adrift, but the American quickly chased back and regained his front position to continue with his focused effort toward the 5,282-foot summit.

Caisse d'Épargne had been doing all the pacing in the peloton, but Pereiro's team was losing numbers and by the Colombière summit the race leader had only one teammate left with him. Barbs were shot later in the Spanish media, with Caisse d'Épargne accusing Sastre's CSC team of not collaborating when they had a chance to pull back Landis earlier in the stage. CSC team boss Bjarne Riis countered that Team CSC—already depleted of Ivan Basso, Giovanni Lombardi, and Bobby Julich—didn't have the numbers to do the heavy lifting. "If we had told our guys to work earlier," Riis said, "it would have blown apart the team."

It wasn't until the gap reached nine minutes, partway down the Colombière descent, that Riis ordered Vande Velde, Jens Voigt, and Stuart O'Grady to increase the speed, while Klöden had his T-Mobile teammates Sergei Gontchar, Matthias Kessler, and Rogers join in the chase. Even so, Landis was still 6:20 ahead when he turned left in the alpine village of Samoëns to start the Tour's final *hors-cat* climb, the Joux-Plane, with 24km to go.

With long stretches at 10 percent and an average of 8.5 percent for its 11.7km length, the narrow Joux-Plane was one of the toughest climbs in this Tour. This is where, in 1987, Irishman Stephen Roche took many risks on the descent to take back vital seconds in his duel with Spaniard Pedro Delgado. That Tour went down to the wire in the final time trial a couple of days later, with Roche emerging as the overall winner by just 40 seconds.

SASTRE'S BID

While Landis continued at his relentless, rhythmic pace, most of the other riders struggled on the bumpy steeps of the Joux-Plane. There was no stopping Landis from continuing his bold bid for glory. Just 500 meters into the 11.7km climb, he dropped his last "passenger," Sinkewitz, despite the German's having sat on his wheel for 70km.

Behind them the chase group crumbled into pockets of ones and twos, when CSC's Fränk Schleck led out Sastre for an impressive attack that left Sastre out alone and striving to gain as much time as possible on race leader Pereiro. The Joux-Plane was Sastre's last chance to make up his 1:50 deficit.

In a Tour of lieutenants, Sastre had stepped into the role of team captain without hesitation. A rider who carved his name racing for stars like Laurent Jalabert, Abraham Olano, Tyler Hamilton, and Ivan Basso, the Spaniard had never been afraid to take the initiative. He did just that at the 2005 Vuelta a España, where his eventual third place became second to Menchov when winner Roberto Heras was disqualified for doping.

At the 2006 Tour, Team CSC was in shambles at the start in Strasbourg following Basso's exit for alleged links to the Spanish doping investigation. Basso's teammates were disillusioned, frustrated, and angry, even threatening to not race at all.

"YOU CAN ONLY GIVE THE MAXIMUM AND NOTHING LESS. I CAME HERE TO HELP BASSO, BUT NOW CIRCUMSTANCES HAVE CHANGED AND HE'S GONE. I WILL DO THE BEST I CAN AND SEE WHAT THE RACE DELIVERS."

As always, Sastre stepped up with a smile and humility that marks the character of this genial man from a small village in the mountains north of Madrid. "You can only give the maximum and nothing less," Sastre said ahead of his prologue. "I came here to help Basso, but now circumstances have changed and he's gone. I will do the best I can and see what the race delivers."

Despite his steadiness, Sastre has never generated much buzz among the hypercritical Spanish press corps. Someone else was always a little more charismatic and a little more dashing. Be it Oscar Sevilla, Aitor González, Iban Mayo, or Alejandro Valverde, Sastre was always being upstaged.

That never stopped him from working hard, but a personal blow following the death of his brother-in-law, Spanish cycling great José Maria Jiménez, in December 2003 sent Sastre spiraling into depression. He struggled through the 2004 season and considered retiring until his podium performance at the 2005 Vuelta.

At this 2006 Tour, Sastre would fare well in the decisive 52km time trial in Rennes, finishing a strong 18th, and he was rock solid in the Pyrénées (where he scored a stage win in 2003) to move into 5th overall only 1:52 behind Landis. Sastre was sounding confident going into the three hard stages in the Alps. With anything possible, he promised he would attack with all he was worth. Though the team didn't play up his chances in public, they quietly believed that Sastre could finish on the podium in Paris, a huge result that would save the Tour for the team.

Sastre's strong position energized his teammates. Vande Velde, riding in his fifth Tour, said, "You can always count on Carlos. He's really easy to work for. He's always relaxed and you always know he's going to do well."

Sastre didn't have his best legs at L'Alpe d'Huez, finishing 25 seconds behind Landis. But Riis was still optimistic. "The next two stages suit Carlos better," Riis said with a shrug. "There are still many climbs to go."

The epic, four-climb stage ending at the La Toussuire saw Sastre at his best, attacking with wild abandon when Landis was dropped. The Tour was suddenly wide open and Sastre was making a dramatic attack to claim the lead. His attack was not quite successful enough, though, so he vowed to try again on the Joux-Plane.

Sastre's move at the foot of the climb ignited a battery of attacks and chases. Soon after Sastre blasted off, AG2R's Christophe Moreau launched a counterattack that was marked by Evans. A few others, including Pereiro, caught them, before another surge came from the young Italian, Damiano Cunego of Lampre, who was caught by Moreau in a rejuvenated effort.

In front, Landis churned away, still more than five minutes ahead of Sastre. Giving everything and riding with his red CSC team jersey unzipped to the waist, Sastre erased his overall time difference on Pereiro and moved into the virtual lead on the upper reaches of the Joux-Plane.

At the summit, Landis led by 5:02 over Sastre, 5:59 over Moreau, 6:19 on Cunego, and 6:52 on Pereiro's five-man group, which had dropped Evans. The Australian was in a threesome that passed the summit 30 seconds later.

Although he seemed headed for the yellow jersey, Sastre revealed a major handicap on the descent. His horrible descending skills cost him about 30 seconds to the hard-chasing Pereiro. So despite finishing second two days in a row and taking the time bonuses that came with it, Sastre fell 12 seconds short of capturing what would have been a well-deserved yellow jersey.

JOINING THE LEGENDS

Almost six minutes clear of Sastre at the line to take his first-ever Tour stage win, Landis ecstatically punched the air to celebrate his amazing coup. His performance in hauling himself back from 11th place overall at 8:08 to 3rd, only 30 seconds behind Pereiro, was sufficient to push this Tour from outstanding to legendary status. "It was epic," stated an awed Horner, who raced with Landis on Mercury. "That's what you come to the Tour for . . . That was an absolutely epic day. Floyd put on a show, man, did he put on a show! That was incredible!"

Praise for Landis was universal. The French sports newspaper *L'Équipe* even said that his 130km breakaway, to single-handedly ride away from the very best riders in the Tour and hold them off over the vicious Joux-Plane with such panache, was the performance of the century. Indeed, it was the most extraordinary turnaround in modern times.

Lim reported that Landis was handed 70 water bottles during his break, with Landis pouring most of the water over his head and torso to prevent his body from overheating. Over the final two hours, Landis averaged a pedal cadence of 89 revs per minute, while averaging a power output of 364 watts. The trainer said Landis had performed similarly in his long training rides through the mountains but had never ridden at that level for such a long time in competition. No wonder his rivals had underestimated him.

Asked about the T-Mobile team's tactics in not starting to chase Landis until it was too late, Rogers said, "I don't think there's any tactics today. What can you do? It's just . . . get to the finish. We're all tired from yesterday. Everyone's tired . . . There's no such thing as tactics on a day like today."

"We knew [Klöden] was having trouble, but who wasn't?" the hardworking Rogers continued. "I was just scraping the bottom of the barrel going up the Joux-Plane. I was totally empty. I couldn't eat the whole day. I kept on vomiting. Just a bad day to have a shit day."

CSC's Vande Velde—who finished in a small group with Voigt, O'Grady, a shattered Leipheimer, and the top three Discovery Channel riders, 21:23 behind Landis—agreed that tactics meant nothing. "The reason we didn't start chasing earlier was Floyd. Everyone thought he would crack," said Vande Velde. "Who would have ever thought that Floyd could have been that strong? I did everything I could. I felt really horrible. I had the chills and I didn't eat, actually nothing, today, so I'm glad we don't have another mountain stage tomorrow."

Tomorrow was still a distant topic for most people. Right now, everyone was talking about Floyd "Superman" Landis.

STAGE 17: ST. JEAN-DE-MAURIENNE TO MORZINE

1. Floyd Landis (USA), Phonak, 200.5km in 5:23:36 (37.175kph); **2.** Carlos Sastre (Sp), CSC, at 5:42; **3.** Christophe Moreau (F), AG2R, at 5:58; **4.** Damiano Cunego (I), Lampre-Fondital, at 6:40; **5.** Michael Boogerd (Nl), Rabobank, at 7:08; **6.** Fränk Schleck (Lux), CSC; **7.** Oscar Pereiro (Sp), Caisse d'Épargne-Illes Balears; **8.** Andreas Klöden (G), T-Mobile; **9.** Haimar Zubeldia (Sp), Euskaltel-Euskadi, all s.t.; **10.** Cadel Evans (Aus), Davitamon-Lotto, at 7:20.

GENERAL CLASSIFICATION

1. Oscar Pereiro (Sp), Caisse d'Épargne-Illes Balears

2. Carlos Sastre (Sp), CSC, at 0:12

3. Floyd Landis (USA), Phonak, at 0:30

4. Andreas Klöden (G), T-Mobile, at 2:29

5. Cadel Evans (Aus), Davitamon-Lotto, at 3:08

CHAPTER 18

Fight for the Podium

The race comes down to the wire.

Floyd Landis wasn't taking any more chances. He even reported early to the start house on stage 19, the time trial that would settle the final destination of a yellow jersey that had changed hands ten times among seven riders since the Tour set off from Strasbourg three weeks earlier. The American did not want to risk an incident like the one that occurred in the prologue: at the last minute, a Phonak mechanic spotted a cut in one of his tires and had to change the wheel, causing Landis to start late by eight or nine seconds. He didn't have much time to play with. Eight seconds was the margin his countryman, Greg LeMond, had when he won the 1989 Tour after coming back from 50 seconds behind Laurent Fignon in the final time trial.

After cruising up the start house ramp in Le Creusot, Landis stepped off his bike, sat down on a small metal trash can, and leaned forward over his time trial machine. For a full minute, he watched Andreas Klöden composing himself before setting off on his time trial. The American remained seated for another two minutes. He then got on his bike, favoring his damaged right hip, and seemed to relax through the one-minute countdown to his 4:09 p.m. start.

"The goal is to do the best time trial of my life," said Landis, who woke up at 6:30 that Saturday morning feeling "a little nervous." He knew he had to be fast out of the gate. The two men who'd be starting three and six minutes behind him, respectively Carlos Sastre and Oscar Pereiro, would do everything they could to stop Landis from gaining the 18 seconds (on Sastre) and 30 seconds (on Pereiro) he needed to win the Tour.

Neither Pereiro nor Sastre, and not even Klöden, had expected to be battling for the podium in this final time trial. And if it hadn't been for Landis's miraculous comeback at Morzine, it would have been the three Europeans going for the overall victory.

Klöden, a close friend of Jan Ullrich, was hit hard when the T-Mobile team leader was banished, and it took the German more than two weeks to find consistent form. Sastre was standing in for the expected CSC team leader, Ivan Basso. And Caisse d'Épargne's Pereiro had started the race in support of Alejandro Valverde. Landis was the only prerace favorite still in contention for the win.

The Phonak team leader, who said he was not fully recovered from "the four-hour time trial I did a few days ago," had a first look at the twisting, rolling time trial course that morning, when his team manager John Lelangue made extensive notes on how to ride through each of the course's trickiest sections. Those notes translated into a constant stream of advice from Lelangue, along with timely words of encouragement, to his rider throughout the stage via radio.

Quickly into his time trial tuck, his hands high and forward like a downhill skier, Landis began very fast. His unofficial time split after 8km was 35 seconds faster than the following Sastre, which already put the American into second place overall. But race leader Pereiro was proving much more resilient. "I started fast," said the Spaniard, "because I wanted to show I was going to ride hard all the way and perhaps demoralize my opponents a little."

By the time the Caisse d'Épargne rider in the yellow jersey sped through the 16.5km checkpoint at Montchanin-le-Haut, after the trickiest part of the course, he was only ten seconds slower than Landis, whose 19:46 split (a 50kph average) was the fastest of the day, even one second ahead of T-Mobile's Sergei Gontchar, who had set the day's fastest time of 1:07:45 two hours before Landis's start.

CLOSE BATTLE

Speeding downhill after the first time check, Lelangue coached Landis, via the team's wireless radio connection, through a chicane over a canal and under a highway bridge, where hundreds of fans had gathered to watch the action and cheer on their favorites. "This is the most dangerous turn on the *parcours*," Lelangue said into the microphone. "Easy, easy, easy. No risk, no risk."

Having gained only ten seconds on Pereiro with almost one-third of the time trial completed, Landis knew he had a fight on his hands. This wasn't a shoo-in. This was more like LeMond putting 58 seconds into Laurent Fignon to narrowly win the 1989 Tour. Based on their first time splits, Landis was on track to take Pereiro's yellow jersey by just four seconds.

It would only take a flat tire (like the one Cadel Evans had in this time trial) or a crash (as suffered by Christophe Moreau), and the Tour would go to the unheralded Spaniard, not Landis. But the course now worked to Landis's advantage. Following the earlier short hills and twisting back roads came 8km of wider, straighter highways, which favored Landis. Not having to worry about turns, he could put his considerable power into churning a huge 54×11 gear at 100 revolutions per minute.

Lelangue had even planned which sides of traffic islands his man should take, shouting instructions like, "That's perfect. Stay on the left. Perfect. Good job, good job."

Landis was 20 seconds faster than Pereiro in those 8km, and suddenly the two were level on overall time. The Spaniard's shoulders, rock steady earlier on, were now rolling from side to side. He would continue to lose time.

Then the American too began to stall. On the course's steepest climb, with 12km to go, Landis was out of the saddle on what was too heavy a gear, as he rode between two walls of fans cheering him on. Over the final 6km Pereiro came back with a stronger effort and was actually one second faster than Landis on this section—probably the extra second Landis used up by coasting across the line, punching the air, and cracking a big smile.

Landis hadn't won the stage; this time it was the whole race. An incredulous Lelangue shouted to himself in his mike: "The Tour de France! The Tour de France!"

Landis was only third in the time trial, 1:29 ahead of fourth-place Pereiro, but that was more than enough to clinch the *maillot jaune*. The American was 30 seconds slower than second-place Klöden and 1:11 behind stage winner Gontchar. "I was surprised to win," said T-Mobile's delighted Ukrainian rider. "I had to take antibiotics during the week. This morning, we were all told to ride hard for the [overall] team classification. I concentrated on pushing hard as possible, staying smooth. The speed then comes naturally."

Gontchar's second time trial win of the Tour was logical enough but he was no less animated, jumping up from the podium and punching his bouquet into the air in celebration. His teammate, Klöden, was equally ecstatic about his second place on the stage (and third place overall). "Today, for the first time in a long time, I finally raced at 100 percent of my capabilities," Klöden said. The skinny German was within seconds of his teammate Gontchar on all four segments of the 57km course from Le Creusot to Montceau-les-Mines, and he finished like an express train as he chased and caught his three-minute man, Evans, in the last few, mainly downhill kilometers.

Evans was satisfied to maintain his fifth place overall with his eighth place in the stage, riding this long time trial only 2:30 slower than Landis. As for Sastre,

the efforts he had made in the Alps seemed to catch up with him, and he placed only 20th on the day, a minute slower than Evans, to end up in fourth overall.

COMING UP SHORT

Gontchar's joy at winning the stage equaled Matteo Tosatto's the previous day. The tall Italian team worker, who was free to try for a win after his leader Tom Boonen quit the race on the first alpine stage, was one of 15 riders to escape 53km into the 187km stage 18 from Morzine to Mâcon.

The breakaway was kept on a tight leash by a peloton led by Saunier Duval, one of the ten teams without a stage win. Another such squad was Gerolsteiner, which had two men in the break, Levi Leipheimer and Ronny Scholz. Leipheimer had come closest to a win at Pla-de-Beret, and he went for broke but came up short on the alpine stage to La Toussuire. The American figured this stage offered him a final chance of glory.

Leipheimer worked hard in the break, and when he saw an opportunity to attack on a short hill 50km from the finish, he went for it. "I was hoping that there were going to be more than two of us when I attacked," Leipheimer said. "It was a hard moment and a lot of riders didn't look so good, and there was still a little bit of climbing ahead. I thought it would be a good chance to make a split. I was hoping more would come with me, but they didn't. At that point I thought, 'Well, I'll go for it.'"

Euskaltel's Iñaki Isasi was the only rider to catch Leipheimer's wheel. As the duo took a 45-second lead, the gap on the peloton grew from three to seven minutes. But the run-in to Mâcon was too flat and straight for two riders to hold off a determined chase. Shortly after they were caught 20km out, Scholz counterattacked, only to be joined by Tosatto and fellow Italian Cristian Moreni of Cofidis.

The three-way sprint was easily taken by Tosatto, who screamed with delight on clinching Italy's and Quick Step's first stage win of the Tour. A great team worker, Tosatto is the regular lead-out man for Boonen and did the same job for Alessandro Petacchi at Fassa Bortolo for six years. Now he had a Tour stage win to add to the one he took at the Giro five years earlier.

"I am a fast rider and I can win sprints in groups of 40 to 50 riders," Tosatto said. "I knew it would come down between me and Moreni. I started the sprint and I didn't make any mistakes. I've won some big races in my career, but this is by far the most important."

Leipheimer earned the day's most aggressive rider award for his efforts in the breakaway, but that was small compensation in view of the big ambitions he had brought into this Tour. The American was the best-placed rider in the breakaway group, and he moved up from 18th to 13th in general classification, but even he admitted he wasn't thinking about that when he joined the break. "I was just going for the stage win," he said. "If I was thinking of tomorrow's time trial, I wouldn't have been in the breakaway today."

Leipheimer would ride only a moderate time trial and did just enough to keep 13th place overall. Surprisingly, he conceded a possible 12th place by just three seconds to the Italian Damiano Cunego of Lampre, who was locked in a tight battle with Leipheimer's teammate Markus Fothen for the white jersey of best young rider.

A FUTURE WINNER?

Italy's Cunego, whose fans call him the Little Prince, wasn't supposed to start the 2006 Tour de France. Like most of his compatriots, the blond-haired Cunego lives and trains for the Giro d'Italia. His overall victory in the 2004 Giro cata-pulted him to stardom, and he subsequently worked hard to live up to high expectations. A solid fourth place overall in the 2006 Giro proved his earlier win wasn't a fluke.

So it was with few expectations and little pressure that Cunego rolled into the Tour's start at Strasbourg. No one put him on any short list of favorites and that was how he preferred it. At 24, Cunego was still a relative youngster on the international scene. Although his *palmarès* reflected a rider with a decade of experience, a Tour rookie has a lot to learn.

"Here you're always jostling for position, always fighting to stay on the wheel in front. All of the best riders in the world are here; it's nervous, everyone is desperate to win," Cunego said, reflecting on the Tour's challenges, two weeks into the race. "You'll be a hundred positions back in the peloton yet the guy next to you will be trying to move up, riding as though it's the last ten kilometers of the world championships."

Cunego survived the first week intact, lost a lot of time in the Rennes time trial as he expected—106th place, 6:22 slower than Gontchar—and struggled through the Pyrénées on climbs he had never seen before. On steep, uneven roads and in muggy humidity that sapped a rider's strength, Cunego described the Pyrénées as "unlike any mountains I've climbed before. They wear you down, make you want to stop. It's then you realize just how hard the Tour is."

By the time the race hit the more familiar slopes of the Alps, Cunego was finding his racing legs just in time to work himself into contention for the white jersey. Through the Pyrénées, German sensation Fothen had taken clear control of the jersey, leading by more than 12 minutes. Fothen is no slouch in the mountains and finished 12th in his grand tour debut at the 2005 Giro, where he rode the final week with a cold that kept him out of a likely top-ten finish. A year later, his Gerolsteiner team was anxious to see its young charge remain in the Tour's prestigious white jersey until Paris.

The tables turned at L'Alpe d'Huez, however, where Cunego got into the day's winning break and finished second to a surprisingly strong Fränk Schleck. Cunego took back five minutes on Fothen with that move, and on the next day's stage to La Toussuire, he pressed ahead with a solid 14th place to chop his deficit on Fothen to 2:42. Then, on stage 17, Cunego finished an excellent fourth into Morzine, to take over the white jersey from Fothen by five seconds.

"The white jersey was never my aim; it just comes automatically as a result of trying to get the most out of my legs every day," he said with a shrug. "I'm taking a lot of positives out of this race." But could he take one more positive and keep his hard-earned white jersey as he raced against the clock in stage 19?

Time trialing has always been Cunego's Achilles' heel, but he had another surprise in store. On a day when most observers expected him to lose minutes to Fothen, the world under-23 time trial champion in 2003, Cunego did what he described as the "best time trial of my life." The young Italian finished an impressive tenth on the stage, a half minute *faster* than Fothen, and increased his hold on the white jersey to 38 seconds. Cunego even finished one spot ahead of time-trial specialist David Millar, who was also finishing the Tour more strongly than he started it.

> "THE WHITE JERSEY WAS NEVER MY AIM; IT JUST COMES AUTOMATICALLY AS A RESULT OF TRYING TO GET THE MOST OUT OF MY LEGS EVERY DAY."

A MESSAGE FROM MILLAR

Two years of hell ended for Scottish rider Millar on the 7.1km of pavement and cobblestones of the Strasbourg prologue. Just days after his two-year racing ban (for taking the blood booster EPO) ended, Millar was back on cycling's largest stage. He was back at the Tour, the event that catapulted him to international stardom in 2000 when he beat Lance Armstrong in the opening-stage time trial.

This time Millar was racing clean, but there was not going to be a Millar miracle in Strasbourg. Riding in the lemon-colored Saunier Duval-Prodir jersey, the tall, thin Brit finished a modest 17th, 14 seconds slower than prologue winner Thor Hushovd. But Millar's ride could have been mistaken for a victory, judging by the way he hugged teammates and coaches as he returned to the team bus after his emotional ride. Once cycling's bad boy, a humbled Millar was born again as a professional cyclist and thankful for it.

"I am happy where I am now. I've worked hard to get here," Millar said. "Obviously it was horrible, but that is part of the punishment. Sometimes you have to hit rock bottom to realize what you have got."

Millar, 29, was more appreciative than any of his current colleagues in the Tour peloton. He was the biggest fish caught up in a 2004 French police investigation into a doping scandal at the Cofidis team, whose top rider was Millar. The police arrested cycling's rock star while he was having dinner in a tony French restaurant in his adopted hometown of Biarritz, on the Atlantic coast of southwest France. Police hauled him off to a jail cell and then searched his home. They found empty EPO vials, which Millar contended he kept as souvenirs to remind him of his errant ways.

The prospect of sitting in a bleak French jail was enough to prompt Millar to come clean. Yes, he said, he had taken EPO. He went on to tell investigators the where, when, and how of his doping experiences. His honesty earned him no leniency. Cofidis fired him and the UCI slapped him with a two-year ban, fined him 2,000 Swiss francs, and stripped him of his 2003 world time trial title, as well as his stage wins at the 2003 Dauphiné Libéré and 2001 Vuelta a España.

Millar lost himself in a haze of drinking and partying to forget his public humiliation. Although he was making an estimated $500,000 a year at Cofidis, Millar had blown most of it, knowing he was still young and had up to ten good racing years ahead of him.

Distraught, he was forced to sleep on the floor of his sister's apartment in London when the money ran out. He faced a future without much hope. "It was very hard," he said. "I lost everything. I made mistakes and I've paid a very high price for them."

Friends encouraged him to start riding his bike to get back into shape if nothing else. Millar relocated to the hills of the Peak District near Manchester, England, and he started to put in some hard miles on the bike. Ripping up and down the steep hills, Millar rediscovered the spark that once made him the most touted young British rider in a generation.

He made a few contacts with friends from the cycling world, including the retired British professional Max Sciandri, who lives in Italy. Word soon leaked out that Millar was training in earnest, and it didn't take long before the news reached Mauro Gianetti, the Italian-based team manager of Spanish squad Saunier Duval-Prodir. The ex-pro thought Millar deserved a second chance and believed Millar's promises to ride clean.

"I saw a guy who made an error, which he paid a very high price for," Gianetti said. "He shouldn't have to pay for the rest of his life."

To his credit, Millar's admission was rare in a sport that is riddled with fallen heroes who search for every excuse under the sun to explain their "adverse analytical findings." Millar promised that he would race clean and serve as a model for new pros.

"I hope the message gets sent out that it is possible to win the biggest races in cycling without doping," he told reporters before the Tour began. "I think the most important thing is to show that to young professionals coming into the sport. I want people to know I am doing this 100 percent clean. As I said, it could take years for people to believe me. But I want what happened to me to be a positive story."

Millar was incapable of delivering the moving, Hollywood-style comeback victory in Strasbourg as many had hoped he could. Instead, he struggled to find his legs. After spending two years out of competition, he returned to the demands of the Tour, hardly an ideal race to mark his comeback. He finished a distant 37th in the Rennes time trial and never worked himself into a decisive breakaway, despite several efforts that included an early attack on stage 18.

Millar felt stronger as the race went on and was excited by his excellent 11th place in the final time trial at Montceau-les-Mines. "It's all been worth it," he said. "It was very hard but I never doubted I wouldn't finish the Tour. This is not the end, it's the beginning."

STAGE 18: MORZINE TO MÂCON

1. Matteo Tosatto (I), Quick Step-Innergetic, 197km in 4:16:15 (46.126kph); **2.** Cristian Moreni (I), Cofidis, s.t.; **3.** Ronny Scholz (G), Gerolsteiner, at 0:02; **4.** Manuel Quinziato (I), Liquigas, at 0:47; **5.** Sébastien Hinault (F), Crédit Agricole, at 1:03; **6.** Jérôme Pineau (F), Bouygues Telecom; **7.** Sylvain Calzati (F), AG2R; **8.** Benoît Vaugrenard (F), Française des Jeux; **9.** Iñaki Isasi (Sp), Euskaltel-Euskadi; **10.** Egoi Martinez (Sp), Discovery Channel, all s.t.

STAGE 19: LE CREUSOT TO MONTCEAU-LES-MINES TIME TRIAL

1. Sergei Gontchar (Ukr), T-Mobile, 57km in 1:07:45 (50.479kph); **2.** Andreas Klöden (G), T-Mobile, 1:08:26; **3. Floyd Landis (USA), Phonak, 1:08:56; 4.** Oscar Pereiro (Sp), Caisse d'Épargne-Illes Balears, 1:10:25; **5.** Sebastian Lang (G), Gerolsteiner, 1:11:03; **6. Dave Zabriskie (USA), CSC, 1:11:20; 7.** Viatcheslav Ekimov (Rus), Discovery Channel, 1:11:27; **8.** Cadel Evans (Aus), Davitamon-Lotto, 1:11:27; **9.** Ralf Grabsch (G), Phonak, 1:11:28; **10.** Damiano Cunego (I), Lampre-Fondital, 1:11:29.

GENERAL CLASSIFICATION

1. Floyd Landis (USA), Phonak

2. Oscar Pereiro (Sp), Caisse d'Épargne-Illes Balears, at 0:59

3. Andreas Klöden (G), T-Mobile, at 1:29

4. Carlos Sastre (Sp), CSC, at 3:13

5. Cadel Evans (Aus), Davitamon-Lotto, at 5:08

CHAPTER 19

Final Flourishes

One last sprint and the podium presentations climax a troubled Tour.

For the eighth year in a row, the "Star-Spangled Banner" boomed out over the sun-drenched Champs-Élysées to salute an American in yellow. Following on Lance Armstrong's seven victories, his former teammate Floyd Landis waved to the crowds massed on the world's most beautiful boulevard, with his wife Amber Basile and their nine-year-old daughter Ryan at his side. They would celebrate later with his faithful Phonak teammates, and then with his close California friends, Amber's stepfather Dave Witt and his wife Rose. And back in Farmersville, Pennsylvania, on that July 23 Sunday, Landis's Mennonite parents would watch their son's triumph on a neighbor's television set after attending morning prayers.

The story of the 83rd Tour de France began in the fallout from a doping scandal and ended, seemingly, in a wonderful, feel-good victory. In between, along 3,657.1km of racing through half a dozen countries, emerged a series of shocks and surprises. The central figure in this was an unpretentious 30-year-old American with a bum hip. One of six children raised in a strict Christian home in rural Pennsylvania, the son of a truck driver, Landis is a guy who refuses to bow to conventional wisdom. That could also be said about the 2006 Tour de France.

Even on the rest day in Bordeaux, Landis pulled a rabbit from the hat by announcing to the world that his wasted right hip joint needed replacement surgery. The Phonak team leader was matter-of-fact about the 2003 crash that fractured his femur and the subsequent calcification, but Christian Vande Velde, one of Landis's U.S. Postal teammates at the time, painted a different picture of Landis's rapid return from the injury.

"He came back *so* fast [from the surgery]," said Vande Velde. "The team was putting a lot of pressure on him, a lot of pressure . . . and good things don't come out of that kind of situation. He was forced to come back directly after the joint surgery. . . . He came off the plane [back from the U.S.] with his leg black and blue; it was a disgusting situation. Not that that was so bad, but more just forcing his body to come back into shape right after that [to ride the 2003 Tour]."

And just as people said there was no way Landis could recover so quickly from that broken leg in 2003, so they said he could not turn his humiliating defeat at La Toussuire into a dramatic victory at Morzine. But he did.

Without that phenomenal turnaround, the winner of the Tour would have been Oscar Pereiro, a "lucky" Spanish rider from Pontevedra, a small port town in Spain's northwestern Galicia region. Pereiro had been lucky because he had finished more than 26 minutes behind Landis in the Pyrenean stage to Pla-de-Beret, and he had come back into the picture only after being allowed to regain 30 minutes in a "no-hope" breakaway across the baked plains of the Midi.

"Oscar was my teammate last year so he's a friend of mine," Landis said later. "But that played a very small part in letting [him] get the lead that day. Had it been someone else 30 minutes down . . . I'm sure we would have done the same thing."

Pereiro deserved credit for the way he became the Tour's key figure in the final week. He raced with resolve and emerged from the Alps wearing the yellow jersey after the dramatic stages that "lost" and "won" the Tour for Landis. The 28-year-old Spaniard then proved his resilience by placing fourth in the final time trial to hold off the late overall challenge from T-Mobile's Andreas Klöden. Although the Tour was full of the unexpected, its final United States-Spain-Germany podium was not wholly unpredictable. It's said that the Tour de France never has a lucky winner; the strongest rider always comes through.

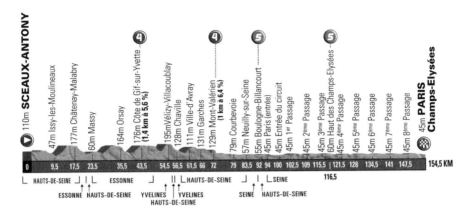

FINAL SPRINT

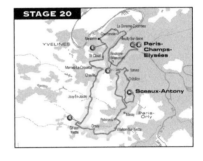

Before the barriers came down on the Champs-Élysées, there was one more stage to race and one more stage win to be claimed. Robbie McEwen had already wrapped up the green jersey competition, but he was still the hot tip to take his fourth stage win of this Tour. After all, three of the fastest sprinters from the opening half of the race—Tom Boonen, Oscar Freire, and Daniele Bennati—had abandoned in the mountains. And the 154.5km stage 20 from Paris's southwestern suburb of Sceaux-Antony was almost certain to end in a sprint on the Champs-Élysées.

After the processional start, after the souvenir photo ops with the winners and the traditional clinking of champagne glasses with the new champion, the racing finally began when the peloton arrived in Paris for eight laps and 52km of ferocious action on a circuit that passed the Arc de Triomphe, the Louvre, and the swank Hôtel de Crillon, where Armstrong was watching the race on a plasma screen TV.

A series of attacks and counterattacks put a mass-sprint finish in doubt for a while. As in 2005, American Chris Horner jumped into the day's biggest break. The 15-man move lasted for two full laps before Horner went ahead with Belgian

201

Philippe Gilbert, only to be swallowed up by the pack with two laps remaining. Horner then went into team-support mode for his Davitamon-Lotto team sprinter McEwen. He pulled the pack up to the Arc de Triomphe for the last time before others took over heading back down the other side of the Champs-Élysées with 4km to go.

Discovery Channel tried a desperate move in the final 2km. Its retiring team member, Viatcheslav Ekimov, led out George Hincapie before teammate Yaroslav Popovych took over in the final kilometer, perhaps hoping that Hincapie could pull off the win. They splintered the peloton, but their impressive push wasn't enough. About 20 riders, including the best sprinters, charged around the final turn for the final 350-meter, slightly uphill cobblestone stretch to the line.

Gerolsteiner's Peter Wrolich went for a long sprint, but McEwen took his wheel and launched his own effort with 250 meters to go. The Aussie looked strong but hadn't reckoned on a challenge from prologue winner Thor Hushovd. The Crédit Agricole rider came from nowhere after his French teammate Sébastien Hinault had taken him through traffic to launch his challenge. Hushovd came charging down the middle of the Champs-Élysées to blast past McEwen and take a glorious win.

Hushovd was thrilled with his triumph. "I showed that I am still a big sprinter," said the Norwegian, flashing his broad, toothy smile. "Having won the prologue, I really wanted to win today to take the first and last stages."

McEwen was typically philosophical about his loss, accepting that he and his team had miscalculated the finish. "[Gert] Steegmans went past everybody on the right and we hit the last corner on the inside," he said later. "We didn't hit the corner well and lost all our speed, and from that moment I thought, this is going to be really difficult. Looking back I should have let Steegmans go into the corner and then come through behind the Crédit Agricole guys.

"I could have changed my line and adjusted my speed through the corner. Instead, I was bogged down and I went from just over 250 [meters] . . . it was too far. One hundred meters to go I was blown."

Second place didn't mean much to McEwen, as he was almost 100 points clear in the points competition, but adding a third green jersey to his career collection confirmed his prowess among the world's top sprinters.

THE POCKET ROCKET

McEwen may not be the best sprinter in Tour de France history or even the most prolific among his contemporaries. But he is arguably the best Tour sprinter of the past few seasons, a designation the Aussie again proved with gusto. Germany's Erik Zabel can count more career scalps—192 race wins to McEwen's 127—and Italy's Alessandro Petacchi boasts more grand tour stage victories—40 to McEwen's 19— but no other sprinter has McEwen's instinct for sniffing out the finish line.

In his prime, Zabel won 12 Tour stages and 6 consecutive green jerseys, but the buzz-cut German's run stalled in 2002 with his final stage win in Alençon. Petacchi, meanwhile, missed the 2006 Tour after breaking his kneecap in the third stage of the Giro d'Italia. Petacchi won four stages of the 2003 Tour, but none since then.

WHEN ASKED BY REPORTERS IF THEY COULD DESCRIBE HIM AS THE GREATEST SPRINTER IN THE WORLD, HE ADDED THE CAVEAT, "AT THE MOMENT," BEFORE ADDING WITH A SMILE, "YOU CAN DO THAT, I DON'T MIND."

By the time McEwen rolled into Paris he had easily made his mark as the best sprinter of the 2006 Tour. No one could argue with that. When asked by reporters if they could describe him as the greatest sprinter in the world, he added the caveat, "at the moment," before adding with a smile, "You can do that, I don't mind."

It took years for the puckish Australian to arrive at this crowning moment. The former BMX racer, known for his crowd-pleasing stunt of pulling wheelies at the end of the Tour's hardest climbing stages, didn't win a Tour stage until his fourth year as a pro, in 1999. It was a doozy, a win on the Champs-Élysées, to announce his arrival in the big time. Or so he thought. McEwen would have to wait three years to win two more stages, the year he ended Zabel's remarkable six-year run in green. In 2003, Baden Cooke snatched the final-day win and the green jersey away from McEwen in a seesaw points battle that came down to the Champs-Élysées.

McEwen found a new gear in 2004, winning two more stages and his second green jersey. The following year, he was relegated for dangerous sprinting in stage 3 after a controversial race jury decision that torpedoed his chances for the green jersey, which eventually went to Hushovd.

A more mature and measured McEwen arrived for the 2006 Tour, and he calmly dominated the first week, racking up three wins in six days to bring his career tally to 11 Tour stage victories and put a stranglehold on the green jersey. "Like I have said before, it is hard getting to the top, but it is harder staying there," he said. "Every green jersey you win is fantastic and a big achievement because you have to do a hell of a lot to get it."

At 34, McEwen was wiser and more calculating in his efforts than before. He never did more than he had to, but always gave the maximum and exploited the weaknesses of his rivals at precisely the right moment. Despite losing his preferred lead-out man, Fred Rodriguez, to a nasty crash in stage 3, McEwen carried on and won two more stages.

"I cannot think of any other sprinter in the peloton that has Robbie's snap and the endurance to be there," Rodriguez said. "If you get him into the 200 meters fresh, there's a good chance he can get around anyone to win. It's mostly genetic; he's a faster-twitch guy and he's just gotten stronger over time."

While the ultimate margin of McEwen's third Tour points victory was impressive—288 points to second-place Zabel's 199—McEwen described his fight for the green jersey as anything but easy. "It has been a big battle," he said. "Most of the battle hasn't been televised. All you see [on television] is a sprint at the finish. But [the battle] is what is happening out there early in the stage.

"There are guys who you can't afford to let go, like Bennati, who you get the whole team chasing after them. Boonen was trying to get into a few breaks as well, because he hadn't won a stage. But with him being that close on points I wasn't going to let him go anywhere.

"It is very aggressive racing. You have to concentrate the whole time. It makes it mentally tiring as well as physically. The hardest work I did was in the second week, and in the transitional stages. In the first week, my teammates were working. They pulled the sprints. In the transition stages I really had to follow the attacks and keep an eye on Bennati, Freire, and Boonen. The three of them were attacking . . . Hushovd too. They were all attacking all the time. I never take a radio with me, but I did have one then. I was going, 'Boonen is going right . . . Bennati is going left.' That was the hardest part of it all, that sort of stuff."

In the end, though, his three main opponents didn't make it through the mountains, and McEwen did what he had to do. He was on cruise control into Paris.

WINNERS AND LOSERS

On the final podium McEwen and Landis were joined by Michael Rasmussen and Damiano Cunego, two riders who also won competitions that award a distinctive jersey. Rasmussen collected his second consecutive red-and-white polka-dot King of the Mountains jersey, while Cunego clinched the white jersey as the highest placed rider age 25 or younger.

Rabobank's Rasmussen cemented his growing reputation as the best climber in the game, but bragging rights don't interest the Dane. When asked if he considers himself the world's best climber, Rasmussen said, "I would consider myself one of the best; maybe in this year's Tour I was the best. Last year I wasn't. It was the guy in yellow [Armstrong], just like the other six years."

Rasmussen said he would show up in Paris in October for the 2007 Tour de France presentation, hoping for a climber's paradise for the next edition, with scores of hard mountain climbs and hilly time trials; or, better yet, maybe even an uphill time trial, such as the long-rumored stage up Mont Ventoux. Asked whether a pure climber could win a modern Tour, Rasmussen said, "I think it's possible . . . if the Tour route is right. But that's something we have to wait and see."

Lampre's Cunego, though, said he wouldn't ride the Tour in 2007. "I'm not going to do the Giro and the Tour in the same year again. It's too much. I think a rider needs to be able to pick out an objective and do everything he can do to achieve it," Cunego concluded. "At the moment I'm thinking that I'll do the Giro, then target the world championships next year, and perhaps do just the Tour in 2008."

By then, the Italian will be 26, too old for the white jersey again. If he wants to get back for another podium view, he will have to fight for a jersey of a different color, most likely the yellow one.

The 2005 white jersey winner, Yaroslav Popovych, also has been favored to win the Tour at some point in his career. His Discovery Channel team was hoping for the Ukrainian rider to step up in 2006. Instead, the whole team fell flat in its first year of not defending an Armstrong Tour title. Popovych did provide the American team's main highlight, a victory in stage 12, but the best the team could do in the general classification was José Azevedo's 19th place.

Team manager Johan Bruyneel said he knew before the Tour was over that changes would have to be made; he was acquiring Gerolsteiner's American team leader, Levi Leipheimer, to head Discovery in 2007.

As for the widely touted George Hincapie, his first Tour in eight years without Armstrong was one he wanted to forget. The Tour also raised questions about his future role on the team. But whether he returned to his long-standing objective of winning classics or aimed high in the Tour, one thing seemed certain: The man with more Tour de France finishes (ten) than any other American would almost certainly be in London in July 2007 for the start of his 11th Tour. He wasn't ready for retirement quite yet.

Before the 2006 Tour's final showdown in Paris, two men who were ending their careers were honored by the peloton. Hincapie's Russian teammate, Viatcheslav Ekimov, 40, was allowed to ride ahead of the pack entering the Champs-Élysées in recognition of finishing his 15th Tour in his final season. Only Dutchman Joop Zoetemelk completed more Tours, 16, including a win in 1980.

The other retiree was Jean-Marie Leblanc, who was leaving Amaury Sports Organisation after 18 years as the Tour's race director. He was presented with a souvenir *maillot jaune*, his image on the front, with a big *merci* signed by all 138 finishers. Leblanc, whose transition to new race director Christian Prudhomme was virtually complete, was also feted at the finish in Paris. After presenting Landis with the final yellow jersey, the former Tour rider and *L'Équipe* journalist was escorted by Prudhomme through a tunnel of applauding ASO staff members.

Leblanc, 63, began his job as race director in 1989 with the eight-second victory of Greg LeMond over Laurent Fignon. The 2006 Tour began on a low note with the sensational banishment of twin race favorites Ivan Basso and Jan Ullrich, along with the exclusions of second favorites Francisco Mancebo and Alexander Vinokourov. The French official didn't pull any punches in his disdain for the man at the center of the *Operación Puerto* doping scandal that caused the rider exclusions.

"Dr. Fuentes has already ruined my final Tour," Leblanc said before the race even began. But by the time it finished in Paris, Leblanc had turned around, just like the race. He wrote in his final editorial for *L'Équipe:* "Thanks to Landis [and the other top performers], I share the delight in this Tour . . . with faith in the sport of cycling that has always inspired me."

Leblanc didn't know that his faith in cycling was about to be tested again. At Châtenay-Malabry, just 3km from where the Tour's final stage had begun earlier in the day, a stage winner's urine sample was waiting to be tested in a French laboratory. A Tour that had been littered with tragedy, subplots, and conspiracy theories was about to return to chaos.

STAGE 20: ANTONY TO PARIS (CHAMPS-ÉLYSÉES)
1. Thor Hushovd (N), Crédit Agricole, 154.5km in 3:56:52 (39.135kph); **2.** Robbie McEwen (Aus), Davitamon-Lotto; **3.** Stuart O'Grady (Aus), CSC; **4.** Erik Zabel (G), Milram; **5.** Luca Paolini (I), Liquigas; **6.** Samuel Dumoulin (F), AG2R; **7.** Bernhard Eisel (A), Française des Jeux; **8.** Anthony Geslin (F), Bouygues Telecom; **9.** Alessandro Ballan (I), Lampre-Fondital; **10.** Peter Wrolich (A), Gerolsteiner, all s.t.

GENERAL CLASSIFICATION
(See complete final standings on pages 227–228.)

CHAPTER 20

Emotions Run High and Low

Only days after his Tour triumph, a new battle begins for Floyd Landis.

Three days after Floyd Landis was crowned champion of the 93rd Tour de France, he was kicking back at a hotel in the Netherlands. Things had never looked better for the American star. The night before, he had earned $75,000 for appearing at the first of a series of exhibition races at nearby Stiphout. He received a huge ovation from fans packed around the short circuit after he won the criterium ahead of the Tour's best climber, Michael Rasmussen. Besides more big paydays at these European criteriums, Landis was scheduled to appear on a spate of U.S. television shows in the week ahead. But then came a phone call from his Swiss team's headquarters near Zürich. It was bad news.

Earlier that same morning, the president of the Union Cycliste International, Pat McQuaid, had driven from his home overlooking Lake Geneva and was about to board a plane for Stockholm. On his agenda was a 50km fun ride with 700 Swedish cyclists, including the famous Petterson brothers, who won three consecutive world team time trial championships in the late 1960s. It would be a pleasant diversion in his hectic life. But as he walked through the Geneva airport, McQuaid's phone rang. It was the UCI antidoping office in Aigle. The "A" sample from a Tour rider's urine, tested at the Châtenay-Malabry lab near Paris, had come up positive for testosterone. What should they do?

McQuaid, a former pro cyclist, was quick to reply. "We decided to make an announcement right away because we have been criticized in the past for not doing so—particularly in the case of an important rider," McQuaid said from Sweden the next day. "Also, we know that the French laboratory [where the testing was done] has a close connection with [French sports daily] *L'Équipe,* and we did not want this news to come through the press, because we are sure they would have leaked it. In this case, we wanted to stop any sort of speculation and rumors that we've been exposed to in the past. So yesterday morning we informed the rider's team, his national federation, his country's antidoping agency, and WADA [the World Anti-doping Agency], and made the announcement to the press in the afternoon."

That announcement stated that a single urine sample from the Tour produced "an adverse analytical finding," a euphemism for what used to be called a "positive" drug test. No names were released, but McQuaid was quoted as saying the news represented the "worst possible outcome" for the Tour.

NOT ONLY DID THE RESULT CAST A SHADOW ON LANDIS'S YELLOW JERSEY, BUT THE SAMPLE IN QUESTION WAS TAKEN ON THE DAY HE SHOCKED THE WORLD WITH WHAT MANY CALLED THE MOST SPECTACULAR SINGLE-DAY PERFORMANCE IN MODERN TOUR DE FRANCE HISTORY.

It was certainly the worst possible news for Landis. After talking with the Phonak boss Andy Rihs, the Tour champion decided to check out of the Dutch hotel, cancel the rest of his criterium appearances, and head back to his European base in Spain. They also agreed on the wording of a team statement that was released the following afternoon: "The Phonak Cycling Team was notified yesterday by the UCI of an unusual level of Testosterone/Epitestosterone ratio in the test made on Floyd Landis after stage 17 of the Tour de France. The Team Management and the rider were both totally surprised of this physiological result."

Not only did the result cast a shadow on Landis's yellow jersey, but the sample in question was taken on the day he shocked the world with what many called the most spectacular single-day performance in modern Tour de France history. Suddenly those (including UCI president McQuaid) who had celebrated Landis's 130km solo ride into Morzine as an antidote to the *Operación Puerto* doping woes were reminded of the suspicion that automatically accompanies "unbelievable" athletic performances.

McQuaid was still treading carefully. "At this point in time," he said, "Floyd Landis has to be given the presumption of innocence. If he is positive then I'm devastated, angry, and annoyed. I will have to deal with the ramifications for the sport immediately."

If the biggest surprise was that Landis had tested positive, the second biggest was that the dope involved didn't make immediate sense. Landis didn't test positive for signs of blood manipulation, use of oxygen enhancers like EPO, or any other method or drug known to boost an endurance athlete's chances of success. Instead, his testosterone-to-epitestosterone ratio (known as the T/E ratio) was seven points above the 4:1 level allowed under the World Anti-doping Agency rules. However, with its inside track to the French lab, *L'Équipe* reported the next day that exogenous testosterone—maybe an artificial steroid—was detected in Landis's "A" sample.

People began to question the benefit that an endurance athlete would derive from short-term use of an anabolic steroid. Testosterone doping is associated with body builders, who use the steroid to grow their muscles to unnaturally large proportions. But testosterone can also promote the quick rebuilding of muscle that is torn down day after day in stage races like the Tour de France. The former Kelme team pro Jesús Manzano—who had revealed insider details of doping methods in a series of paid interviews with a Spanish newspaper in 2004—argued that testosterone can be taken during competition with a nearly instantaneous result. "Its effects are felt almost immediately," Manzano wrote. "It gives you a lot of force and produces a sort of euphoria."

Others disputed that claim, including Landis, who began a series of telephone conference calls and live press conferences with reporters to defend himself and deny wrongdoing. "Unfortunately, I don't think it's ever going to go away no matter what happens next," Landis said about his "A" sample's positive result. "It appears as though this is a bigger story than winning the Tour."

THE DAY OF THE TEST

In the media feeding frenzy that followed initial disclosure of the "adverse analytical finding," Landis attempted to present his side of the test result. During a live satellite interview with CNN's Larry King from Madrid the day after the disclosure, Landis mentioned possible sources of the skewed testosterone result, including prescription hormones for an overactive thyroid and cortisone injections for his degenerative hip. The UCI had given Landis its approval for both medications. It seemed possible, said some experts, that the rider's efforts on stages 16 and 17 could have caused traces of the artificial steroids contained in these products to surface and affect his testosterone or epitestosterone levels. But how would Landis prove it?

What is known is that Landis was tested two days before the stage 17 test (at L'Alpe d'Huez) and two days after it (at Montceau-les-Mines). Neither test showed abnormalities, nor did any of the other four urine samples and two blood samples that Landis supplied during the Tour. So what happened on stage 17 that could have changed his testosterone parameters for that day?

He began stage 17 in an angry mood—angry about letting his team down and being written out of the race. "I woke up and read the *Dauphiné* newspaper and [the headline] said, 'Landis Out,'" he said. "And that made me mad. Because I may be down, but I'm not out."

Instead, Landis came out of his corner swinging. He spoke to his eight teammates, saying their efforts over the past weeks hadn't been in vain. "I told them that the only chance we have to win the Tour is go from the beginning," Landis said. "It was a long shot, but I figured we had nothing to lose. We came here to win the Tour, and that was the only chance. We didn't have any other options."

After word about his plan got around the peloton, Landis was asked not to exhaust the field over a "lost cause" after two extreme days in the mountains. "A few people told me it was crazy, and please don't do it," Landis said. "And I said

'Go drink some Coke, because we're leaving on the first climb if you want to come along.'"

Landis shattered the field on that first climb and then drove on like a man possessed, to show that he was the strongest rider in the Tour. He shocked everyone by keeping the field at bay for 130km, winning the stage and riding himself within 30 seconds of the yellow jersey. Taking back eight minutes on a field of the sport's best riders was something Landis was able to visualize and turn into reality.

"Knowing Floyd the way I do, I wasn't surprised to see him come out fighting," said Lance Armstrong. "His ride was epic. He showed a champion's resolve." If anyone would know, it would be Armstrong. Landis trained and raced with Armstrong when they were both on the U.S. Postal team, and Landis helped Armstrong win three of his seven Tour victories. Armstrong understood that the 2006 Tour was won inside Landis's head.

"We knew Floyd was very good," Armstrong said at L'Alpe d'Huez, two days before Landis's epic stage 17 ride. "When he came on the [U.S. Postal] team we realized that he was not only good, but extremely tough—very, very tough. He will not quit. Floyd is as hardheaded as they come, and I mean that as a big compliment."

FOLLOWING THE DREAM

Landis's 30-year journey from a modest household in Farmersville, Pennsylvania, to the Tour de France podium on the Champs-Élysées is the stuff of legend. And true to Landis's character, his Tour victory was the culmination of a series of departures—of tough decisions to leave his comfort zone, even when it meant leaving behind those closest to him.

His parents Paul and Arlene Landis are strict Mennonite Christians who reject modern amenities such as televisions or computers. When Landis was in his teens, he would sneak out at night to ride his mountain bike, wearing long sweatpants in accordance with a religious stricture not to show his legs. When he told his parents that he wanted to become a professional cyclist, they weren't keen on that modern concept either.

"It's true that at the beginning we wanted, as many parents do, for him to be able to support his family," said Landis's mother. But her son had fallen in love with cycling. After winning the 1993 national junior cross-country championship in Traverse City, Michigan, at age 17, he left home against his parents' wishes and moved to California to pursue a career in mountain bike racing.

Landis raced as a semipro mountain biker for three years. Then his team lost its sponsor. Without a travel budget, Landis and his teammates looked at local alternatives. They started competing in California road races, usually criteriums, and took pleasure in burning off the front to upset the roadies. After one such race in February 1999, the Mercury pro road team director, John Wordin, who had also competed in the event, told Landis he was impressed by his strength, despite Landis's choppy, unrefined mountain-bike pedal stroke. Wordin knew right away that Landis was "an exceptional rider" and offered him a place on his team. "He didn't have any money, didn't have a job," Wordin said. "He was on the point of ending everything to work at a friend's restaurant in San Diego." Landis signed on the dotted line.

Near the end of Landis's first season with Mercury, Wordin took him to France to race in the prestigious Tour de l'Avenir, a ten-day stage race for young pros and amateurs that is seen as a stepping-stone to the Tour de France. Landis had never heard of the event. "I begged John Lelangue [who was then working for ASO, many years before he became the Phonak team manager] to take Mercury for the Tour de l'Avenir," Wordin recalled. "I told him, 'You'll see, one day Floyd will win the Tour de France.' At the start Floyd was always riding at the back. He was losing time every day. I said to him, 'You didn't come to Europe just to ride around, so just do something.' And the next day he did an incredible ride to take the yellow jersey."

Landis eventually finished the 1999 Tour de l'Avenir in third place and had a taste of winning in Europe. He said a few years later, however, that pulling on that yellow jersey wasn't the beginning of a bigger dream. "I've had a career that's had progressive steps," he said. "I've always had the dream, I've always thought about the Tour de France, even when I was mountain biking. It's the biggest show there is in cycling."

Landis's wife, Amber Basile, confirmed Landis's boundless confidence. Asked when Landis first told her he believed he could win the Tour, Basile answered, "I think he's always said that, at least for the last five years. He's known for a long time that he could; it's just been a long journey getting there. He makes his own destiny. He sets his mind to it and knows what he wants to do. It might take him a while, but he does it."

Landis had hoped to get a shot at the Tour with the Mercury team, and in 2001, Wordin signed Greg LeMond to be a team consultant in return for his bringing the team a major sponsor, Viatel. The big plans folded when Viatel's telecommunications business went down the drain and the team stopped paying the riders. Landis was newly married to Basile, who had a four-year-old daughter, and went heavily into debt. That's when Armstrong's U.S. Postal team started showing an interest in Landis.

Speaking in early 2006, Landis remembered that difficult period of his life. "Probably anyone with any sense would have quit cycling before they got into debt," he said with a nervous laugh. "But I was sure that I could make it. I wasn't in debt because I couldn't manage money. I was in debt because I believed that I could make it in cycling, and that was my only choice. I didn't get paid for a year [by the Mercury-Viatel team] and I wasn't a high-paid rider to start with. So the only way for me to get through the rest of the year to where I was on [Lance's] team, and actually getting paid, was to get myself into a lot of debt. Okay, it was a big risk, but I think it's actually evidence of the confidence I had in myself."

That confidence paid off when Armstrong took a personal interest in Landis and helped him become a better bike racer and helped him pay off his credit card debt. "I was in a completely different place in my life than he was in his," Landis continued, "and he helped me a lot. He was a hero of mine to start with because, obviously, he had won the Tour three times before I even met him. So just being able to be there and train with him was motivation enough for me."

INNOCENT OR GUILTY?

Given their long-standing relationship, even though it turned sour for a while when Landis left U.S. Postal for Phonak, it was not a surprise to hear Armstrong phone in to *Larry King Live* on July 28 and say, "I still believe in Floyd and I believe him to be innocent."

As for Landis, he said it would make no sense for a rider to try to gain a short-term benefit from testosterone. He was at a loss to explain why his T/E ratio came in high and how a subsequent carbon isotope ratio test confirmed the *L'Équipe* leak, that some of his testosterone came from exogenous sources. But Landis said he had no reason to believe the counteranalysis of his "B" sample would reverse the result of the "A" sample. On August 5, the UCI announced that the second test did indeed confirm the result of the first.

The Phonak team—which had been plagued by doping cases for more than two years—immediately cut formal ties with its Tour winner. "Landis will be dismissed without notice for violating the team's internal Code of Ethics," Phonak announced, adding that while the team would support Landis's right of appeal in the case, "this will be his personal affair and the Phonak team will no longer be involved in that."

In the days that followed, Landis could not explain why one of his test results turned up positive. He also offered the possibility that his sample had been tampered with. "I'm beginning to wonder about this myself after the way the situation's been handled . . . [After] I give them the sample, I don't know where it goes," he told Jay Leno on the August 8 *Tonight Show*.

In addition, Landis raised serious concerns about the number of leaks that had followed news of the initial "A" sample result, charging that the UCI and WADA were unable or unwilling to follow confidentiality provisions spelled out in the UCI's own rules. "I've been catching a lot of grief in the press: 'Floyd has a new excuse, a new reason for what happened.' This is a situation where I'm forced to defend myself in the media," Landis told *USA Today*. "It would never have happened if UCI and WADA had followed their own rules. There's some kind of agenda there. I just don't know what it is."

The UCI does release information regarding positive tests if the governing body and the race organizer—in this case ASO—deem it necessary to preserve the integrity of the sport. Chapter 12 of the UCI antidoping rules states, "The Anti-Doping Commission and the National Federation of the License-Holder who is asserted to have committed a violation of these Anti-Doping Rules may make public statements and identifications they deem appropriate under the circumstances." Rules also state that such discussion should not come "earlier than the moment of sending the notification" to the affected rider.

McQuaid cited a commitment to transparency as the reason the UCI made its announcement as soon as it learned the result of the "A" sample. "The Landis affair carried . . . a clear and strong message for those who had the intelligence to decode it," he explained. "For the UCI, the time for facile excuses or for pardoning [people] is definitely past. This is a war without concessions against doping."

For Landis, who was about to embark on a long appeals process, the war had just begun. After the initial damaging revelations and his muddled responses, Landis assembled a defense team headed by Howard Jacobs, a Los Angeles lawyer. Jacobs has defended many athlete clients involved in doping cases, including Landis's friend Tyler Hamilton, who preceded Landis as team leader at Phonak but was the subject of a positive blood-doping test and later received a two-year suspension from the sport.

Hamilton's case was complicated. He was the first athlete ever accused of homologous blood doping—being transfused with someone else's blood. The test was under development in the months before Hamilton's alleged positive result, and, due to the lengthy process of hearings and appeals, his suspension was not confirmed until 18 months after the initial test.

There was a possibility that the Landis case too could take many months to play out, particularly as no testosterone "positive" has been upheld since Dutch cyclist Gert-Jan Theunisse lost his fourth place at the 1988 Tour de France. The reasons for that 18-year hiatus include the doubts experts have raised concerning the methodology of both testosterone tests: the one for detecting the T/E ratio and the carbon isotope ratio test.

Since testosterone is a natural hormone, doping controls have a more difficult time determining abuse than with a substance like cocaine, which could only show up in an athlete's urine or blood if externally sourced. Doping controls employ a two-headed method to catch athletes using testosterone. First, a screening test compares the ratio of testosterone to epitestosterone, which also occurs naturally. Normal males have a ratio up to 2:1; the UCI's legal limit is double that. Anything above this means that a second test is used, the isotope ratio mass spectrometry test, which studies the testosterone at a molecular level to determine its composition and then compares it to the body's cholesterol. If natural, the two should match in their ratio of carbon-13 to carbon-12 isotopes. If an IRMS test is performed correctly and two differing populations of testosterone are discovered, the one plausible explanation is that the testosterone that does not match the body's cholesterol profile has been externally sourced.

HIGHS AND LOWS

When Landis walked up the steps to the Tour podium in Paris, he was suffering. Since his hip joint began degenerating because of lack of blood supply, he has walked with a limp that he disguises as a strut. Since breaking his leg in 2003, he had been riding in pain, hence the constant grimace and unusual time trial position. His coping mechanism is sheer willpower.

"I forget that he has a problem because he doesn't talk about it," said his wife, Amber. "He never complains about it. Ever. I tell him sometimes, I wish you'd complain about it more, so I knew what the hell is wrong with you. Tell me that your hip hurts. But he never complains, never. You'll never hear him say that something is wrong. He'll never make excuses for anything."

One-on-one or in a small gathering, Landis is friendly and affable. Almost universally liked by teammates and rivals alike, Landis said he received condolences and encouragement from other riders at the start of stage 17, when they believed he had lost the Tour. "I should apologize to them for leaving them behind," he joked later, "because they were all very nice to me."

But Landis also exhibits a fierce, angry side reminiscent of his former boss, Armstrong. At the stage 17 finish line in Morzine, Landis's winning salute—a flexed arm and pumped fist—showed more anger than elation. In the seconds that followed, television pictures showed an almost violent Landis, arms extended, screaming at the scrum of cameras and microphones.

"When he crossed that finish line and punched his fist, you could see that was not for the love of the sport, that was to show the world that he was the strongest guy in the race," said Robbie Ventura, Landis's friend and coach. "I think a little anger drives him."

Like his Girona, Spain, roommate Dave Zabriskie, Landis is transformed in front of microphones and cameras. Usually sporting a backward-turned hat and rock star sunglasses, Landis becomes reserved when all eyes are on him, and he often provides vague, smart-alecky answers, sometimes with an expression that is equal parts smile and snarl.

At his final Tour press conference, Landis got increasingly testy when asked about the doping scandal that rocked the first week of the race. The first time the subject came up he didn't do himself any favors by answering, "I don't know anything about that."

Again he was asked if he had benefited from the absence of Ivan Basso and Jan Ullrich, and whether there should be an asterisk in the record books next to his Tour win. Landis snapped. "Since you really want a quote on what happened in the beginning of the race, and you won't stop asking those questions, I'll say that it was an unfortunate situation for all of us," he barked. "And none of us, in any way, got any satisfaction out of the fact that they're not here. Anyone have any questions about something else?"

The topic came up a third time when Landis was asked how he felt about being a role model to young cyclists around the world. Somehow the question struck a chord, and this time he answered more thoughtfully. "I think it's up to every child's parents to explain to them when they're watching the race what the best decisions in life are about," he said. "My parents taught me that hard work and patience are some of the most important things in getting what you want. That's the way my parents raised me, and I think that's not a bad way to do it."

Of all the riders in the pro peloton, Landis is closest to Zabriskie. "You can't be as good as he is and be laid back," Zabriskie said. "Floyd's always thinking of a way to get better."

In addition to his coach, Ventura, Landis works intensively with Allen Lim, a Ph.D. in exercise physiology from the University of Colorado. "I found that Floyd is one of the most meticulous people, in terms of his training diary and note taking, as any athlete I've ever worked with," Lim said. "That was a huge benefit to me. His notes go back to when he first started riding a bicycle. It's a decade's worth of notes. The guy hasn't missed a single day. There's one thing you have to be to succeed in anything—you have to be a student of the game that you play, and Floyd is a student of the sport. He doesn't miss anything." Ventura added that Landis "doesn't trust everybody," but stressed that he's got a "humongous heart."

"If Floyd cares about you, he'll go to the ends of the earth, he'll do everything he can to help you out," Ventura said. "I think he projects this image of being angry, but he smells the roses. He enjoys life. He's just really private. He's got this small group of people that he shares with. He's really a kind, caring, special guy. When he gets on his bicycle, and is in the bike-racing environment, that angry image kind of comes out a little bit."

After winning the Tour in Paris, Landis received a call from President Bush, who invited Landis, his wife Amber, and their family to visit the White House—a visit that was put on hold after Landis's doping violation gave him a different kind of notoriety. Landis is a man who needs to live a simple existence on his own terms. When asked before the Tour ended how he thought his life would change, Landis said, "If my life will change or not, I don't know. I hope it doesn't change too much, because I'm a pretty happy person in general."

Earlier in the year, Landis confided in a journalist, "There's times when I don't like [cycling], but there's times like that in any job. You don't stop and just give up; you go on because sometimes those end up being the parts you remember—the miserable parts."

Landis will always remember the "miserable parts" he experienced in the final days of July 2006. From the high of winning the Tour to the low of that "bad news" phone call less than three days later, few athletes have ever experienced such extremes of emotion.

Being such a buoyant character, Landis recovered his usual optimism within days. But his doping problem was kicked into insignificance on August 15. Just after he had written an open letter to his team, which ended with the sentence, "thank you all for your support and courage as I embark on this journey to restore my name, the team's name, and the image of cycling," Landis received devastating news. His wife's stepfather, David Witt, who was with them on the Champs-Élysées three weeks earlier, was dead from an apparent suicide. The San Diego Police Department reported that Witt, 57, was found in his car in a North Park parking garage close to the restaurant, Hawthorns, that he and his wife owned. Witt died of gunshot wounds to the head. The Landis-Basile family went into mourning.

Eleven days before that tragedy, Landis had posted the following message about the doping accusations on his Web site:

Keep the Faith

In the past week, I have gone from the "Top of the World" to the depths of scandal. I have been thrust into the international spotlight and am being asked to defend myself against something that I did not do, for reasons that I do not understand. Although this has been a hard time for my family and me, we are confident that I will be vindicated. I am innocent of any wrongdoing and want to take an opportunity to clear up some misconceptions that exist regarding the situation.

It is widely known that the test in question, given as a urine sample after my victorious ride on stage 17 of the Tour de France, returned an abnormal T/E ratio from the "A" sample. I want to be entirely clear about one point of the test that has not been fairly reported in the press or expressed in any statements made by international or national governing bodies; the T value returned has been determined to be in the normal range. The E value returned was LOW, thus causing the skewed ratio. This evidence supports my assertion that I did not use testosterone to improve my performance. I emphatically deny any claims that I used testosterone to improve my performance.

Much has been speculated about the presence of exogenous testosterone in the "A" sample. Together with some of the leading medical and scientific experts in the world, we are reviewing the documentation about the "carbon isotope ratio test." All I can say at this time is that I did not take testosterone, so there must be another reason for the result, as leaked by the UCI.

Beyond the specifics of the testing, however, I am particularly troubled by the actions of the UCI. Information about an "adverse analytical finding" was prematurely released by the UCI in order "to avoid a known leak" within the lab. A direct statement followed from UCI president Pat McQuaid that left little to infer as to whose test was in question.

I was notified of the "A" sample results while attending post-Tour criteriums in Europe. As a result of these breaches in protocol, confidentiality, and disregard for due process, I view this as a clear violation of my rights as a professional racer licensed by the UCI.

I became the center of media attention with little time to understand the nature of the "A" sample results, possible causes or explanations. As I tried to come to terms with the situation, my statement and attempts to understand the results were interpreted as "excuses" before I had time to fully grasp the facts of the case. The inappropriate actions of the UCI has caused undue, and potentially irreparable, harm to my reputation and character. I feel I am being prosecuted without regard to my basic rights.

It is now my goal to fight to clear my name and restore what I worked so hard to achieve. I am a fighter. I did not give up during the Tour and I won't give up now, no matter what the results of the "B" sample are.

Keep the Faith,
Floyd

POSTSCRIPT

By early September 2006:

Jan Ullrich had been fired by his team, T-Mobile, and his case was being investigated by Swiss Cycling for a possible doping suspension after his dossier from *Operación Puerto* was passed on by the UCI.

Ivan Basso was suspended by his team, CSC. Bjarne Riis, team manager, said he would not take back the Italian star if it materialized that Basso had lied in saying he had no connection with *Operación Puerto* or Dr. Eufemiano Fuentes.

Alexander Vinokourov was on his way to winning the Vuelta a España with his Astaná team after helping his Kazakh teammate Andrey Kashechkin finish second at the Tour of Germany.

No word has been heard from **Francisco Mancebo** since he said he was quitting cycling the day before the Tour start.

After recovering from his broken collarbone, **Alejandro Valverde** was heading for second place overall at the Vuelta a España.

After recovering from his broken wrist, **Bobby Julich** finished 69th in the Tour of Germany. He then quit the Tour de Benelux, saying he was frightened of crashing again.

Since abandoning the Tour de France, **Iban Mayo** returned to racing by winning the five-day Tour of Burgos, and was considered one of the favorites at the Vuelta a España.

After quitting the Tour, **Tom Boonen** won three stages of the Tour de Benelux before preparing for the defense of his world title in Salzburg, Austria.

Since finishing 32nd at the Tour, **George Hincapie** went on to win the time trial stage of the Tour de Benelux, but lost the overall title by one second after another rider caused him to crash 50 meters from the finish line of the final stage. He returned home to win the 2006 U.S. pro road championship in Greenville, South Carolina.

After winning a mountain stage of the Tour of Germany but finishing second overall to an inspired **Jens Voigt** of CSC, **Levi Leipheimer** signed a contract to lead the Discovery Channel team at the 2007 Tour.

Saying he was tired after finishing sixth at the Tour, **Denis Menchov** began the defense of his Vuelta a España title on August 26, but abandoned on stage 10.

After placing an excellent fifth in his second Tour, **Cadel Evans** finished tenth at the Tour of Denmark, and second at the Tour of Poland.

Carlos Sastre started his third grand tour of the year on August 26 by leading his CSC team to first place in the stage 1 team time trial at the Vuelta a España, to wear the yellow jersey for a day.

After finishing on the Tour podium, **Andreas Klöden** went on to win the five-day Regio Tour ahead of his teammate **Michael Rogers**, but his T-Mobile team did not re-sign Klöden after he publicly defended his friend Ullrich in connection with *Operación Puerto*. Klöden will race with his former teammate Vinokourov on the Astaná team in 2007.

On hearing about the Floyd Landis positive, Tour runner-up **Oscar Pereiro** said he would not feel like the winner if awarded the title by default. He later changed his mind to say, "I now feel like the winner of the Tour de France." He then entered the Vuelta a España to help his team leader Valverde.

Floyd Landis mourned the death of his stepfather-in-law, while his legal team prepared to defend Landis in proceedings by the U.S. Antidoping Agency, which was likely to recommend a two-year suspension from cycling for his positive test for testosterone at the Tour de France. Upon receipt of more than three hundred pages of documentation from the lab that performed the tests, Landis said his legal team was confident he would be cleared of the violation.

Full Results of the 93rd Tour de France

YELLOW JERSEY: FLOYD LANDIS

The results of the 93rd Tour de France will be confirmed only when ongoing proceedings into the possible disqualification of Floyd Landis are completed. This is how the race finished:

FINAL STANDINGS: **1. Floyd Landis (USA), Phonak, 3657.1km in 89:39:30 (40.784kph); 2.** Oscar Pereiro (Sp), Caisse d'Épargne-Illes Balears, at 0:57; **3.** Andreas Klöden (G), T-Mobile, at 1:29; **4.** Carlos Sastre (Sp), CSC, at 3:13; **5.** Cadel Evans (Aus), Davitamon-Lotto, at 5:08; **6.** Denis Menchov (Rus), Rabobank, at 7:06; **7.** Cyril Dessel (F), AG2R Prévoyance, at 8:41; **8.** Christophe Moreau (F), AG2R Prévoyance, at 9:37; **9.** Haimar Zubeldia (Sp), Euskaltel-Euskadi, at 12:05; **10.** Michael Rogers (Aus), T-Mobile, at 15:07; **11. Fränk Schleck (Lux), CSC, at 17:46; 12.** Damiano Cunego (I), Lampre-Fondital, at 19:19; **13. Levi Leipheimer (USA), Gerolsteiner, at 19:22; 14.** Michael Boogerd (Nl), Rabobank, at 19:46; **15.** Marcus Fothen (G), Gerolsteiner, at 19:57; **16.** Pietro Caucchioli (I), Crédit Agricole, at 21:12; **17.** Tadej Valjavec (Slo), Lampre-Fondital, at 26:25; **18.** Michael Rasmussen (Dk), Rabobank, at 28:33; **19.** José Azevedo (P), Discovery Channel, at 38:08; **20.** Marzio Bruseghin (I), Lampre-Fondital, at 43:05; **21.** David Arroyo (Sp), Caisse d'Épargne-Illes Balears, at 44:00; **22.** Patxi Vila (Sp), Lampre-Fondital, at 44:28; **23.** Patrik Sinkewitz (G), T-Mobile, at 49:01; **24. Christian Vande Velde (USA), CSC, at 50:19; 25.** Yaroslav Popovych (Ukr), Discovery Channel, at 52:02; **26.** Giuseppe Guerini (I), T-Mobile, at 57:59; **27.** Eddy Mazzoleni (I), T-Mobile, at 1:02:40; **28.** José Luis Arrieta (Sp), AG2R Prévoyance, at 1:03:00; **29.** Pierrick Fédrigo (F), Bouygues Telecom, at 1:05:27; **30.** Vladimir Karpets (Rus), Caisse d'Épargne-Illes Balears, at 1:07:18; **31.** Axel Merckx (B), Phonak, at 1:09:28; **32. George Hincapie (USA), Discovery Channel, at 1:11:14; 33.** Xabier Zandio (Sp), Caisse d'Épargne-Illes Balears, at 1:16:47; **34.** Sylvain Calzati (F), AG2R Prévoyance, at 1:20:26; **35.** Iker Camano (Sp), Euskaltel-Euskadi, at 1:21:34; **36.** Mikel Astarloza (Sp), AG2R Prévoyance, at 1:24:26; **37.** Stéphane Goubert (F), AG2R Prévoyance, at 1:28:33; **38.** Laurent Lefèvre (F), Bouygues Telecom, at 1:30:24; **39.** Benoît Salmon (F), Agritubel, at 1:30:55; **40.** Christophe Brandt (B), Davitamon-Lotto, at 1:34:24; **41.** Christophe Rinero (F), Saunier Duval-Prodir, at 1:34:59; **42.** Egoi Martinez (Sp), Discovery Channel, at 1:35:12; **43.** Ivan Parra (Col), Cofidis, at 1:37:09; **44.** Cristian Moreni (I), Cofidis, at 1:38:07; **45.** Sylvain Chavanel (F), Cofidis, at 1:40:05; **46.** Ruben Lobato (Sp), Saunier Duval-Prodir, at 1:40:52; **47.** Georg Totschnig (A), Gerolsteiner, at 1:42:55; **48.** Patrice Halgand (F), Crédit Agricole, at 1:43:03; **49.** Alexandre Botcharov (Rus), Crédit Agricole, at 1:44:46; **50.** Iñigo

Landaluze (Sp), Euskaltel-Euskadi, at 1:48:22; **51.** Matthieu Sprick (F), Bouygues Telecom, at 1:48:31; **52.** Sergei Gontchar (Ukr), T-Mobile, at 1:49:22; **53.** Jens Voigt (G), CSC, at 1:50:41; **54.** Matthias Kessler (G), T-Mobile, at 1:52:03; **55.** Stefano Garzelli (I), Liquigas, at 1:53:55; **56.** David de la Fuente (Sp), Saunier Duval-Prodir, at 1:55:19; **57.** Salvatore Commesso (I), Lampre-Fondital, at 1:56:55; **58.** David Moncoutié (F), Cofidis, at 2:03:10; **59.** David Millar (GB), Saunier Duval-Prodir, at 2:04:10; **60.** Gilberto Simoni (I), Saunier Duval-Prodir, at 2:07:18; **61.** Moises Duenas (Sp), Agritubel, at 2:07:59; **62.** Koos Moerenhout (Nl), Phonak, at 2:09:03; **63.** Thomas Lövkvist (S), Française des Jeux, at 2:12:13; **64. Chris Horner (USA), Davitamon-Lotto, at 2:12:25; 65.** Pavel Padrnos (Cz), Discovery Channel, at 2:16:45; **66.** Sebastian Lang (G), Gerolsteiner, at 2:25:15; **67.** Alessandro Ballan (I), Lampre-Fondital, at 2:26:34; **68.** Fabian Wegmann (G), Gerolsteiner, at 2:27:17; **69.** Sandy Casar (F), Française des Jeux, at 2:28:34; **70.** Paolo Tiralongo (I), Lampre-Fondital, at 2:32:08; **71.** Iñaki Isasi (Sp), Euskaltel-Euskadi, at 2:32:36; **72.** Juan Manuel Garate (Sp), Quick Step-Innergetic, at 2:32:47; **73.** Didier Rous (F), Bouygues Telecom, at 2:32:54; **74. David Zabriskie (USA), CSC, at 2:33:46; 75.** Gorka Verdugo (Sp), Euskaltel-Euskadi, at 2:33:52; **76.** Christophe Le Mevel (F), Crédit Agricole, at 2:34:24; **77.** Carlos Da Cruz (F), Française des Jeux, at 2:40:01; **78.** Francisco Ventoso (Sp), Saunier Duval-Prodir, at 2:41:22; **79.** Simon Gerrans (Aus), AG2R Prévoyance, at 2:46:33; **80.** Manuel Quinziato (I), Liquigas, at 2:47:33; **81.** Björn Schröder (G), Milram, at 2:47:48; **82.** Juan Antonio Flecha (Sp), Rabobank, at 2:49:5; **83.** Jérôme Pineau (F), Bouygues Telecom, at 2:51:22; **84.** Viatcheslav Ekimov (Rus), Discovery Channel, at 2:51:33; **85.** Joost Posthuma (Nl), Rabobank, at 2:52:00; **86.** Erik Zabel (G), Milram, at 2:52:13; **87.** Benoît Vaugrenard (F), Française des Jeux, at 2:52:31; **88.** Anthony Geslin (F), Bouygues Telecom, at 2:52:31; **89.** Thomas Voeckler (F), Bouygues Telecom, at 2:52:57; **90.** Manuel Calvente (Sp), Agritubel, at 2:53:27; **91.** Stuart O'Grady (Aus), CSC, at 2:55:25; **92.** José Luis Rubiera (Sp), Discovery Channel, at 2:55:44; **93.** Pieter Weening (Nl), Rabobank, at 2:56:03; **94.** Bram Tankink (Nl), Quick Step-Innergetic, at 2:57:02; **95.** Cédric Vasseur (F), Quick Step-Innergetic, at 2:58:55; **96.** Ronny Scholz (G), Gerolsteiner, at 3:00:48; **97.** Alexandre Moos (Swi), Phonak, at 3:01:34; **98.** Riccardo Ricco (I), Saunier Duval, at 3:01:37; **99.** Marco Velo (I), Milram, at 3:02:09; **100.** Nicolas Portal (F), Caisse d'Épargne-Illes Balears, at 3:02:20; **101.** Luca Paolini (I), Liquigas, at 3:04:18; **102.** Ralf Grabsch (G), Milram, at 3:04:21; **103.** Nicolas Jalabert (F), Phonak, at 3:05:05; **104.** Christian Knees (G), Milram, at 3:05:58; **105.** Gustav Larsson (S), Française des Jeux, at 3:06:14; **106.** Mario Aerts (B), Davitamon-Lotto, at 3:06:26; **107.** Bert Grabsch (G), Phonak, at 3:08:23; **108.** Bernhard Eisel (A), Française des Jeux, at 3:08:59; **109.** Daniele Righi (I), Lampre-Fondital, at 3:12:51; **110.** Philippe Gilbert (B), Française des Jeux, at 3:13:03; **111.** Walter Beneteau (F), Bouygues Telecom, at 3:15:41; **112.** Johan Vansummeren (B), Davitamon-Lotto, at 3:18:44; **113.** Sébastien Hinault (F), Crédit Agricole, at 3:19:15; **114.** Anthony Charteau (F), Crédit Agricole, at 3:20:29; **115.** Vicente Garcia Acosta (Sp), Caisse d'Épargne-Illes Balears, at 3:20:32; **116.** Robbie McEwen (Aus), Davitamon-Lotto, at 3:21:01; **117.** Eduardo Gonzalo (Sp), Agritubel, at 3:21:27; **118.** Michael Albasini (Swi), Liquigas-Bianchi, at 3:21:34; **119.** Matej Mugerli (Slo), Liquigas, at 3:21:48; **120.** Samuel Dumoulin (F), AG2R Prévoyance, at 3:22:15; **121.** Thor Hushovd (N), Crédit Agricole, at 3:23:52; **122.** Victor Hugo Peña (Col), Phonak, at 3:24:36; **123.** Stéphane Augé (F), Cofidis, at 3:25:19; **124.** Bradley Wiggins (GB), Cofidis, at 3:25:32; **125.** Matteo Tosatto (I), Quick Step-Innergetic, at 3:25:54; **126.** Christophe Laurent (F), Agritubel, at 3:26:23; **127.** Unai Etxebarria (Ven), Euskaltel-Euskadi, at 3:30:12; **128.** Julian Dean (NZ), Crédit Agricole, at 3:30:33; **129.** Patrick Calcagni (Swi), Liquigas, at 3:33:28; **130.** Arnaud Coyot (F), Cofidis, at 3:35:34; **131.** Christophe Mengin (F), Française des Jeux, at 3:35:52; **132.** Kjell Carlström (Fin), Liquigas, at 3:35:53; **133.** Filippo Pozzato (I), Quick Step-Innergetic, at 3:37:06; **134.** Cédric Coutouly (F), Agritubel, at 3:39:00; **135.** Peter Wrolich (A), Gerolsteiner, at 3:39:20; **136.** Aitor Hernandez (Sp), Euskaltel-Euskadi, at 3:50:16; **137.** Gert Steegmans (B), Davitamon-Lotto, at 3:59:16; **138.** Jimmy Casper (F), Cofidis, at 4:00:05; **139.** Wim Vansevenant (B), Davitamon-Lotto, at 4:02:01.